ALSO BY KARL GERTH

China Made: Consumer Culture and
the Creation of the Nation

AS CHINA GOES,
SO GOES THE WORLD

AS CHINA GOES, SO GOES THE WORLD

How Chinese Consumers Are Transforming Everything

★

KARL GERTH

 HILL AND WANG

A DIVISION OF FARRAR, STRAUS AND GIROUX

NEW YORK

Hill and Wang
A division of Farrar, Straus and Giroux
18 West 18th Street, New York 10011

Library of Congress Cataloging-in-Publication Data
Gerth, Karl.
    As China goes, so goes the world : how Chinese consumers are transforming
everything / Karl Gerth.— 1st ed.
        p.   cm.
    Includes bibliographical references and index.
    ISBN: 978-0-8090-3429-1 (hardcover : alk. paper)
    1. Consumption (Economics)—China.   2. Consumer behavior—China.
3. Economic history—21st century.   I. Title.

HC430.C6.G469 2010
339.4'70951—dc22

                                                        2010012647

Designed by Jonathan D. Lippincott

www.fsgbooks.com

2   3   4   5   6   7   8   9   10

For my parents,
Judy Valentine Gerth and Roger Andrew Gerth

CONTENTS

AS CHINA GOES,
SO GOES THE WORLD

INTRODUCTION

When I first traveled to China in 1986 to spend a year studying at two Chinese universities, I was surprised to find myself immediately transformed from a poor college student with barely enough money to buy the odd pizza and six-pack of beer in the United States to a "rich foreigner" with much more to spend than my Chinese classmates. The problem with this elevation of my fortunes, I soon discovered, was that outside the fancy new hotels catering to foreign tourists, there were few places to shop and not much to buy. This was a China very different from the one most visitors find today. Now luxury cars, fashionably dressed Chinese, and omnipresent advertising fill cities that resemble endless strip malls with street after street of stores big and small.

It's difficult to convey how quickly consumer lifestyles have taken hold throughout China since the market reforms initiated at the end of the 1970s. Today any visitor can see that the newly middle-class urban Chinese consumers are clearly catching up with their counterparts in wealthier countries. Although China's total consumer spending of $4 trillion is still less than half that of the United States, it has surpassed consumer spending in Japan and is closing in on that of the European Union. It has taken China just a few years to learn what took these consumer countries decades: how to spend. Chinese have already become the world's largest consumers of everything from mobile phones to beer; they have embraced consumer habits that see them increasingly living in large single-occupancy homes, shopping in chain stores, and eating meat-based diets served in fast-food outlets. Chinese consumers are also spending on new leisure activities, from vacationing in exotic locations to attending professional sports events. Even rural Chinese, long the laggards of Chinese consumerism, are buying more cars and larger houses, and filling the latter with computers and televisions.

Although China remains a nominally socialist country, consumerism is now deeply entrenched in all areas of Chinese life. Perhaps my favorite example is the growth of the personal grooming industry. When I first began to travel to China, a consumer had little choice. One could find few beauty products and even fewer places outside the grungy state-run shops to get a haircut, much less a facial, pedicure, or scalp massage. Even state-run shops were hard to find, operated by unmotivated workers, and open only during the regular business day. Two decades later, cosmetics and beauty sales in China have skyrocketed, from $24 million in 1982 to over $168 billion in 2009; such products are now available in more than 1.6 million hair salons, department stores, and boutiques. A country that a few decades ago was full of socialist citizens sporting unisex baggy Mao suits and blunt haircuts now has more than 11 million people generating billions of yuan in profits by thinking all day, every day, about other people's hair, nails, and faces. From just fifty companies manufacturing soap and shampoo in the late 1970s, the growing personal grooming industry now includes some four thousand cosmetics companies and six hundred beauty-related professional training institutes. Every major global cosmetics and hair care brand now sells in China. In 1981, Japan's largest cosmetics manufacturer, Shiseido, was the first international firm to enter the Chinese market; three decades later, it has five thousand boutiques there. The beauty industry—perhaps the ultimate consumerist industry and one unthinkable in China thirty years ago, when Maoists derided personal adornment as "bourgeois"—has now become the fifth largest sector of the massive Chinese economy, trailing only property, cars, tourism, and information technology.

But as Chinese consumers attempt to catch up and overtake their counterparts in the leading consumer countries, the consequences are radically transforming their society and the world. The rise of the Chinese consumer is first and foremost a story about changes in China over the last three decades. But to borrow from the old Pogo cartoon, we have met the enemy and he is us. Without question, Chinese culture shapes and explains many of the impacts of the rapidly expanding Chinese consumerism, but the reason that traveling Americans, Europeans, and Japanese now feel so at home in Beijing and Shanghai is because, in an essential sense, they are. The same brands, stores, and, broadly speaking, shopping experiences they are accustomed to back home now await them in China as well. (Including, unfortunately, many of the same negative consequences, such as increased pollutants, waste, disparity, and obesity.) While the United States and the rest of the world certainly stand to reap benefits from China's heady embrace of consumerism, including a new and expanding market for their products, nobody yet fully understands just what they might be sowing, for the Chinese or for the rest of the globe, by continuing to insist that the Chinese consume more and more.

So what are the *collective* implications of *individual* consumer choices for China and the rest of the world? While many journalists, scholars, and critics have already found much to worry about as China joins the industrialized family of nations—the outsourcing of manufacturing jobs, competition for oil, human rights violations, growing Chinese military budgets, and rising carbon emissions—they have generally overlooked the effects of something subtler but equally profound: China's rapid development of a consumer culture. This book makes the case that Chinese consumers, with help from their counterparts in other industrialized countries, are already shaping the future we will all share.

From Communism to Consumerism

To better understand China's decision to follow this course and its commitment to making it succeed, you might find a bit of historical perspective helpful. With the establishment of the People's Republic of China in 1949, Mao Zedong announced that China had "stood up," meaning that the country, which had been dominated by foreign imperialist powers for the previous hundred years, would now control its own destiny. For its first thirty years, as market economies from America to Japan were developing modern consumer societies, the PRC tried to develop its industrial economy with as little integration into those capitalist economies as possible, and exercised its sovereignty by pursuing policies to limit the availability of consumer goods and to channel scarce resources to heavy industry. The state's priorities at this time were *productivist*: to make or facilitate the making of things that make more things ("producer goods" such as steel and chemicals) rather than things that could be used directly ("consumer goods" such as bicycles and toothpaste). The Chinese leaders and bureaucrats making choices on behalf of the country chose to restrict consumer spending by limiting consumer goods. Consequently, the Chinese found little to buy.

But this all changed with the death of Mao and the rise of Deng Xiaoping in 1978. Now China's leaders decided that "opening to the outside world" (meaning the capitalist world) was essential to securing the technology and investment necessary to develop its economy.

The Mao era's go-it-alone approach had, they decided, outlived its usefulness, and the risks of creating inequality within China and dependence on capitalist countries were outweighed by the potential gain: China's recovering its historical place as a wealthy and powerful nation. Since 1978 and the start of the Reform Era, which continues down to the present, China, in exchange for money and know-how from capitalist countries, has had to gradually cede control over its foreign and domestic trade policies, a process culminating in its decision to join the World Trade Organization in 2001. Things were changing before then, but after 2001 nothing would be the same. With WTO membership, China has had to grant foreign companies greater access to potential Chinese consumers, and the process has accelerated tremendously. While international trade organizations and foreign governments pushed these policy changes on China, the decision to embrace them began a shift that has moved China ever closer to a market economy and the Chinese increasingly toward modern consumer lifestyles.

This shift from a centrally controlled command economy toward a consumer economy was not merely another imposition of imperialism from abroad. This time China actually welcomed and encouraged foreign influences, or at least resigned itself to playing by the rules of the major market economies, most notably the United States. With Deng's rise to power, the country's leaders began to dismantle the state-controlled planned economy to prepare the soil in which foreign investors were invited to plant the seeds of market-led growth. Following the examples set by Japan, Taiwan, Chile, South Korea, and Singapore, Deng created a market economy mixed with authoritarian centralized control that he called "socialism with Chinese characteristics" (but that might more accurately be called "privatization with Chinese characteristics"). The massive expansion of industrialization that quickly developed was nurtured by a reliance on exports, an opening to foreign investment, and support for technology transfer to China through joint ventures with foreign companies. But China's leaders still attempted to restrict access to imported consumer goods and limit the influence of consumers on economic growth. This was born of a desire not so much to limit consumerism as to channel it, to ensure that the result was long-term growth in national wealth rather than an outrush of Chinese capital to pay for ephemeral consumer delights.

Despite continued limitations on outside access to Chinese consumers, the developed nations were not only welcome but eager partners as they sought access to cheap labor and to a vast emerging market for their products. For decades investors from around the world have rushed to invest hundreds of billions of dollars simply on the promise of breaking into the Chinese market and gaining access to these potential consumers. The reasons are clear: the country has hundreds of millions of not only new middle-class consumers but also first-time buyers in any number of product categories who haven't yet established brand preferences. In that sense, Chinese consumers are like the golden demographic for marketers in the United States: youngsters with disposable incomes who are just learning to prefer Pepsi or Coke.

As Chinese become more like consumers in developed nations, we forget just how recent the Chinese policies designed to promote consumer spending are. Since the 1990s, the country's leaders have understood that the massive budget and trade deficits of its biggest trading partner, the United States, were unsustainable and have wanted to decouple their economy from an overreliance on economic growth fueled by exports. Even before the 2008 global economic crisis, they recognized that it was only a matter of time before the American and European consumer markets were saturated with inexpensive Chinese imports and heavily indebted Western consumers were less and less able to pay for lifestyles based on consuming more and more. Chinese leaders now began to view stimulating consumer desire as not a wasteful endpoint, the death of production, but rather the starting point of production.

These policies actually reflected a remarkable shift from the export-led growth model promoted by earlier policy makers such as Zhao Ziyang in the late 1980s. The often-used metaphor of "unleashing the Chinese consumer" mistakenly assumes an inherent desire among Chinese consumers and overlooks that Chinese politicians have actually been *pushing* their population to consume more. Rather than depend on the buying habits of foreign consumers, China decided to become its own best customer and to teach its citizens to consume more like Americans. It is true that when the going gets tough, as with the economic crisis that began in 2008, Chinese leaders tend to revert to familiar productivist habits, namely, the use of state demand to revive the economy by channeling resources into state-owned enterprises and endless infrastructure projects such as roads and airports. But this does not diminish their commitment to increasing the country's annual average consumption rate from 33 percent of GDP (the lowest of any major economy) to something closer to the U.S. and world average of 70–80 percent. That's immeasurably more consumer desire translated into a lot more air-conditioners, automobiles, bottled water, and vacations.

The 2008 global financial crisis has only increased the urgency of the calls of political and business leaders around the world for Chinese consumers to rescue the global economy by saving less and consuming more—much more. At the height of the crisis in late October of 2008, for instance, the *New York Times* editorial page, under the heading "As China Goes, So Goes . . ." urged the Chinese government to stop "clinging to the old export strategy" and to encourage its consumers to spend more. Then-president George W. Bush also urged the Chinese government to further stimulate domestic consumption, hoping out loud "that China changes from a saving society to a consuming society." The Obama administration has pursued much the same policy. In a speech at Beijing University in 2009, treasury secretary Tim Geithner praised China's leaders for recognizing that "sustainable growth will require a substantial shift from external to domestic demand, from investment and export driven growth, to growth led by consumption."

These and similar calls by the European Union and Japan for China to reduce its massive trade imbalances by increasing imports and consuming more are based on hopes that Chinese consumers will become the new motor of global economic demand and growth. Most mainstream economists and policy makers argue that Chinese consumption may in fact save the global economy, that Chinese demand for American and European high-tech goods, financial services, and other products will create jobs and economic growth in the United States and other leading economies and lead to a stable, increasingly capitalistic, and eventually (though this is touted less often nowadays) democratic China. In short, China's consuming more will prove a panacea for all that ails the leading economies. The implication, pressed to a logical extreme, is that China can save the world by doing its part to consume goods and resources faster.

The Chinese leadership has its own reasons for wanting to promote domestic consumption and to shift China from a producing to a consuming society. In 2008, Li Keqiang, a rising political star, voiced the conventional wisdom among top Chinese policy makers that "boosting domestic demand is essential for propping up growth," especially in the face of global economic weakness. To provide customers for all those Chinese products previously bound for saturated American and other developed markets, China's leaders have implemented policies to dismantle barriers to increased Chinese consumption, including making it easier for banks to lend money by easing credit and reserve restrictions, and discouraging savings by lowering interest rates. Recognizing the vast potential consumer market living outside its cities, Chinese officials have also attempted to stimulate rural consumption by improving the power grid and subsidizing the cost of cell phones, washing machines, and flat-screen televisions. To indirectly encourage consumers to tap into their "rainy day savings," they have also begun to restrengthen social welfare provisions by introducing health insurance and ensuring state-mandated minimum incomes.

And they have implemented these policies with their own growing sense of alarm. Wanting to avoid the stagnation experienced by other Asian export-led economies such as Japan, Korea, and Taiwan, Chinese leaders have identified domestic demand as the key to long-term economic growth. To China's leaders, promoting domestic consumption and modern lifestyles is seen as a way—perhaps even the only way—for China to build national wealth and international power and to ensure the leaders' own power domestically. Thus, as political scientist Patricia M. Thornton suggests, there are political as well as economic motivations for the promotion of consumerism and the conversion of the activist revolutionary masses of the Mao Zedong era into the more atomized and politically passive consumers of the contemporary Reform Era.

Creating Consumers

But prodding Chinese consumers to spend much more faces many hurdles, not the least of which is one often forgotten amid all the discussions of Chinese consumerism: China remains a very poor country. Hundreds of millions of China's 1.3 billion "consumers" include the rural poor, who spend too little and have too little to spend. While it's obviously hard for Chinese consumers to spend what they don't have, more liberal financial policies have begun to make it easier for middle-class urban consumers to borrow to buy more now. China's personal loan market, established only in 1997, is growing quickly, with mortgage lending expanding by an average of 80 percent annually. Another challenge has been the traditional thriftiness of the Chinese, who save, on average, anywhere from a quarter to a half of their income (a sharp contrast to the U.S. rate, which hovers above 1 percent in 2010, one of the lowest rates in the world). Worry over potential health care costs, retirement, education, and housing expenses, all once covered by the socialist state, currently preoccupies most Chinese and creates policy challenges for the government. The global financial crisis has only added to this new era of job insecurity.

Still, the Chinese are indeed learning to buy much more. The new opportunities to borrow are quickly reversing China's culture of saving, and as the Chinese borrow more they are becoming, in popular parlance, mortgage slaves, car slaves, credit card slaves, and a new class of young big spenders that has become known as the "tapped-out-by-the-end-of-the-month clan." In late 2009, 30 percent of Chinese families were spending more than half of their income to pay back loans. Government and business policies have also begun to ease constraints on spending by offering limited pension plans and health insurance. Such policies have also increased buying power by giving civil servants pay raises, increasing personal income tax exemptions, abolishing agricultural taxes, and allowing the Chinese currency to appreciate (within limits).

The Chinese government has also enacted specific policies to promote leisure spending as it has tried to move its economy away from an overreliance on polluting and energy-intensive heavy industry. China has implemented weekends, also called "double leisure days," and the forty-hour workweek. To vacation is promoted as patriotic. The government's intention, as announced by former vice premier Wu Yi at the 2006 Hangzhou World Leisure Expo, is to see that lei-

sure does not become "the privilege of a minority of people" but popular and widespread. The most high profile of these efforts was the
creation of Japanese-style "Golden Weeks," three seven-day annual
national holidays around the Chinese Lunar New Year, Labor Day,
and National Day Golden Week (commemorating the establishment
of the People's Republic of China on October 1, 1949). These holidays
provided a huge boost to domestic tourism, so much so that the government eventually discontinued them in an attempt to spread the
times the Chinese traveled more evenly throughout the year (the
equivalent of the U.S. government's abolishing the Thanksgiving and
Christmas holidays to more evenly distribute spending and travel).
Promoting vacation days has led to the overnight creation of a massive
tourist industry in China, now a critical and deeply entrenched part of
the economy. Travel agencies (like barbershops, previously few and
state-run) have become ubiquitous. Similarly, the province of Hainan
Island, once a sparsely populated and underdeveloped hinterland off
the coast of Vietnam, is becoming for the Chinese what Hawaii is to
Americans.

Loosely defined, consumerism has been around in China for hundreds and arguably thousands of years. But the fundamental transformations necessary to produce the defining attributes of modern
consumerism have in fact been under way since around 1900. This
nascent consumer culture included the spread of mass-produced goods
and their display and discussion in newspapers, which began to spread
in China around that time. Then as now, people used these new goods
to communicate to the world who they were. Of course, the possessions that define a Chinese person as prosperous have changed dramatically over time. In the early twentieth century, electric fans, lightbulbs,
and even something as basic as a Western-style bowler hat set one
apart. During the Maoist era, Chinese consumers sought four functional status symbols: bicycles, watches, sewing machines, and radios,

known as "the four things that go 'round." As expectations rose in the 1980s, Chinese hoped to purchase "six big things": videocassette recorders, televisions, washing machines, cameras, refrigerators, and electric fans. By 2000, consumers desired even more expensive items, with air-conditioning units becoming the most sought after product by consumers in the country's eleven largest cities. Demand also rose for personal computers, mobile phones, color televisions, microwave ovens, and video equipment. In the countryside, motorcycles topped the shopping lists of ten million Chinese as motorized vehicles increasingly replaced human- or animal-powered transport such as bicycles and donkey carts. Since then, modern Chinese consumer desire has expanded to the consumption of experiences, such as education, leisure travel, and cultural events such as the Beijing Olympics.

Today as many as a third of the population, or 430 million Chinese, could be classified as middle class (the core consumer class), which is defined as any household with at least six of such electronic products as TVs, refrigerators, washing machines, telephones, mobile phones, stereos, DVD players, air-conditioners, and microwaves. By another measure, about 13 percent of China's population, more than 150 million people, can afford to own some luxury goods such as designer clothes, expensive handbags, and brand-name watches. That's a lot of people at the grassroots level—and not just politicians and business leaders—with a vested interest in the new economic and social order of consumerism and the politics that promote it.

Yet *consumerism* implies more than the increased purchasing of more goods. It refers as well to the orientation of social life around consumer products and services, to the entrenchment of consumerism into the everyday life of a society in which one converses and communicates with others through things bought in markets (where "Would you like a Coke?" replaces "Would you like a sugar water?"). In a consumer culture, individuals define themselves not only through their ancestry, accent, job, hometown, or religious affiliation but also through things—the way driving a gas-guzzling Hummer conveys something different about a person from owning a fuel-efficient Prius does. Consumerism thus refers to the ways individuals, groups, and nations have increasingly come to define their identities through the consumption of mass-produced and mass-discussed goods and services.

Consumer culture changes the ways we experience the world. Once you have had your hair styled in a clean, air-conditioned salon by a trained and courteous professional, it becomes harder to imagine returning to the state-owned barbershops. Likewise, once you are accustomed to using a private bathroom in the comfort of your own home rather than a shared neighborhood public toilet, it is hard to go back to squatting next to your neighbors. As a twenty-five-year-old woman from Nanchang recounted, "I used a public toilet when I was a child. At that time everybody did because we didn't have a private one in our home. I can't imagine going back to the time when tens of households had to share the same restroom; it would be too inconvenient and too embarrassing."

As China Goes . . .

Before consumers can appreciate an advertisement contrasting Coke versus Pepsi and learn to prefer one to the other, they need to learn to desire Coke or Pepsi rather than water or tea. On April 15, 1981, at the official opening of Coca-Cola's first bottling plant in China since the Communist Revolution in 1949, company chairman Roberto C. Goizueta claimed that date might well "be one of the most important days in the history of our company, and, in more ways than one, in the history of the world." We may be tempted to dismiss this claim as the boast of a world-class marketer. But the return of Coke to China symbolized the endorsement of unabashed consumerism in the largest nation on earth. Now nearly all the key issues facing China, and to some extent the planet, revolve around Chinese consumers, from the political legitimacy of the Communist Party to the radical transformation of the everyday lives of a fifth of the world's population, from the health of the global economy to the environmental welfare of the planet.

To promote consumerism, China's leaders must continue their remarkable shift away from an obsession with state-controlled production and an export-led growth model that depends on overseas consumers. In its place, they must enact policies that allow—and even prod—consumers to drive the economy. Clearly its earlier emphasis on production served China well, as confirmed by even a cursory inspection of the products surrounding everyone in countries that have been consuming cheap Chinese goods for decades. But it's now obvious that the world has at least as much reason to care about Chinese consumption as about Chinese production. Even if Chinese consumers manage to spend enough to rescue the world economy, what are the global implications of the Chinese driving more cars, eating more beef, and going on more vacations? And what are the political implications of growing economic inequality, corruption, and new consumer activism? The changes described in this book, good and bad, are already well under way. Millions of Chinese *have* gone from poor to middle class; the Chinese *do* have access to a broader range of goods, conveniences, and experiences than ever before—benefits that have improved their lives in innumerable ways and that consumers in developed nations have long taken for granted. At the same time, China *is* already the largest greenhouse gas emitter; new Chinese diets *are* endangering species; fake Chinese drugs and airplane components *are* sold around the world; Chinese companies, backed by their powerful government, *are* starting to buy out or challenge established global brands, renewing and deepening the world's commitment to consumerism.

The consequences, intended and unintended, of this transformation in China are changing the world in significant but often unidentified ways. What is certain is that China's future and the future of the world will be profoundly shaped by China's rush toward consumerism. As the following chapters show, as China goes, so goes the world.

1 ★ NO GOING BACK?

China Creates a Car Culture and Economy

Today's China sounds different. Back when I arrived in Nanjing for my junior year in college in 1986, one of the first things that struck me was the absence of car noise, signaling, of course, the absence of cars. As I rode the Communist-era bus from the airport, aside from the growl of its engine and the tooting horns of a handful of trucks and cars, the air was instead full of the ringing of bicycle bells and the whirring of their wheels.

Determined to hit the ground running, the next morning, as the other students slept, I got up early to change money, finding my way to the brand-new luxury hotel towering over the heart of the city. Built to comfortably house foreign businesspeople, the hotel did not admit Chinese. That morning a dozen stood at its entrance simply gawking at their city's first high-rise. I marched right in, along with a group of Chinese teenagers sporting Nikes; only much later did I learn that the hotel guards identified overseas Chinese and allowed them entry by looking at their shoes—most local Chinese were still wearing either cloth or inexpensive leather. After changing money, I set off by bus across town to the Friendship Store, where foreigners, and Chinese with a special currency, could buy Chinese trinkets and hard-to-find imported items. The bus chugged along as an ocean of bicycles as far as the eye could see floated past, carrying an army of Chinese pedaling their way to work and weaving back and forth in front of the bus as if to assert the self-evident fact that the road was theirs.

Safely delivered to the store, I browsed a little and selected a bike. Its most distinguishing feature was the lack of any—namely, it looked like a shinier version of the thousands of bicycles I had already seen on China's roads, and so seemed to promise that it would carry me around this new and exciting city. But to my surprise, the store clerk wouldn't allow me to buy it. I had assumed that all I needed to buy something was enough of the right kind of money. I had had only a year of college Chinese, barely enough to correctly pronounce the tones of my Chinese name (Ge Kai, two characters pronounced with tones that each rise and fall), so it was hard to follow what the problem was, but I eventually figured out that I needed a ration coupon from my employer, or "work unit." The store workers (they could hardly be called "salespeople," as they did not seem very interested in selling anything) realized the absurdity of the situation, but it took some lengthy deliberations and a few phone calls, for reasons still unclear to me, before I could buy the bike.

I rode off triumphantly back toward campus, anxious to share my victory with my American classmates (who were later taken en masse to the same store, where they bought bicycles without incident). Along the way home, though, the bicycle began to disintegrate, as parts started to come loose, and finally, as I rounded a corner, the bell fell off and tumbled down the street. I later learned that new Chinese bikes only *looked* assembled. Every part required additional tightening and, as one Chinese friend told me, a good rainstorm to rust the parts together. Chinese bicycles were notoriously poorly built and required constant maintenance. The following semester, when I was studying at Beijing University, one student taught me a local expression: "Every part of a bike makes noise except the bell."

What made the joke work, of course, was the fact that in 1986 you could still hear bicycles. Today, they are overwhelmingly drowned out by the rumble of car engines. The change was so abrupt—in less than ten years—that the brains of those familiar with China before its rapid embrace of a car culture still haven't quite adjusted to the difference in sounds. In fact, a distinguishing feature of China's embrace of consumerism is its headlong nature—what Western consumers took decades or a century or so to adopt, Chinese are managing in mere years. By any measure, the accomplishment is impressive. It also defies controls and begets consequences that beget yet more consequences. I treasured my bicycle because it gave me mobility without the need to rely on the slow and extremely crowded buses. (To this day, after my experiences pushing my way onto China's overcrowded buses, I still see an elevator as always having room for one more.) My bicycle allowed me to explore the city and to do so relatively safely, as there were very few private cars, and the noisy, slow-moving buses posed little threat. Getting a taxi was expensive and difficult—you had to order one or find a queue at a hotel for foreigners. That was in 1986. Jump forward two decades. Today cabs are so common I grow impatient if I have to wait more than a few minutes to hail one. Those cities that once hummed with the sound of tiny bicycle bells now roar with the sound of endless cars pushing through ever-heavier traffic to hotels where even the locals can enjoy the luxury of plush lobbies and feather beds.

This change is what makes the story of the car in China so important. In the early 1980s, China had only one car or truck for every 1,200 of its 800 million people; for local transportation, the vast majority of Chinese relied on bicycles. Indeed, the bicycle—the manufactured product most closely associated with Mao's China—had served as an iconic image of China for over half a century. While the decade that followed my first visit to China saw a steady increase in the number of motor vehicles on those once blissfully quiet roads, at the end of the

1990s China's car industry went into overdrive, and within a decade China overtook the United States as the world's largest market for cars and also one of the world's largest manufacturers of cars. This was no accident, nor a mere "correction" in the market, but the result of deliberate policies.

Why did China's leaders elect to build a car industry and culture almost overnight, thereby making their economy and society—like ours in the industrialized world—highly dependent on cars? Consider that Chinese grade-school students in the mid-1990s were still being taught the dangers of an American-style car culture; state-approved textbooks told them that America's car culture was unsafe, polluting, and wasteful of natural resources. At the same time, the country's top scientists were advising against going down this route. They cited the inevitable accompanying need to import massive amounts of oil and the country's resulting loss of energy independence and urged the government to develop a massive public transportation network instead. Nobody can argue that China didn't understand the downside to embracing cars, but the perceived upside was more compelling. To grow and to compete in world markets on terms partially dictated by others, China decided to embrace cars and encourage its population to desire and buy them.

As with its decision to embrace consumerism itself, Chinese leaders didn't think they had a choice. China decided to join the World Trade Organization in the mid-1990s to gain expanded access to global markets for its exports, a decision that required the country to play by WTO rules and relinquish some control over its own markets. The race was on. Before imports stormed into the previously protected market once full membership took effect in 2001, the country's leaders recognized that they had less than a decade either to quickly develop a domestic car industry or to surrender the domestic market to foreign companies, perhaps permanently. China wanted to introduce cars on its own terms—namely, it wanted to have a domestic car industry rather than ceding a key industry to foreigners. To develop its domestic car industry in time, it would have to ease barriers on imports just enough to create an internationally competitive car market and entice foreign investment and technology from global car manufacturers. Efforts to create domestic demand worked. The resulting price cuts, access to world-class car models, and easier credit from state-owned banks quickly led to soaring demand on the part of Chinese consumers, most of whom just a few years earlier had never dreamed of riding in any car, let alone one of their own. That soaring demand soon made China the world's largest car market, surpassing the United States in 2009. In one of countless estimates regarding China that proved to be *under* rather than over expectations, the rise of the Chinese car market to world supremacy occurred six years ahead of earlier projections. The strategy also created a massive domestic car industry, with the country manufacturing some ten million cars a year, contributing to a global car glut that threatens to bankrupt its American competitors. As in the United States, the Chinese government and, of course, car manufacturers now practically beg citizens who two decades earlier could only aspire to own their own bikes to desire and buy cars, regardless of the environmental and geopolitical consequences.

No aspect of China's consumer revolution occurs in isolation. The emergence of a vast market for cars is simply a part of many simultaneous and reinforcing changes, each change having its own far-reaching effects. The Chinese state itself is behind many of the changes promoting car use. Until the late 1990s, most urban residents worked in state-owned factories and lived in company-owned housing nearby, meaning they could easily walk, ride a bike, or take public transportation from home to work and back. But as increasing numbers of state-owned enterprises were closed and others relocated to the suburbs, workplaces became less accessible and a new commuter culture emerged. In place of mixed-use development, where people live and work in the same neighborhood, city centers across China are being razed and rebuilt into central business districts of gleaming office skyscrapers, pushing affordable housing out to distant suburbs. None of this is occurring without the implicit and explicit support of the state; all of it carries as a consequence the demand for more cars.

Like their counterparts around the world, Chinese consumers now not only want to own cars but also "need" private transport. The country adds an estimated 12,000 to 14,000 cars to its streets every day, for a total of more than 35 million—a number expected to grow to more than 150 million within ten years. In 2006 alone, Chinese consumers purchased 6.8 million vehicles, overtaking Japan as the world's second largest car market, and at the start of 2009, China became the world's largest such market, selling more than 12 million cars annually. In a 2002 survey of families in Beijing, Guangzhou, and Shanghai, 70 percent reported that they planned to buy cars for personal use within five to ten years; in 2005, two fifths of Chinese respondents reported that owning an automobile was their grandest dream.

The successful drive to get the Chinese to buy cars has paved the way for the arrival of such other icons of American-style consumerism as shopping malls on city outskirts, suburban gated communities, leisure homes in the countryside, and weekend holidays. For a country set on stoking domestic consumer demand, all of these are positive developments. Yet the car craze has also led to a number of more troubling and largely unanticipated consequences. These problems are most visible in China's major cities, where the majority of car ownership is concentrated. In 2009, Beijing alone had four million cars traveling its heavily congested roads, triple the number a decade earlier, and even with the continual addition of new and wider roads, the city cannot confiscate land, demolish residential buildings, and build roads fast enough to accommodate them all. These cars spew thirty-six hundred tons of pollutants into Beijing's air every day, making it one of the most polluted cities on the planet, with air pollution five to six times higher than World Health Organization safety standards. Leading up to the Olympics in 2008, Beijing took extraordinary measures to curb this pollution; in a bid to reduce the number of cars by one million, only cars whose license plates ended in an even number were allowed on the road one day, odd-numbered-license-plated cars the next. In 2008 Beijing ranked thirteenth in the table of most polluted cities—behind six other Chinese cities. In Shanghai, where earlier efforts to control its notorious traffic jams and pollution have failed, authorities recently tried to limit car consumption by raising registration fees to nearly $5,000, a sum twice the per capita annual income in the city. There has also been a belated rush to expand the public transportation system with new subways.

But the genie is out of the bottle.

China Builds a Car Culture

The Chinese now desire cars. Just as significantly, China needs its citizens to want cars and has consciously created policies to promote private car ownership. This is a dramatic change. Since its victory in 1949, the Communist Chinese government has pursued a flourishing domestic vehicle industry as a symbol of economic power and self-sufficiency. But until the mid-1990s, "vehicles" were seen as the means to transport necessary goods and troops, not for city dwellers to travel to suburban malls. Mao's government gave no thought to manufacturing cars for private consumers or building roads for the recreation of its citizens. Chinese manufacturers had the technical capacity to make cars for private consumers, but weren't allowed to by the state.

This bias against consumers continued even after the Mao era. At the start of the Reform Era, state-owned Shanghai Automotive decided to seek a joint venture with a foreign partner to manufacture 150,000 cars a year, but it was looking to export the majority of them. During the cold war, China feared attack by the Americans, Russians, or both, so to protect critical industries, it created a highly dispersed motor vehicle industry. No single enemy nuclear strike, it was reasoned, could destroy all the country's modern industry. This policy left 1,950 factories sprinkled across the country and collectively producing some 160,000 vehicles each year. But only a few thousand of these were cars. As late as 1990, passenger vehicles still represented just 8 percent of the 520,000 vehicles produced annually in China, hardly an ideal starting point for creating consumer demand, national brands, or economies of scale.

Eventually the demand for taxis to serve foreign tourists, whom the government began to court as a desirable source of hard currency, drove the introduction of more cars. At first, imports filled this demand, and their numbers grew from just 52 sedans in 1977 to nearly 20,000 by 1980. But by 1984, the anxiety of Chinese officials about squandering precious hard currency on imported consumer goods finally led them to approve a joint venture between Beijing Automotive and American Motors Corporation and to allow, if not yet encourage, private ownership of cars. But the path was not smooth and never quite as advantageous to the U.S. firms as they had imagined; the joint venture to produce the Beijing Jeep is a case study in how China emerged having acquired the new technology it needed at virtually no expense. No matter. The siren song of the size of the Chinese market proved, repeatedly, too hard to resist. Soon joint ventures with other foreign automakers such as GM and Ford followed, and a Chinese automobile industry was finally under way. Yet to stem the outflow of foreign currency, Beijing still tried to limit the availability of consumer goods, particularly imports, by imposing licenses, quotas, and high tariffs on foreign-made vehicles. During the 1990s, for instance, consumers paid a 220 percent tariff on full-size passenger cars, among the highest in the world. At the same time, China's leaders attempted to boost domestic production by forcing multinational car companies to use more domestic parts ("local content") and domestic labor ("value added"). This was the start of the government's drive to promote domestic desire for increasingly domestically produced cars and, eventually, Chinese-owned car brands.

Since then, car production has become an employer of some two million in China and an important engine of economic growth. Although in 1993, China still had only 37,000 private cars, a visual revolution in Chinese cities was under way. A population that was accustomed to seeing very few of the same-looking drab cars on its streets was suddenly exposed to a variety of colorful new models. By the early 1990s, China was producing one million vehicles, including trucks, buses, and passenger vehicles. Cities vied to become China's Detroit, and local politicians actively promoted locally produced cars.

In the Eighth Five-Year Plan published in 1990, the national government designated the automotive industry as a pillar of the economy. To compete with international companies, Beijing consolidated domestic automobile makers into a half-dozen giant conglomerates (called *jituan gongsi* or *jituan qiye,* modeled after Japanese *keiretsu* business groupings and Korean *chaebol*). Each conglomerate had a foreign partner who controlled no more than 50 percent of the new company. The goal was not simply to have the Chinese manufacture cars for GM and other international companies but to create Chinese-owned brands competitive at home and in export markets. And to boost Chinese demand for "Chinese cars," Beijing also pushed banks to lend to private consumers and pressured provincial and local governments to divert public transport funds into building roads.

In addition, the government finally recognized that domestic production required domestic demand. Its most significant change in policy was the decision to encourage domestic private ownership. The promise of a huge Chinese market for cars lured some $60 billion in Chinese and foreign capital into automotive production—sixty times what the partnering U.S. companies had invested over the previous four decades. In 2000, the decision to promote private ownership was, for the first time, explicitly included in the proposals for the Tenth Five-Year Plan.

The desire to own a car now permeates Chinese life. As a leading academic authority on cars in China, Li Anding, put it, "The desire for cars here is as strong as in America, but here the desire was repressed for half a century." Until the late 1990s, government ministries purchased some 80 percent of all passenger cars sold in China, and nearly all the rest were bought by private enterprises and foreign companies; individuals accounted for only 1 percent of sales. But by 2000, 30 percent of the 600,000 passenger cars sold in China were bought by individual consumers, a percentage that doubled by the end of the decade. The rise of this new consumer market pushed manufacturers to start catering to consumers' tastes for a broader range of models, colors, and features. Like car owners elsewhere, the Chinese see their vehicles as symbols of personal success and view driving as a right. When pressed to explain their desire for cars, Chinese consumers offer up the same reasons as consumers around the globe: status, independence, and privacy. And, increasingly, they consider Chinese cars a source of collective national pride and patriotism. Models such as the poetically named Chang'an Zhi Xiang Hatch ("the Will to Soar") reflect a new energy and aspiration among Chinese consumers. Companies such as Chery Automobile are producing their own models, though often through reverse-engineered carbon copies of their foreign competitors. Its QQ model is similar to the Daewoo Matiz/Chevrolet

Spark mini car, for instance, and the Oriental Son, a midsize sedan, is a reworking of the Daewoo Magnus.

How Car Culture Is Changing China

As China's citizens have come to equate car ownership with personal freedom, prestige, and success, the social pressure to possess a car has become increasingly difficult to resist. A prominent Shanghai historian recently told me that although he can afford a car, for environmental reasons he has made the principled decision to instead take public transportation. All well and good, except that his apartment complex comes with an allotted parking space, which of course stands empty, prompting his friends and neighbors to begin asking uncomfortable questions about his financial well-being.

As the Chinese have become more automobile savvy, not just the fact of owning a car but one's car's price and appearance have become new ways to determine an owner's social status. As one popular saying has it, "if you want to know a man's tastes, you just need to look at his watch and car." According to a GM spokesperson in Shanghai, the car's actual performance is often less important to Chinese consumers than features such as video displays on seatbacks, wooden fittings, and leather upholstery that their friends and family can readily see. And German car manufacturers add length to their models to appeal to Chinese consumers. At one end of the status scale, owners of inexpensive cars tell stories of being ridiculed and denied valet parking; at the other, luxury models have become a handy way for kidnappers to identify potential upper-class victims. (In Guangdong province, for instance, one gang used state vehicle registration rolls to target BMW owners.)

Along with desiring and driving cars, traffic jams are another new experience for Chinese consumers, as increasing numbers of them trade the slow, plodding, but dependable bicycle or public transport for the uncertain, traffic-dependent progress of the car. It is not unusual to sit in a queue for an hour to make a left turn just so you can zip across the city on an elevated highway. But no one is getting anywhere as fast as they once did. A decade ago, for instance, the average speed on Beijing's Third Ring Road was forty-five kilometers per hour. It's presently twenty, and often as slow as seven at busy intersections. Private automobiles, in other words, bring mobility in principle but uncertainty in practice.

At the same time, it may be difficult for most Westerners to appreciate the extent to which private automobiles represent a new era of mobility for Chinese consumers. Until the 1990s, travel within China was highly restricted. A Chinese traveler needed a letter from his or her work unit to buy a plane ticket, a comfortable seat on a train, or a room in one of the few decent hotels. For those with enough money, the personal car, of course, pushes against all such strictures and consequently has become a powerful symbol of individual freedom and status, despite the difficulties of urban traffic jams.

Cars have also transformed the experience of walking in China's cities. Western pedestrians are by now well familiar with the kinds of signals, barriers, and conventions necessary to coexist with speeding urban traffic. In China, however, the requirement that one cross streets within set times and at specific locations as determined by traffic lights is new, and pedestrians and drivers alike routinely ignore the rules. The Chinese media, evoking speed and efficiency as measures of modernity, have begun accusing pedestrians of bad manners by crossing streets too slowly. Raising the complaint to a question of national character, they observe that the Chinese take longer to cross a street than their counterparts abroad. (This is not unique to China. Korean media have carried similar stories, contrasting the relative chaos of Korean queues and traffic with those of the highly disciplined Japanese.)

Chinese pedestrians, the accusation runs, tend to watch cars rather than signals and, when they grow impatient with lights timed to facilitate vehicle flow, attempt to cross the street anyway. One local TV station ran videotapes of pedestrians who ignored signals and even stopped to chat with friends in the middle of the road.

Concern over breaking in pedestrians to the new rules of the road underscores the obvious: cars bring danger as well as mobility. Collisions between pedestrians and bicycles or even donkey carts were rarely fatal, but not so with cars. The death rate on China's roads is one of the highest in the world, even though it has started trending downward. In 2007, it dropped to 90,000 fatalities for the year, and dropped again in 2008 to 73,000; before that, however, somewhere between 100,000 and 200,000 people died each year in fatal car crashes. On average, 680 Chinese died and 45,000 were injured due to car accidents every day during the first five years of the twenty-first century. By comparison, the United States, which is much more heavily motorized, saw 115 deaths a day; Britain, fewer than 10. Most of China's automobile accidents occur outside cities, where rural pedestrians and cyclists must battle with cars, buses, and trucks for space on older, narrower roads. The effects are also unequally distributed by class: in collisions between bicycles and cars, the cyclist is much more likely to die or be injured than the driver, and the wealthy can afford safer and more dependable cars. Paradoxically, perhaps, the increased risk of death has likewise increased the demand for automobiles. Just as many Americans switched to more expensive and fuel-hungry SUVs because they perceived them as safer, many Chinese (even the reluctant historian alluded to earlier) see cars as dangerous but safer than walking or riding a bicycle.

Cars are also becoming the focus of middle-class leisure activities. Shanghai, in addition to pouring billions of dollars into creating a car industry in the new "International Automobile City" in its Jiading District, has also built a car culture center replete with the country's first Formula One racetrack. In 2004, when the $320 million state-of-the-art facility opened its 5.4-kilometer track, 150,000 people attended the first race, paying at least 1,800 yuan each. The Chinese state and private investors have funded not only Jiading's research, development, and production facilities but the racetrack and an adjacent $50 million car museum to encourage consumer celebration of the car as an accoutrement to leisure. Their aim, according to one official, is to build in three years what "took Detroit a hundred."

Newsstands across China are stocked with dozens of glossy car magazines. A 500-car, six-screen, American-style drive-in movie theater opened on the outskirts of Beijing in 1998. The archetypical car-related leisure business, drive-through dining, has also appeared in China. The first McDonald's drive-through restaurant, in the central business district of Dongguan, Guangdong, features an enormous, fifty-space parking lot. Seeing the drive-through as "the next generation of McDonald's restaurants in China," the chain has opened ninety in Shanghai, Beijing, Tianjin, Guangzhou, Shenzhen, and dozens of other cities and is considering an alliance with Sinopec, which runs 30,000 gas stations throughout China. Chinese consumer culture is quickly catching up with international "best practices."

Another odd import, the vanity license plate, has melded with Chinese superstitions, proving that Chinese markets are more finely tuned for many things than in other countries, especially when it comes to numbers. When Chinese buy a new phone, for instance, they aren't randomly assigned a number as they are in the U.K. and the United States, but rather buy a specific number, which can range in price from a few to thousands of dollars. The luckier the number (such as eight, which sounds like the word for "become wealthy"), the higher the price; unlucky numbers (especially four, which sounds like the word for "death") command lower prices. A Chinese regional airline, for instance, paid

$300,000 for the phone number 8888-8888. When a southern Chinese city auctioned off license plates with lucky numbers, the highest, AC6688, sold for $10,000; the auction raked in $366,500. A secondary market for desirable plate numbers has also emerged; one enterprising man in the southern city of Hangzhou, for instance, offered to sell his plate number, A88888, for $140,000. (This culture of license plate numbers has led some consumers to go to extremes. Parents, for instance, have reportedly refused to allow their children to take taxis with unlucky license plates to their college entrance exams.) This market for automobile plates reflects not only superstition but conspicuous consumption; those with several eights inform onlookers that the owner is wealthy.

Car clubs have sprung up throughout China. Beijing alone has over a hundred, primarily organized around travel, such as touring, but also around maintenance and dating. These clubs are run by car dealers, owners of specific models, or even travel agencies. The largest touring club in China is affiliated with the Beijing traffic radio station FM 103.9 and offers the usual assortment of services, such as group insurance rates and, within the city, emergency roadside service. Their primary mission is to organize the popular "self-driving tours" in which groups of car owners drive in convoys, with places to eat and sleep arranged in advance. Clubs will even take their own mechanic along. Other car clubs create their own subcultures around brands, such as the Beijing VW Polo Club; the wedding of one member even included a procession of thirty-two of these super-mini cars through the streets of Beijing.

The ripple effects of the advent of China's car culture have ironically recast that onetime icon of Chinese basic transportation, the bicycle. As car traffic, and in some cities outright bans on bicycle riding, have led many Chinese to abandon bikes, the new middle class is starting to embrace cycling as a leisure exercise. Once, bikes were prized, difficult-to-obtain family possessions; now China produces seventy million bicycles a year and more than a thousand brands. Although tradi-tional brands such as the Tianjin-based Flying Pigeon (Feige) and the Shanghai-based Phoenix (Fenghuang) and Forever (Yongjiu) remain popular, particularly with older consumers, younger cyclists prefer the fashionable, lighter Taiwan-based Giant, the number-one brand in the country. The types of bikes now for sale in China reflect all the major transnational bicycling trends: mountain bikes, road cycling, and bi-cycle motocross, known as BMX. Bicycles now convey status among teenagers in a way that mirrors that which cars impart to their parents. As one thirteen-year-old boy admitted, "I was heartsick and envious at the sight of my classmates on their stylish bicycles, but my parents wouldn't buy me a new one until I promised to get better grades." The competition at one middle school in Shanxi province got bad enough that the school prohibited students from riding bikes costing more than 300 yuan to campus.

How Chinese Car Culture Is Transforming the World

China's production of cars for its domestic consumption is also fueling a boom in car use around the planet. Chinese automobile manufac-turers excel at producing cheap "gateway cars," cars for first-time buy-ers. In 2007, Chinese automakers built 8.8 million cars, and by the end of 2010, Chinese automakers expect to sell 10 percent of their production to the international market. If this persists, China may do for the car industry what it did for other consumer goods such as plas-tic lawn chairs and electronics: greatly reduce their entry-level price and make them ubiquitous across the globe. Certainly, the Chinese state is actively promoting the exportation and international consump-tion of Chinese cars. Even as the government backed away from extending easy credit for domestic car purchases starting in 2004—

spurred on by fears that state-owned banks were overexposed to bad loans—China's Ministry of Commerce adopted measures such as financial and export credits to encourage Chinese automakers to export vehicles with Chinese brand names to the international market, where automobile sales make up a tenth of the world's total trade volume. Chinese companies such as Geely, Chery, and Lifan not only compete with foreign brands domestically but sell their cars in Africa and other developing markets, and recently made international news with their decision to aim for the European and American markets. And if Americans prove hesitant to embrace Chinese brands, there is always the expediency of buying a brand Americans already buy, as they tried to for the first time with the purchase of GM's Hummer truck unit by Sichuan Tengzhou, a previously unknown Chinese heavy industrial company.

The state-supported development of the Chinese auto industry has led to massive overcapacity (a capacity that may reach 10 million units per year by 2010) and a consequent intensifying pressure to promote exports. In 2005, China for the first time exported more automobiles (170,000) than it imported. If this trend continues, Chinese cars may transform consumer consciousness around the world, including in established auto markets such as the United States and Europe. China's brands may enter American consciousness in the same way that Japan's Toyota, Honda, Lexus, and Mazda and Korea's Hyundai and Daewoo did. Chinese-branded cars and trucks have already entered more than 170 countries, up from only a few dozen in 2000.

There are many Chinese contenders. The next Asian car brand to enter popular Western consciousness may be Qirui (Chery), which has ambitious export plans and a bold track record. Chery initially succeeded with its QQ, which apes the Daewoo-GM car the Chevrolet Spark. Chery's QQ, which went on sale in 2003, beat GM to the market and undersold the Spark by a fourth. At just $7,000, it gained a place in the low-end market, making cars affordable to many more consumers. By 2005, Chery was exporting nearly twenty thousand cars and has ambitious plans for expansion into Middle Eastern and Russian markets. While its initial flirtation with the American market hasn't been reciprocated, it won't be the only such overture.

Chery is a state-owned company with self-proclaimed plans that reflect China's national mission to own and export world-class brands. A sign at the entrance of the QQ assembly plant reads: "We Need Not Only to Work Hard, We Must Also Be Diligent, and More Important We Must Have a Sense of a National Mission." That mission, shared by other Chinese automakers such as Great Wall and Geely, includes exporting cars in large numbers. Although the auto industry is not a zero-sum game, it's close. The ascendancy of Chinese brands means the decline of someone else's, first in China and then around the world, including in the United States.

The spread of car culture to China, and from there outward to the rest of the world, confirms a key argument of this book: Chinese consumers are becoming the new vanguards of global consumerism. Because of the size and growth rate of the Chinese automobile market, all the leading international manufacturers are designing cars specifically for the China market. In just a few decades, Chinese consumers have gone from settling for older technologies and weaker brands to becoming a proving ground for the latest brands and technologies. For instance, in honor of the sixtieth anniversary of the founding of the People's Republic of China, which fell on October 1, 2009, BMW rolled out a special edition of its ultra-luxurious, twelve-cylinder turbo sedan. And when Volkswagen decided to export its first gasoline-electric hybrid vehicle, it decided to do so in China, not the United States. Chinese consumer choices may soon determine the car options available around the world.

Even as the car culture creates new industries and jobs in China, it is also consuming massive quantities of oil, in the process transforming China's foreign relationships. Private cars now consume a third of all oil imports in China, and surging car use is pushing up that demand. Already China accounts for roughly 12 percent of the world's demand for energy, and its consumption is growing at more than four times the global rate. By the early 1990s, China had lost its energy independence and needed to import a majority of its crude oil, a whopping $130 billion in oil in 2008. This demand has huge international implications as China competes around the globe with other advanced economies, most notably the United States, to buy and control nonrenewable resources. Consequently, Americans, Europeans, Japanese, and everyone else who relies on oil imports to meet their energy needs are paying more.

As with many other countries before them, China's reliance on oil has forced its government into unsavory international relationships. On the eve of the Beijing Olympics, for instance, China was importing 6 percent of its oil from Sudan, accounting for 60 percent of that country's exports. These purchases were highly controversial. International human rights campaigners argued that Chinese oil purchases were directly underwriting genocide in the Darfur region, and rebranded the games the "Genocide Olympics." The point isn't that the West has been able to avoid the same compromised relationships, but instead that Chinese consumer demand for cars, and energy more broadly, directly strengthens the hands of anyone sitting atop oil reserves.

This car culture is also gobbling up China's valuable agricultural land. Perhaps the most economically unfair impact of China's embrace of cars is its effect on food prices. Poor people around the world are paying more for food because of cars. Cars are driving this increase not only by competing for crops to produce biofuels but also by swallowing up millions of acres of cropland for roads and parking lots. As Lester Brown, founder of the Earth Policy Institute, observes, "There's no such thing as free parking." Countries such as China and

India that have only begun to embrace the car have likewise only begun to pave over their lands. As asphalt becomes China's number one crop, the world's poor—and everyone else—will pay more for food.

But they are paving, nonetheless. Twenty years ago, my classmates at Nanjing University and I headed out for a field trip to the historic city of Yangzhou. As the bus made its bumpy way out of the city while dodging chickens, bicycles, tractors, and donkey carts, I remember wondering how long we would have to endure the ill-kept local roads before reaching the highway. But we never got on a highway—there were virtually none then. Now China is devoting billions of private and state dollars to building roadways. China's first modern expressway, a tollway linking Guangzhou and Shenzhen, was built by Hong Kong tycoon Gordon Y. S. Wu in the 1990s. Between 2000 and 2004, the country doubled the length of its motorways to 34,000 kilometers (21,000 miles) and has the third most roads in the world—44 percent of them built since 1990. Nor will it stop there: China plans to double again the length of its motorways by 2020.

China's leaders, however, are aware of the myriad and often unwanted consequences of encouraging a desire for cars. Indeed, they have taken steps to slow China's growing dependence on imported oil even as they have continued to encourage the development of a car culture. In 2005, China imposed new fuel economy standards for cars and trucks that are far more stringent than those of the United States. The following year, the central government began promoting smaller, lower-carbon-emitting cars, calling on eighty-four cities across the nation to repeal bans on small cars (originally intended to limit noise and air pollution, reduce fatalities, and remove unattractive vehicles from the streets). They also took other regulatory measures such as lowering parking fees for smaller cars and allowing their use as taxis. Cities such as Beijing, where 10 percent of households owned cars by 2005, are going even further by capping the number of license plates issued each month.

And the government, recognizing the unanticipated implications of having supported cars over public transportation, is finally spending billions to improve public transportation in the big cities. By 2008, Beijing had 200 kilometers of underground track for its subways, doubling their length in just three years. Shanghai expanded its underground railway from 80 to more than 420 kilometers in 2010, when the city hosted the World Expo; by 2020, the plan is to have 810 kilometers, twice the length of London's subway system.

Beijing officials, facing rising pollution along with the increase in car ownership, also periodically make gestures to fight for the ever fewer number of "blue sky days" in the city, which had fallen to only fifty-six in 2006, down sixteen days from 2005. Under pressure to live up to its promise to hold a Green Olympics, Beijing tried instituting "Car-Free Days," modeled on a program begun by thirty-four French cities, to alleviate pollution and traffic jams. Beginning in June 2006, more than a quarter million Beijing residents agreed to avoid driving their cars to work once a month; the gesture, however, had no discernible effect on air quality or traffic jams. On the other hand, a new regulation allowing cars into the city only on alternating days, based on odd and even license plate numbers, led to the creation of carpooling arrangements by drivers with complementary plate numbers. Indeed, the practice has expanded beyond sharing rides to work to sharing rides to school and even vacation travel.

In the spring of 2006, the Chinese government also tried to dampen the demand for passenger cars and imported oil by imposing a luxury tax on cars with larger engines, which included nearly all imported cars. Yet the new tax failed to slow the shift in the market toward American-style larger, less efficient cars, in part because a growing production glut has kept prices low, and in part because people will pay more for status. For instance, the price of Shanghai VW's most popular model, the Santana, dropped from 124,000 yuan in 2001 to 76,000 yuan in 2005.

More so than their Western counterparts, China's leaders were deliberate about this transition to the automobile. They also knew they faced a choice, though arguably a poor one. Thirty years ago, in the spring of 1979, the American magazine *Mother Jones* ran an article about China titled "The First Post-Oil Society?" The article predicted that "the likelihood that Shanghai will become the Detroit of the Far East seems, at this point, remote." If an industrializing China continued to have a mere 100,000 cars in the entire country, China could create "the world's first post-petroleum culture." However laughable now, those expectations also remind us that there once were compelling reasons to think China might travel a different route than its neighbors and the West. But today China is finding itself trapped by the same economics and politics that have made changes in transportation policy difficult in the United States and Europe. Far from saving the world, Chinese car buyers by the millions are committing their country to a problematic developmental path.

China's centralized state has proven remarkably good at certain things. As planned, the automobile industry has become a major part of the Chinese economy, employing several million people and bringing in large tax revenues in Beijing and Shanghai. The success of the auto industry also offers the possibility of increasing Chinese exports and trade surpluses with leading Western nations. All of these were consequences sought when China set out to create a domestic car market. But whereas a factory can be opened or closed, taxes and tariffs imposed or lifted, the unleashed hopes and dreams of the consumer—without whom the launch of any new market is a nonstarter—are not so readily restrained. Perhaps the most important consequence of

China's embrace of a car culture is that car ownership has now become part of the Chinese middle-class dream. Reining that in has now become all but impossible.

Like the United States and the European Union, China, too, is trying to have it both ways—promoting a car-dependent culture and economy while blunting its inevitable negative consequences. Indeed, China is doing more than the United States to mitigate the consequences of cars. At forty-three miles per gallon, for instance, China's minimum fuel efficiency standards are now already higher than the U.S. standard of thirty-five miles per gallon, which will not even go into effect until 2020. Likewise, Chinese manufacturers are racing with other world car manufacturers to produce electric, low-carbon-emitting cars. They have already introduced China-made plug-in hybrids into the market in their own country and should have them in the United States shortly; fully electric cars are coming. But in a country where coal-powered plants produce almost 70 percent of the electricity, clearly resolving the fundamental contradiction between cars and the unfolding environmental calamity described in Chapter 8 will take more than simply replacing the tens of millions of new petro-powered cars with electric vehicles. The world now needs to ask of China what it has consistently failed to do itself: embrace cars without producing negative consequences.

2 ★ WHO GETS WHAT?

The Creation and Implications of China's New Aristocracy

Back while I was a university student in Beijing in the mid-1980s, I traveled with a Chinese classmate to his hometown, a dusty coal mining city in northwest China. His family worked for the railway, and so his wearing a rail worker's jacket and flashing an ID meant we rode overnight for free. There we visited his girlfriend, the daughter of the city's Communist Party secretary. I had expected the family of the highest Communist Party official in town to live lavishly. But the only apparent benefits of the secretary's position were a slightly larger apartment in a new building plus a car and driver. The black sedan, from whose windows I was given a tour of the historic city, was a particularly nice perk. As the party secretary's driver drove in the middle of the road, gigantic trucks overflowing with coal hastily moved out of our way. Although power had its advantages, they were modest.

Since the shift to a market economy, however, this has changed radically. Ever greater numbers of Chinese are living lavishly, and publicly so. Now government officials can directly—or indirectly via their friends, family, and even mistresses—convert political power into wealth and live much more comfortable lives. In contrast to the Mao-era revolutionary ideology of equality, in which displays of wealth were at times deemed crimes against the state, the accelerating economic reforms of the past three decades have produced a new class of rich Chinese, and with it an increasing demand for luxury products. Unlike the ranks of the rich in America and Europe, most of the wealthiest Chinese are not rags-to-riches entrepreneurs or the beneficiaries of inherited wealth, but rather political insiders who have peddled their influence to gain new affluence. While the desire for consumer goods has rapidly grown among all Chinese as economic reforms help millions escape poverty and many move into the middle class, the rise of what the Chinese call their "new rich" (*xin fu*) and "new aristocracy" (*xin gui*) has led to both envy and resentment. As a thirty-two-year-old middle-class man put it, "The first barrel of gold of most rich people could never survive serious scrutiny." The growing inequality in income and consumption that has accompanied the emergence of these new mandarins may prove to have serious consequences for China's future, even as it reflects the vast and rapid changes wrought by the economic reforms of the last three decades.

Lifestyles of the Rich and Infamous

Despite their origins, China's wealthy have become larger-than-life symbols of the consumer lifestyles now being encouraged by the Chinese government. For many middle-class Chinese consumers, they also serve as the lodestar of their own ambitions. China's new wealthy have become the focus of many television shows and magazines, the popular cultural equivalents of the 1980s American television show *Lifestyles of the Rich and Famous*. As a twenty-six-year-old woman from Sichuan explained to me, "I watch the Travel Channel a lot. There are a bunch of TV shows about the lifestyles of the upper class. Someday I want to be as rich as they are. Then I can eat French dinners, wear Chanel perfume, carry Louis Vuitton handbags, and travel anywhere in the world, like those rich people do. How great would that be!" Despite popular opinion that blames the wealthy for enriching themselves at the expense of the many, often through illegal activities, her sentiment is as ubiquitous as the automobile now displacing China's bicycles.

As a consequence, in less than a decade China has gone from an almost insignificant consumer to a key consumer of global luxury brands. Wealthy Chinese are at the forefront of a new society and economy dependent on cars, tourism, meat-based diets, and other forms of consumption that were once prohibited or at least tightly regulated. The pace of this transformation has been stunning. Even twenty years into the Reform Era, mainland Chinese buyers accounted for a mere 1 percent of global sales of luxury handbags, shoes, jewelry, and perfume. But by 2005, the Chinese had become the world's third biggest buyers of such goods, with more than 12 percent of global sales, well behind Japan (41 percent) but gaining on the United States (17 percent); by one prediction, in 2015, China will overtake Japan and become the top market for luxury goods. By 2005, Chinese tourists had also become the biggest spenders of all nationalities, averaging nearly $1,000 on shopping per trip abroad and nearly double that amount when shopping in Europe. Such statistics have led global luxury producers to see Chinese shoppers as the successors to the free-spending Japanese of the 1980s and to overextended U.S. and European consumers.

The Chinese consuming classes have become increasingly status-conscious. Take, for example, the fact that by 2003, China had become the world's largest consumer of the world's most expensive car, a 728 Bentley stretch limo, with a $1.2 million price tag; Cadillac is opening forty showrooms in China. Chinese yuppies, dubbed Chuppies by some, also bought 23,600 BMWs in 2005, up 50 percent over the previous year. In short, China has become the world's largest consumer of luxury cars, with more than 5 million potential luxury car buyers.

As those car sales indicate, China's luxury market is booming. Since the economic reforms, the country has spawned nearly a million millionaires. Yang Qingshan, secretary-general of the China Brand Strategy Association, estimates that 13 percent of the Chinese, or 170 million people, can afford luxury items—a number that has been growing at 12 percent a year. The *China Daily* estimated that by 2010, as many as 250 million Chinese would be able to afford luxury goods. For obvious reasons, purveyors of the world's most famous luxury brands are flocking to China. As late as 1992, China had few places outside of five-star hotels to buy luxury brands. Now malls carry the latest in Louis Vuitton, Calvin Klein, Armani, Prada, and Omega products. By 2005, ninety pairs of Lotos sunglasses, each costing between $100,000 and $600,000, were spotted in a Wangfujing shop in the center of Beijing. International luxury brands are opening scores of stores in dozens of cities across China, including even grittier cities such as Shenyang in northeastern Liaoning province. The French luxury jeweler and watchmaker Cartier has thirty stores in China, a footprint second only to that in the United States. Even the U.S.-based kitchen and bath appliance manufacturer Kohler has been aiming for the high-end Chinese market, with four hundred stores spread over a hundred Chinese cities. Just as in the West, Chinese consumers have learned to view their bathrooms not simply in utilitarian terms, but as broadcasting status and comfort.

Awareness of and preference for global luxury brands is omnipresent. In 2006, the *Hurun Report*, a Shanghai-based magazine that covers the lives of the wealthy, interviewed six hundred Chinese millionaires to identify their preferred brands. Christie's was voted the best auctioneer; Vacheron Constantin, the best watch; Davidoff, the best cigar; Giorgio Armani, the best designer; Hennessy, Chivas Regal, and Dom Pérignon, the best liquors; Princess, the best yacht; and Ferrari, the best sports car.

Despite their preference for Western brands, the Chinese do not merely covet foreign luxury goods but adapt them to their own tastes and traditions. Although China has emerged as the fastest-growing market for the finest whiskies of Scotland, these are popularly used to create a fashionable concoction of ice, whisky, and green tea that would make many purists cringe. Chinese also consume fine wines differently, often mixing them with carbonated drinks. This doesn't bespeak the missteps of parvenus. No less than their counterparts in the West, Chinese consumers perceive wine as a symbol of upper-class identity.

By 2005, China had also become the world's third largest market for jewelry, behind the United States and Europe, with $10 billion in sales. De Beers, the largest diamond seller in the world, entered the Chinese market only in 1993, but through extensive marketing campaigns has created the emotional association between diamonds and love that it so successfully established in the West. Within a decade, the Chinese market was worth billions. Likewise, since easing regulations on the import of gold jewelry, China has become the world's fourth biggest market, after India, the United States, and Turkey. In 2005 alone, Chinese consumers bought more than 250 tons of gold, a metal now associated with the Spring Festival, the country's most popular gold-buying season. By 2006, China had overtaken Japan as the world's largest consumer of platinum, the metal of choice for wedding rings.

However significant the emergence of China's hundreds of new millionaires, their true influence is on how they inspire a broad-based cultural obsession with luxury consumption, particularly among China's urban salaried workers. In fact, most of China's luxury consumers are the young and middle-aged (rather than the middle-aged and elderly, as in developed countries). As one newspaper noted, "The imported ideology of consumerism has greatly stimulated the Chinese desire to spend. This phenomenon is especially apparent among the young, who want to be 'in' and think buying more luxury goods will help." According to one friend in this demographic, the peer pressure to keep up with the number of luxury possessions is tremendous: "If my colleagues have four Louis Vuitton bags, I am supposed to have five better and bigger LV bags." Part of the allure of "LV bags," she tells me, is the conspicuous size of their logo.

China is importing not only international luxury goods but also the international leisure preferences of the wealthy. For most of the twentieth century, economists measured China's attempt to "catch up" with the industrialized world by its levels of production in steel and grain, but as Chinese policy makers promote the transition from a heavy reliance on manufacturing to a more service-oriented economy, "catching up" now refers to matching the range and availability of consumer experiences. In the mid-1990s, Yabuli, in northeastern Heilongjiang province, which was built for the 1996 Asian Winter Games, was the only large ski resort in China. Ten years later the country had more than two hundred ski resorts hosting three million visitors. Thirteen trendy new ski villages have sprung up in Nanshan, a ten-slope resort area located ninety minutes by car from the capital. When a ski slope opened outside of Beijing in 1998, it attracted only thirteen thousand people its first year; eight years later, it was attracting nearly two million visitors a year. This despite the fact that, with the Gobi Desert quickly encroaching it, Beijing is arid, sits only 140 feet above sea level, and has unpredictable winter weather; the necessary snow-making machinery consumes as much water yearly as would 42,000 people. To overcome such weather and environmental limitations, investors have begun to build indoor slopes, including the Qiaobo Ski Dome. According to the Chinese Ski Association, ten million Chinese will visit its slopes by 2010, a godsend to the international ski apparel and equipment industry, which is facing oversaturated markets in Europe and the United States. The owners of luxury brands, such as those in so many other industries, now look to China to save their profit margins.

Golf is the luxury leisure import that conveys the greatest status in China. Although some Chinese claim that their country invented a golf-like game over a thousand years ago, the British imported the modern Scottish game to China in the nineteenth century. Banned during the Communist era, golf was one of the first leisure activities reintroduced during the Reform Era, right after five-star hotels. The sport quickly became the quintessential symbol of wealth and power in China; its imagery appears repeatedly in television commercials, in magazine spreads, and on highway billboards. Since 1984, when China opened its first course since the Communist Revolution in 1949, the country has added another 350, most in the past decade. And there are as many as 1,000 more under construction, including in smaller cities in such less affluent provinces as Yunnan, Hebei, Hunan, and Shandong. From just 1,000 or so golfers in the mid-1990s, China now has over 1 million. As of 2005, it even had its own developmental pro tour, sponsored by Omega, to train players for the international tours that now routinely visit China's links.

Golf is limited largely to China's highly affluent. The country boasts only a couple of public courses, while a top club such as the Tomson Shanghai Pudong Golf Club, just twenty minutes from downtown and site of the BMW Asian Open since 2004, costs more than $100,000 to join. Golf complexes such as Shenzhen's Mission Hills, which with ten courses and two thousand villas is the nation's largest, have imported not only courses designed by international celebrity golfers such as Jack Nicklaus, Ernie Els, and Vijay Singh, but an entire way of life, including elaborately landscaped gated communities filled with multimillion-dollar luxury villas and condos, clubhouses, and spas. Indeed, Chinese and foreign investors often see golf courses as simply a pretext for turning cheap land into expensive gated communities, which has led to a glut. The sheer number of courses is itself predictive that very soon golf may be the next luxury activity of the affluent to be claimed by middle-class consumers.

As with elites in many other countries, the game's popularity has spread in the classic fashion of emulation: first China's affluent emulated their Hong Kong, Taiwanese, Japanese, and international counterparts and learned to play; then their underlings followed, with the less well heeled having to settle for less expensive courses and driving ranges. As one young golfer practicing his swing at a two-story driving range in Shanghai's financial district put it, "Golf is like social status. People play because they think they're rich, or because they want you to think it." Xiamen University administrators made golf lessons mandatory for their management, law, economics, and software engineering majors and available to all students. University president Zhu Chongzhi justified this decision by claiming that competence in golf would help a student's career and, in a somewhat circular argument, that "first-rate universities should cultivate the elites of society." In 2006, an elementary school, the Shanghai Yangjing-Juyuan Experimental School, teamed up with its neighbor, the Lujiazui Golf Club, to be the first in the country to offer golf lessons to primary school pupils, for 4,800 yuan a term.

The spread of luxury brand consumption has not proceeded unhindered, however. China remains nominally a Communist country with both a tradition of embracing frugality and a Maoist era disdain for consumerism. The consumption of imported luxury items remains controversial. In response to the statistic that 64 percent of the world's most expensive cognacs are sold in Asia, and the vast majority of that in China (where sales have grown by 146 percent in ten years), one chagrined official remarked, "How can a country where the annual income is less than $400 import so much cognac?" Similarly, golf's association with luxury and elitism seems to have unsettled CCP officials, who a few decades earlier had transformed a British colonial golf course in Shanghai into a public zoo. Unlike their counterparts in the United States, Chinese government leaders are not routinely photographed playing golf. In 2003, former premier Zhu Rongji even tried to limit golfing by public officials after a leading member of a Communist Party county committee in Hunan province died while playing; although officials claimed he was on government business, the public wondered why he was working on the weekend and suspected he was on holiday at taxpayers' expense. And when the *Beijing Youth Daily* published an editorial stating that "promoting aristocratic sporting activities in universities is a vulgar pursuit of lucre," Beijing University canceled its plans to add a campus driving range.

But shopping sprees, ski trips, and golf rounds aren't the only aspects of wealthy lifestyles emulated by the middle class: mistresses have once again become status symbols in China. For centuries, concubines were treated like any other product: traded, sold, or used to close business deals. The practice was virtually stamped out in the Maoist era as decadent and bourgeois. In the early years of the Reform Era, however, the revived practice quickly spread in Guangdong with the arrival of Hong Kong and Taiwanese businessmen. By 2000 there were anywhere from hundreds of thousands to millions of such mistresses across China. In places such as Guangzhou, one fourth of those polled said they personally knew someone who had or was a mistress. The practice of keeping "second wives" (*ernai*, or literally "second breasts," and often in the North called *xiao laopo*, or "little Mrs.") is so widespread that apartment complexes in prosperous areas of cities such as Dongguan, Chengdu, and Shanghai are popularly known as "concubine villages."

These second wives play a complex role in China's consumer marketplace. They represent the top end of a market for sexual services that ranges from full-time street workers to factory employees who occasionally swap sex for money to the many levels of hostesses working in massage parlors, karaoke clubs, and upscale bars. Even within the second wife category there is a taxonomy of prestige based on looks, education, and place of origin or ethnicity that ranges from the inexpensive and accommodating to the expensive and demanding.

As with so many other new consumer activities in China, having a second wife has gone from a discreet to a highly conspicuous practice. Indeed, being conspicuous is part of the mistress's job. One of the numerous tongue-in-cheek online "contracts" for second wives stipulates the expected benefits for each side: sex and "face" for the man, and a luxurious lifestyle for the woman marked by the consumption of high-class, sexually provocative, well-known designer clothing and shoes. Likewise, married men show off their wealth and taste by bringing their mistresses to trendy night spots, while less expensive second wives are often employed in place of personal assistants.

In rare cases, these relationships enable second wives to accumulate enough capital to grow wealthy with their own investments. In other cases, mistresses can wield some power over their patrons. The political career of a Communist Party chief in the city of Baoji, in Shaanxi province, known locally as "Mayor Zipper," was destroyed by the disclosures of one of his eleven mistresses. Yet acquiring wealth and consumer goods through work as a second wife remains dangerous. As Rachel DeWoskin observes, *ernai*, like other sex workers, "are vulnerable to abuse, unprotected by degrees, careers, or backup plans, and often deserted in their thirties. An increasing number of notable ernai now lead lives complicated by corruption and scandal. They are forbidden by law but flaunted in practice, socially both celebrated and condemned, just as concubines have always been."

The biggest opposition to the free market in mistresses, however, has come from the government, which often turns a blind eye to prostitution but has an interest in limiting the reach of the burgeoning market in mistresses, especially after a 2000 report revealed that over 90 percent of corrupt male cadres kept one. Chinese media and gossip networks are rife with notorious cases of officials using ill-gotten gains to support second (and sometimes third and fourth) wives. The practice is so widespread, according to anti-corruption activist Li Xinde, that it has given rise to a common saying: "Behind every corrupt official, there must be at least one mistress." Government studies confirm this bit of folk wisdom. In a review of 102 cases of corruption in Guangdong cities in 1999, every one included an illicit affair.

Legal wives now have the right to all the family resources when husbands are convicted of maintaining second wives, though few cases make it to court. In perhaps the most famous such case, in January 2008 the popular Chinese television personality Hu Ziwei stormed onto the set of a live broadcast of CCTV's official launch of a new Olympic sports channel to castigate her handsome and popular sports anchor husband for having an affair, even implying that China would never be a great power if it accepted such marital infidelities. Yet another example of the ripple effect caused by rapidly expanding consumer markets is private investigators who specialize in catching cheating husbands. In Chengdu, a divorced woman established one such agency, Debang, which has since established branches in other cities and employs more than a hundred people. The refusal to accept infidelity is one reason that divorces rose to 1.4 million in 2007, a rate of around 20 percent and a fivefold increase since the Reform Era began.

Effects on Social Attitudes, Mobility, and Consumerism

As noted earlier, the simple existence of the new aristocracy reflects a profound transformation in China. Twenty years ago China was among the world's most egalitarian but desperately poor countries; as a result of the economic reforms, the rise of this new elite has now made it one of the most unequal. In addition to the proliferation of Chinese millionaires and multimillionaires, before the start of the financial crisis of 2008, the country boasted more than a hundred billionaires, second only to the United States. Moreover, this inequality has grown very quickly. In the late 1990s, having a net worth of $6 million earned one a spot on *Forbes* magazine's list of the wealthiest Chinese; five years later it took at least $150 million. Another way to measure this inequality is the Gini coefficient, a standard international measure that ranges from 0 (perfect equality: everyone owns the same amount) to 1 (absolute inequality: one person owns everything). China's Gini coefficient has increased by more than 50 percent in the past two decades, with urban dwellers currently earning more than 4 times the income of rural residents. By 2009, China's coefficient was 0.46, meaning that it was more unequal than many Latin American and African countries. The inequality represented in the lifestyles of China's rich and famous also raises troubling consequences for social stability and the future development of a consumer-driven economy in China.

It is ironic that while hundreds of millions of people have been lifted out of poverty in record time, giving the CCP one of the greatest triumphs in modern governance, China is also creating one of the most unequal societies in history. Even as tens of millions of Chinese have gained access to previously unimaginable material pleasures, hundreds of millions still have not. The social and economic implications of this shift should make the Chinese uneasy. It certainly does among the Communist Party's top leaders, who now talk endlessly of "building a harmonious society" as they try to devise new strategies to spread the wealth. After all, "boosting domestic consumption" is a strategy not simply for economic growth, but also for maintaining political power and support.

In the face of this inequality, China's new aristocrats seemingly walk on the razor's edge, their wealth and consumption inspiring both emulation and deep animosity. A surprising 65 percent of the Chinese polled by *Beijing Youth Daily* admit to despising the wealthy; the most common words used to describe the new rich were *corrupt* and *greedy*. Most Chinese assume that the wealthy amass their fortunes through corruption. According to a 2006 survey of multimillionaires by the respected Guangzhou-based newspaper *Nanfang Weekend*, Chinese millionaires felt insecure and troubled that their wealth was considered not a validation but rather an indictment. When Rupert Hoogewerf, the founder of *Hurun Report*, compiled his first list of China's richest people in 1999, he encountered resistance; few people wanted to cooperate, and many of the people he identified as wealthy thereafter became targets for tax officials, the media, corporate blackmail, and even kidnappers.

The prevalence of billionaires who owe their fortunes to corruption doesn't mean there haven't been rags-to-riches stories. The thirty-something billionaire game developer Timothy Chen embodies the possibility of a new class of admired wealthy. Chen's company, Shanda Network Development, which he hopes will become China's Walt Disney, overcame the two limitations of gaming growth, payment and piracy, by locating his games almost exclusively online. Teenagers who log on and pay to play can avoid their parents' oversight by playing in Internet bars, and piracy actually serves to add new players. The company is currently worth billions. Tellingly, Chen lives modestly. He claims to own only one apartment in Shanghai, and his parents exhibit the traditional suspicion of wealth. "If I was a very low official, they would be proud of this," he has revealed, "but as a rich man, they don't want to introduce me to their friends."

A folk expression derived from Confucius's disciple Mencius holds that "one cannot become wealthy without being unjust." Chinese culture, rich in aphorisms, is full of similar sentiments underscoring the fundamental incompatibility between the righteous (*yi*) and the profitable (*li*), and between the public (*gong*) and the private (*si*). Examples include "Just as there is no such thing as an honest official, there is no such thing as an honorable merchant," and "For one family to prosper, ten thousand families must suffer to death." China's continued if increasingly nominal status as a socialist country heightens this historical antagonism. During the Maoist era, capitalists were vilified and, in the late 1950s, liquidated as a class. State workers had good reason to believe that they were, as Communist propaganda promised, the masters of Chinese society. Their work units provided them everything: salaries, housing, health care, and education. At retirement, they could count on a pension and continued housing and medical care and usually assured employment for a son or daughter in the same unit. They could reasonably come to see their workplaces as collectively owned by the members of their unit. In sharp contrast, the various forms of privatization that followed often benefited the few at the expense of the many.

There are four primary groups among China's newly rich, each emerging at a different stage of the reforms and each increasingly offensive to ordinary Chinese. The first group to appear was the small-scale individual entrepreneurs (*getihu*), who sprang up in the early years of the Reform Era, toward the end of the 1970s, and led China's initial retailing revolution. As nearly twenty million young people "sent down to the countryside" during the Cultural Revolution returned to Chinese cities seeking work, to absorb the unemployed the central government sanctioned the establishment of small-scale businesses with fewer than eight employees. By 1988, urban China had more than three million such enterprises, employing almost five million people. Roadside bicycle repair shops, food stalls, and fruit vendors appeared everywhere. In the countryside, home to three fourths of these new enterprises, individuals set up fishing ponds and other small businesses. According to the sociologist Thomas Gold, who conducted interviews with the proprietors, most "had little confidence in the life expectancy of the policy that spawned them. They therefore earned as much money as they could, consuming it aggressively in the expectation that their halcyon days were numbered." This newly affluent group was awarded very low social status, and while some became comfortable and better off than state workers, very few are part of the new aristocracy today.

A second and more successful group among the wealthy emerged with the reforms of 1985, when the government allowed state enterprises to sell their surplus products and keep the profits. This promptly created a dual-track price structure for commodities: a lower price for quotas earmarked for the state, and a higher market price, often inflated by 200 or 300 percent, for sale for profit. Tens of millions of Chinese exploited these price differentials, the most successful being the politically connected, especially the children of high-ranking officials or "princelings" holding provincial and national offices who used their connections to gain control over public resources and ensure state buyers even for bad products. Such speculation within this dual-track price structure became known as "official racketeering," and its practitioners were labeled profiteers or wheeler-dealers. During the 1980s, this racketeering generated as much as 600 billion yuan in profits, but those who got rich by it were seen as parasites responsible for the rapid inflation that followed the price reforms of the late 1980s. Indeed, it has long been overlooked that profiteering, rather than a lack of political freedom and "democracy," was the primary complaint fueling the Tiananmen Square demonstrations of 1989.

But those wheeler-dealers were poor compared to the land speculators who gained their riches in the late 1980s, and became China's first billionaires and even trillionaires. As with official profiteering, land speculators relied on political connections to gain the right to purchase choice parcels of land and secure loans from state-owned banks. Chinese land developers are seen by most Chinese as completely dependent on state connections, from expropriating the land of urban residents and rural farmers to obtaining unsecured low-interest loans from state banks to finance construction. According to one report, 90 percent of

China's billionaires (measured in yuan) are princelings, including nearly all of the richest developers in China—nine of the top ten real estate magnates and thirteen of the richest fifteen owners of construction companies in Shanghai. Many Chinese blame this group for the inflation of the late 1980s and the inflated Chinese housing market, which has made home ownership prohibitively expensive and slowed the spread of a broader, middle-class consumerism.

The final, largest, and most reviled category of the new rich are former managers of state-owned enterprises (SOEs) who became wealthy during the rapid and notably corrupt conversion of public enterprises into private and stockholder-owned companies beginning in the late 1990s. Having bought shares cheaply from the state to become major shareholders, once their enterprises were privatized they often sold this stock at a high profit, fired workers, and profited from the liquidation of enterprise assets, especially land, which was often located in city centers. The size of individual fortunes is often proportional to how callously state workers were dispossessed—the more ruthless the manager was, the wealthier he is. Moreover, these individuals still maintain their ties to the Communist Party: two thirds of the six million or so owners of private firms are former state officials, and about the same number are currently party members.

Although not technically a part of the new aristocracy, another group of business leaders owe their position, wealth, and privilege to the state: the managers of the remaining state-owned enterprises. After all, the Chinese state still owns the country's largest companies, thereby maintaining monopolistic control over the "commanding heights" of the economy, including key industries such as energy, transport, banking, and communications. The top twenty companies in China in terms of revenue are state owned (including such companies as Sinopec, China Mobile, China First Automobile, and China Minerals). And even the twentieth largest state-owned company (the Internet provider China

Netcom) has more revenue than the largest private company (the electrical appliance company GOME). The state companies are either monopolies or oligopolies, and very profitable. All their senior and even mid-level executives are appointed by the CCP, and as a consequence, when they embezzle and misappropriate company funds, it's deemed "corruption," a direct fleecing of the public rather than stealing from private stockholders.

In one way, then, China decidedly differs from most industrialized countries. As the sociologist Xiaowei Zeng puts it, "Ordinary people in the PRC have better reasons than their counterparts in non-socialist societies to believe that the rich are rich because they have taken from the state and the people"—which explains why envy is matched by popular animosity toward the new aristocracy, having even spawned a neologism, "hatred of the rich," and a pop-psychological condition known as "the mentality of hating the rich," both widely used since 2000. Notably, the Chinese generally despise the rich not for their extravagant or wasteful consumption, but because their wealth was acquired dishonestly. As a male bank employee from Beijing put it, "I could also become rich if I were heartless and ignored laws and ethics like rich people do. But I don't think I can, because my heart is too soft. It isn't worth it."

Wealth inequality and resentment are also blamed for a rise in petty crimes. In 2003, the media attributed an increase in the number of high-end automobiles being vandalized to increasing hatred of the rich. Other reported forms of hostility directed toward the affluent included "bullying, exclusion, harassment, pranks, conspiracies to entrap, and even a prevalent public attitude of hatred," the aim of which is simply to bring a wealthy person down a peg or two, to cause him or her to "experience a bit of suffering." The Chinese media have linked such hatred to much more horrific crimes as well. The year 2003 saw a spate of highly publicized murders of wealthy Chinese, including Li

Haicang of Shanxi, who was shot in his office; Liu Qimin of Fujian, who was stabbed to death by four employees; and Zhou Zubao of Beijing, who was murdered while visiting his rural hometown. The reaction on the Web was overwhelmingly uniform, with comments such as "he deserved to die" and "the murder was nicely done."

The Reform Era has also witnessed the emergence of kidnapping and extortion targeting businesspeople, celebrities, and their children, many organized by sophisticated criminal gangs such as the Xinjiang Gang in Shanghai, the White Shark Gang in Guangdong, and the Wolf Gang in Shanxi. In the country's wealthier coastal provinces, there are at least ten such crimes a day. From a handful of cases in the early 1980s, by the turn of the century there were thousands—at least a third more than in Colombia, which is notorious in international business circles for the widespread practice. Many other kidnappings are related to labor and land disputes. When Hong Kong factory owner Lau Siufan visited his bicycle parts factory in Shenzhen in early 2006, for instance, he was abducted by thugs sent by a scrap metal vendor who demanded millions of yuan. Local police, viewing the matter as a business dispute, refused to intervene.

As one market begets another, the newly rich increasingly hire bodyguards, thereby creating another wealth-related industry. As many as five thousand men now work as bodyguards in Guangzhou alone, and double that number in Shenzhen. The wealthy often send their children to British boarding schools, transfer assets overseas, live a less conspicuous lifestyle, or relocate to cities such as Shanghai and Beijing, where conspicuous consumption is safer. One shoe factory owner reported that rather than provide a sense of security, his wealth had forced him to "transform his house into a fortress." After the father of a rural entrepreneur was abducted ten times, each time requiring a ransom of 80,000 to 100,000 yuan, he took out a special insurance policy. When another factory owner's son was kidnapped and the family forced to pay 300,000 yuan, neighbors blamed the victim's family for conspicuously living in a luxurious house and driving a Mercedes-Benz. Indeed, such crimes are commonly seen as a form of wealth redistribution—or, as a popular expression puts it, "robbing the wealthy to aid the poor."

A dramatic increase in charitable giving by China's well-to-do may be in part an attempt to counter such widespread hatred. At the start of the twenty-first century, the new aristocracy in China were routinely criticized by the media, government, and intellectuals as selfish, leading the government to call on wealthy companies and individuals to use more of their wealth to help the poor. After a brutal series of natural disasters in 2005, for instance, the vice-minister of civil affairs, Li Liguo, made a direct appeal to the wealthy to donate more, and policy makers have created tax breaks for charitable donations. As with every other aspect of China's emerging markets and wealth, the change in philanthropy happened quickly. The 2007 *Hurun Report* list of Chinese philanthropists noted that thirty of the nation's hundred wealthiest individuals were also among the top hundred most philanthropic, up from twenty the previous year, and that many of China's wealthy were contemplating establishing their own charitable foundations. Shenzhen hotel entrepreneur Yu Pengnian gave away 2 billion yuan, mostly to pay for cataract surgery for 100,000 people. The effort seems to be working, with other philanthropists such as Huang Rulun and Li Jinyuan regularly garnering favorable press.

The simultaneous creation of a consumer culture and monetization of political power have spread the desire for new consumer lifestyles but not necessarily the means for attaining them, as new forms of corruption have made upward mobility increasingly difficult. According to the outspoken journalist He Qinglian, now in exile in the United States, before 1978 the state monopolized all three forms of power—political, economic, and cultural/educational—and the Chinese enjoyed few material goods aside from basic items such as furniture and clothing. But market reforms enabled the politically powerful to gain control of formerly public assets through privatization and to manipulate their public offices for private gain, leading sociologist Sun Liping to conclude, "if a middle class has had difficulty emerging in China, it is partly because so many of the resources necessary for one have already been cornered." In truth, the problem facing China is less that a middle class has failed to emerge than that its ranks may have difficulty expanding.

He Qinglian identifies three layers or classes within contemporary China: a small elite, a much larger middle class, and an assortment of laborers and marginalized groups at the bottom. The political and economic elites comprise some seven million people, or 1 percent of the employed population. The economic elite is made up primarily of families who have profited from what is popularly known as a "one family, two systems" arrangement, in which the parents work for the state and the children are in business. (The phrase itself is a play on "one country, two systems" used by the Communist Party to describe their flexible political approach toward incorporating Hong Kong into Chinese rule.) The elite also includes newcomers who have cultivated government ties and others, though a distinct minority, who have succeeded by seizing early market opportunities, especially in the high-tech sector. These subgroups share a lifestyle that, according to He Qinglian, includes "high-speed living, limited spare time, abundant consumption and similar tendencies in their leisure pursuits and sexual proclivities." The arrangement is also inherently limiting: there are only so many effective ties to government and influence to be exploited.

As He Qinglian points out, the difficulty of moving into China's new elite restricts the potential size of the new Chinese middle class and curtails their ability to buy and consume, thereby limiting the formation of the very class that Chinese and foreign political and business leaders are looking to become the new global economic motor.

At the top of the current middle class are "well-paid intellectual work-ers, managers of middling and small enterprises in the state sector, private owners of middling and small firms, white-collar employees of firms with foreign investment, [and] employees of state monopolies," which constituted somewhat more than twenty-nine million people, or about 4 percent of the workforce. Below these are "specialized technicians, scientific researchers, lawyers, teachers in higher educa-tion and middle schools, rank-and-file employees in the arts or media, average functionaries in government, middle- and lower-level man-agement in state enterprises, [and] upper-level self-employed and traders," who together comprise about eighty-two million people, or almost 12 percent of the workforce. Although the makeup of these middle-class groups is much the same as in Western countries, it in-cludes a much smaller proportion of the entire population.

The government's attempts to create a broad consumer society are being obstructed by China's having not only a small middle class but an entrenched working class. The Chinese workforce, represent-ing many millions of potential consumers, faces massive unemploy-ment and underemployment, especially since the privatization push of the late 1990s left millions unemployed, what is euphemistically called "off-post." By the end of that decade, the official jobless rate was over ten million, although the actual number was undoubtedly much higher. This doesn't even take into consideration the hundreds of millions of poor Chinese, many of them farmers. In the earliest years of the Reform Era, when farmers were allowed to sell their sur-plus, those near major cities were the first to become wealthy, a trend of rural enrichment that failed to continue. Now farmers face many burdens. Although the land tax was reduced and then abolished in 2006, farmers face endless levies and other forms of indirect taxation and local corruption. Chinese agriculture remains largely unindustri-alized and inefficient, keeping incomes down. In 2008 the number of poor receiving government assistance was at least thirty-five million, the unemployed were as many as one hundred million, and poorly paid migrant laborers were at least another hundred million. This major reduction in the middle layers of Chinese society and rapid expansion of its lower layers, according to He Qinglian, creates a surefire formula for social instability. She for one is skeptical that the global trade opportunities provided by China's joining the WTO in 2001 will solve these problems. WTO members cannot force China to eliminate official corruption, and membership may actually have exacerbated social polarization between elites and the rest of society and between wealthier coastal provinces and poorer interior ones.

And yet China's creation of a Western-style consumer culture, right down to SUV ownership and exotic foreign golf holidays, shows no signs of abating. The complaint that officials are using public money for expensive hobbies such as golf is very different from the complaint that the growing desire to play golf is inherently bad or unfair. While many Chinese may resent the way the wealthy have obtained their wealth, they also endorse and desire the lifestyles of China's newly rich and famous, which results in a further entrenchment of consumer culture. Although corrupt politicians may come and go, the new affluent lifestyles they have helped create—the pinnacle of consumer culture—have become only more firmly fixed. As Sébastien Noat, the manager of Block 8, a luxury night-life complex in Beijing that caters to the capital's new class of young urban professionals, summed up the reason for such luxurious lifestyles in China: "The owners of America live here." And while these new "owners of America" may now primarily emulate the lifestyles of their foreign counterparts, as they and China grow wealthier, they have also begun to redefine international luxury standards and what it means to be wealthy.

3 ★ MADE IN TAIWAN

Taiwan and the Shaping of Chinese Consumerism

Much of popular understanding of modern history is based on photogenic turning points. One such moment was in June 1987, when U.S. president Ronald Reagan stood in front of the Berlin Wall that separated Communist East Germany from capitalist West Germany and famously challenged Soviet leader Mikhail Gorbachev to "tear down this wall." Yet at about the same time as Reagan's telegenic dare, far from the glare of the cameras a less sensational but perhaps even more significant barrier separating Communist China from capitalist Taiwan was beginning to crumble. Nowhere, perhaps, was the cold war better represented than in the division of the Chinese nation into two blocs separated not only by a mass of water but by ideology—by communism and capitalism at their most strident. But starting the same year as Reagan's memorable speech, the potent pull of shared economic interests and shared history would lead to a gradual thaw between the two places that would dramatically transform China's consumer culture. Although this shift may not have been as obvious as in Eastern Europe—where following the collapse of the Soviet Union throngs of formerly captive consumers drove their Trabants and other jalopies into Western countries looking for things to buy—it was just as real, and arguably more influential.

There was a time, not that long ago, when Chinese youth dreamed of a life in the United States enjoying the vast variety of fast-food restaurants, dance clubs, shopping malls, concerts, and everything that a cosmopolitan city with a lively nightlife could offer. Today, the consumer options available in Shanghai would put most American cities to shame. Some Chinese living in the United States now even refer to returning to America after a visit in China as "going back to the countryside from the city." When a Chinese friend returned to the southwestern Chinese city of Kunming from her home outside San Francisco, she reported to me that her Chinese friends teased her about being an "American peasant" for being so unfashionably dressed. So how have Chinese cities—and especially Shanghai—created such dynamic consumer cultures so quickly? The answer is simple: Taiwan.

To understand the impact of Taiwan on this transformation, it helps to understand the origins of the Chinese cold war that preceded it. In 1911, Sun Yat-sen, known as the father of the modern Chinese nation, led the overthrow of the Qing Dynasty. He established the Republic of China (ROC) the following year, co-founding the Chinese Nationalist Party (Guomintang) and serving as its first leader. This new state comprised most of mainland China and Mongolia and, with the surrender of Japan at the end of World War II, was joined by the island of Taiwan. This was followed by civil war between the Western-backed Nationalist Party, now led by Chiang Kai-shek, and Mao's Communist Party. When the Nationalist Party lost that war in 1949, they retreated across the Taiwan straits to the island of Taiwan and established Taipei (Taibei) as the supposedly temporary capital of the republic, which early in the cold war was recognized by many Western nations and the United Nations as the sole legitimate government of all of China. On the mainland, the Communists founded the People's Republic of China (PRC). When he fled, Chiang Kai-shek took with him his soldiers, members of his Nationalist Party, and perhaps most important, many Chinese intellectual and business leaders—some two million refugees in all. Many of the exiles who would help Taiwan prosper and grow, however, had been forced to leave families and friends behind, dividing not only Chinese culture but hundreds of thousands of families.

For those transplanted to Taiwan and their descendants, the mainland just a few miles away was shrouded in mystery and the anti-Communist propaganda avidly spread by the Nationalists. There was, indeed, so little contact between the two that when I dropped out of college for a year and supported myself by teaching English in Taiwan, students and adults who knew I had traveled in mainland China would routinely ask me what it was *really* like (and, of course, which place was better). Military tensions between the countries ran high well into the 1980s. In the center of Taipei, giant placards proclaimed the national goal: "Retake the Mainland!"

It wasn't the Taiwanese military but rather a political decision that profoundly transformed Taiwan-China economic and cultural relations and accelerated the restoration of China's consumer culture. In 1987, Taiwan's Nationalist government lifted martial law and eased restrictions on contact with the mainland. The result was the massive increase in the flow of capital, products, and eventually people between Taiwan and China. The oft-used metaphor of "flows" makes this China-Taiwan exchange sound natural, as though a current gently moved capital, pop culture, and people across the strait. In reality, the exchange was driven by political decisions on both sides, although Taiwan's comparative advantage in human and material resources and Chinese demand for those resources determined the content and volume of the flow. As China's economic reforms advanced, more and more mainland Chinese consumers realized that rather than "duties" they had "needs" that the Taiwanese were best able to meet. And as Taiwan's industrial sector became less competitive internationally, its deindustrializing economy needed to find new markets; its workers, new jobs.

The profit motive led the way; manufacturers and business owners followed. As a consequence, China has received massive quantities of Taiwanese investment. Indeed, one could argue that Taiwanese investments have financed the transformation of China. Of an estimated $700 billion invested directly and indirectly by foreigners in China by 2006, $100 billion came from Taiwan. This is all the more remarkable considering the size of Taiwan and that the two nations remain technically at war. Taiwanese investments have gone into tens of thousands of projects all over China, even in Nanchang, the birthplace of the Communist state. Today, more than seventy thousand Taiwanese companies have investments in the mainland.

Trade between the two countries now breaks new records yearly and has amounted to over $2 trillion since 1987. In 2002, China replaced the United States as the top market for Taiwanese goods. In 2005, Taiwan sent $50 billion worth of goods to China—everything from electronics to fruit—and received $20 billion worth of goods in return. And this total doesn't include trade via Hong Kong, which, because Taiwan had banned direct exchanges with the mainland for decades, re-shipped tens of billions from Taiwan to China and helped Taiwan generate a $60 billion trade surplus. But these figures represent not simply commodities traveling back and forth but a transformation of ordinary lives. They reflect a sea change from millions of girls standing in rows in identical Mao suits shouting Communist slogans to those same girls wearing the trendiest fashions and singing the latest pop tunes from Taipei while walking down streets full of restaurants and clubs.

Perhaps as important as this resumption of trade was Taiwan's partial lifting of a travel ban to China upon the death of Chiang Kai-shek's son Chiang Ching-kuo. This led to an informal cultural exchange as families divided for decades after the civil war were reunited, bringing with them a tide of cultural influences. Those driven into exile by the civil war and their children now became agents of new consumer lifestyles as they traveled back and forth between the two countries, taking their new customs and tastes with them. After decades of separation, Taiwanese travelers not only got to learn about contemporary China firsthand but also taught the Chinese much about being consumers through everyday interactions, arguably doing more than any other group to directly transform Chinese consumer culture at the local level. Although their visits usually lasted only a few days or weeks, their gifts and their attitudes stayed behind.

Take, for example, the father of one of my former Taiwanese students. When he traveled to see his relatives still living in his ancestral homeland in rural Henan province, he didn't arrive empty-handed. Like tens of thousands of other Taiwanese visitors, he returned to China with lavish presents. Indeed, he had intended to give his mainland relatives a color TV, one of the most coveted and difficult-to-obtain products in China at the time, but they had begged him not to. Such a gift would not only elicit envy but force his mainland relatives to host TV parties for family, friends, and hangers-on. Others were less cautious, accepting not only TVs but washing machines, motorcycles, and cash. The gift giving became so common and the items so predictable that enterprising Taiwanese stores made the whole process easier by allowing travelers to purchase the gifts in Taiwan and then pick them up in China.

This exchange has accelerated Taiwan's profound influence on consumer lifestyles in China. In the decades since those gift-giving reunions, Taiwan has shaped a rapidly growing consumer culture directly through its pop culture, which was quickly and enthusiastically adopted in China. A mainland county-sized city such as Dongguan suggests the feedback loop at work. Located on the Pearl River Delta,

Dongguan is now one of China's most important industrial cities. First came the Taiwanese-financed factories, which provided higher wages and standards of living for local Chinese. Then Taiwanese investors brought new consumer products and services, initially targeting Taiwanese transplants but then the newly affluent Chinese.

While political sensitivities and the use of tax havens make it difficult to accurately measure the extent of Taiwanese monetary investment in China, it is undoubtedly vast. Intracultural flows are even harder to quantify. Of course, this is not only a Taiwan-China problem. I grew up in America shortly after the so-called British Invasion of U.S. pop culture of the late 1960s, which included the biggest rock bands of the day, the Beatles, the Who, Led Zeppelin, and the Rolling Stones. While it is relatively easy to track how much those groups earned from concerts and record sales, that leaves unaddressed how "British" my own pop cultural sensibility is and whether this music was even "British" or a re-imported (and whitened) version of American blues, jazz, and rock. In the case of Taiwan's influence on China, we can find both obvious influences, those known and sold as "Taiwanese," and more subtle ones, through consumer goods such as instant noodles and practices such as Japanese karaoke, introduced through Taiwan without necessarily being identified as such.

From Mainland Fervor to Shanghai Fever

Since the first major wave of Taiwanese businesspeople arrived during the "Mainland Fever" following the lifting of martial law and relaxation of the travel ban in 1987, more than a million—known in China as Taishang—have relocated to China and established several tens of thousands of businesses. Taiwanese who had previously and illegally arrived in China and invested their money had usually settled in areas where they could continue in low-tech, labor-intensive "sunset" industries such as shoes and bicycles. Taiwanese investors helped turn places such as Dongguan from a rural fishing area into a city of seven million and the country's third largest exporting city—now also home to the second largest shopping mall in the world. Dongguan was an obvious choice for factories because it is close to Hong Kong, which, along with nearby Macao, offered the only direct flights to Taiwan. In the early years, Taishang were mostly men relocating on their own. But by 2000, more than 100,000 Taiwanese entrepreneurs lived in Dongguan and another 300,000 Taiwanese workers and family dependents had settled in the rest of Guangdong province.

Like the treaty ports that had facilitated the introduction of the mass-produced material culture of the industrial age into China in the early twentieth century, these initially small Taiwanese communities in China became conduits for introducing new jobs and professions along with new consumer lifestyles. The town of Houjie was one of the first within Dongguan prefecture to receive Taiwanese investment. In the 1980s, small-size shoe factories began relocating there to save on labor and production costs. As more Taiwanese arrived, Taishang began to cater to their tastes with modest Taiwanese restaurants and papaya milk shops. These were soon followed by other Taiwanese chains, such as Yon Ho Soybean, Mentor hair salons, and an ever-increasing number of clothing stores. By the mid-1990s, Taiwanese retailers shifted their attention from simply serving fellow Taiwanese transplants to wooing the increasingly affluent Chinese host community.

As China's economic reforms advanced, China offered the Taishang short- and long-term economic opportunities that no longer existed back in Taiwan. Take the case of Min, a businessman interviewed by sociologist Ping Lin. With his business drying up on Taiwan, Min went to China in the early 1990s to design and construct buildings for transplanted Taiwanese businesses dissatisfied with the quality of mainland builders. Once there, he traveled around China looking for other opportunities to make a quick buck. Seeing that Beijing fashions lagged behind those in South China, he bought fashionable pants in bulk in the far southern province of Guangdong and resold them in Beijing. Introducing the concept of marketing to Communist China, he hired several beautiful women to walk around the streets modeling the clothing. Suddenly, young Chinese girls became aware of a new "need," and the models told them where they could fulfill it. Min promptly sold out his stock, and the erstwhile builder ended up making his fortune selling pants. In China, the Taiwanese also found that they could afford more comfortable lifestyles than they could back at home. As one Taishang explained, by living in Dongguan he could afford a more beautiful girlfriend, a bigger house with servants, and meals at any restaurant—"even the cost for prostitutes is much cheaper." Other Taiwanese began visiting China to shop for both goods and services, taking advantage of the lower prices.

A new phase of Taiwanese investment and immigration to China began with the 2000 election in Taiwan of the independence-minded Democratic Progressive Party (DPP) candidate Chen Shui-bian to the presidency. Fearing increased political instability, Taiwanese businesses succumbed to "Shanghai Fever." The media saturated Taiwan with images of the opportunities and quality of life (all maintained by a stable state) available across the water, and books on investing and living in Shanghai by Taiwanese businessman Chen Bin became bestsellers. The old image of China as backward was replaced by that of a cutting-edge Shanghai portrayed as a land of "eating, drinking, playing, and pleasure." Within five years, more than 12,000 Taiwanese businesses and between 300,000 and 600,000 Taiwanese had set themselves up in Shanghai and the surrounding areas of the Lower Yangzi River Delta.

Unlike their earlier counterparts, this new wave of Taiwanese businessmen brought their wives and children with them, creating entire communities with their own neighborhoods, schools, and social scenes. They also shifted from light manufacturing to high-tech and high-fashion, and to service industries such as banking, consulting, medical services, education, and real estate. For instance, Kunshan, an hour's drive from Shanghai, now resembles Taiwan's high-tech industrial zone and is known as Little Taipei. Although it may have been faddish to relocate to Shanghai, many Taiwanese businesspeople felt they had no choice. Transplanted wives also enjoyed a better quality of life, with increased purchasing power. But Shanghai Fever differed from earlier migrations of Taiwanese to the mainland in that it included not just mid-level managers but also Taiwanese cultural leaders and visionaries. These transplants helped remake Shanghai to accommodate a global middle and upper class accustomed to luxury condos, elevated highways, international schools, supermarkets with favorite imported foods, restaurants with international cuisines, KTV (karaoke bars) programmed with familiar pop songs, and bookstores stocking the latest foreign bestsellers. As China's recent transformation establishes itself beyond any shadow of doubt, consumerism begets more consumerism.

These new migrants have already begun to redefine Shanghai and China as a destination for global consumers. Tourists come to China no longer just to experience Mao's "Revolutionary China," but also to shop, seeking a wider and less expensive variety of consumer goods and experiences. As a tourist destination, China offers visitors from elsewhere the experience of feeling wealthy. Ten or twenty years ago, comparative wealth wouldn't have meant much, as there wasn't much to buy. But now urban China resembles a giant open-air mall. For those who move to China, the promise is an immediate upgrade in class status. "You can have as many housemaids as you want," as one Taiwanese housewife living in China put it. "You can't have this kind of life in Taiwan or in the U.S."

By 2005–2006, the very media that had fueled Shanghai Fever were now full of stories about broken dreams and lost fortunes. Nonetheless, the Taiwanese keep coming. Most feel they have few options. As put by one reporter's Taiwanese friend, "Unemployment in Taiwan has risen and hundreds of thousands have not only lost their jobs but also their dreams. But now New Shanghai has become a place where many people think they can change their fortunes, especially those 'New Shanghaiese' from Taiwan who are willing to take a bold chance and work hard." A new generation of Americans and Europeans has begun to follow on their heels. Thanks largely to the Taiwanese, an expanding infrastructure of consumerism will already be there to greet these new expats and fulfill their needs.

Catering to Chinese Tastes

The profound influence that the Taiwanese have had on the leisure culture on the mainland is especially evident in Chinese cuisine and restaurants. Initially there to serve other Taiwanese, Taiwanese companies providing everything from fast food to high-end delicacies have opened branches throughout China, introducing the mainland to such Taiwanese foods as egg pancakes and bubble tea. Taiwanese fast-food chains such as Yon Ho Soybean and Yonghe King have popularized Taiwan-style beef noodle soup. Fashionable Shanghai districts around The Bund, Nanjing Road, and Huaihai Road have opened Taiwanese-style coffee shops, shaved ice and bubble tea shake shops, teahouses, and even branches of high-end restaurants such as Ding Tai Fung, ranked by the *New York Times* as one of the world's best. The biggest Taiwanese success story in sheer volume may be Master Kong–brand instant noodles, which sells over six billion packages in China per year.

All of which underscores that Taiwan has taught China a great deal about modern food retailing, a key to the successful introduction of consumerism. Take Yonghe King, one of the first Taiwanese restaurant chains in China. In 1995, Li Yulin, like tens of thousands before her, visited Shanghai from Taiwan to look for business opportunities and exploit the gap between Taiwanese and mainland Chinese consumer lifestyles. She soon found that the two most popular Taiwanese breakfast options, soybean milk and deep-fried dough sticks, were sold out of unhygienic street stalls and were not as good in China. "At the very least," she observed, "I knew that Taiwanese living in Shanghai would welcome the opportunity to buy better-tasting soybean milk, fried dough sticks, stove-fried bread, and riceballs and enjoy them in cleaner, friendlier surroundings." So she and co-investor Li Youao opened a very modest shop of 120 square meters, hiring Li Yulin's own father to cook. (He would later be immortalized as the KFC Colonel Sanders–like face on the company logo.) Within three years, the original partners had taken on additional investors and opened 18 shops on the mainland. Within a decade, the chain had 120 restaurants in 10 cities, making the brand a household name and creating a 24-hour fast-food dining experience. A few years ago Li Youao decided to make the company the "Chinese McDonald's" and teamed up with the Philippines' largest fast-food chain, Jollibee (founded by an ethnic Chinese), to open 1,000 new restaurants in China. In a stroke of marketing genius, the chain aimed to set up branches next door to every McDonald's.

In Shanghai, Yon Ho Soybean is another Taiwanese chain offering what the proprietors bill as a "Chinese-style" fast food. The chain began in the Taiwanese town of Yungho and initially marketed soymilk concentrate to small breakfast restaurants. The company branched out into other products, and in 1997 it ventured into China. Encountering supply-chain problems and finding it difficult to collect bills, in 1999 it changed its strategy and opened its first restaurant in Shanghai's Pudong district. But rather than concentrate on city centers, where competition was fiercest, the company decided to expand into outlying areas and rely on licensees, opening nearly a hundred stores in secondary markets across China. The company has become so successful that Yonghe (a different spelling of Yon Ho, which means "eternal peace") has almost become a generic term for fast food, sometimes making the company a victim of its own success. According to company estimates, more than a hundred fast-food outlets in Shanghai alone use the two characters that make up the company's name, forcing it to file an endless number of trademark infringement lawsuits. It also responded to this threat by importing another mass retailing practice, creating a mascot—a baby scarecrow—and placing it, like the Ronald McDonald clown, at the entrance to stores to reassure consumers that they are in the right place.

Taiwan exerted an early and very powerful influence on the spread and growth of Chinese consumerism. What's important to keep in mind here is that, as with cars, this brought a cascade of consequences. China wanted Taiwanese investment dollars, technology, and expertise—so it opened the door. Taiwanese spied an opportunity and charged through it. But China didn't bring in the Taiwanese in expectation of building a market for bubble tea. If you take billions of dollars of Taiwanese investment dollars, it turns out you also get better fried dough sticks and bubble tea, which sets off new desires and market competition. Suddenly the issue isn't if you drink coffee, but what brand and where.

Pop Music Makes Pop Commodities

Once, everywhere you went in China you were greeted by the strains of martial music and patriotic songs blaring out from public address systems. But now China's youth have discovered that they need pop music, which is perhaps the most ubiquitous Taiwanese consumer product in China and now as unavoidable as the Mao-era songs once were. The Taiwanese-dominated world of "mandopop," or Mandarin Chinese–language pop music, is not simply diluted Western pop but, in the words of anthropologist Marc Moskowitz, "a new sonic ethos—a blend of traditional Chinese, Japanese, Taiwanese, and Western musical styles into something new and delightful for Chinese-speaking audiences." This sonic ethos has been enormously successful in China, accounting for 80 percent of Chinese-language music sales in the country.

This pop revolution started in the late 1970s with the arrival of Taiwanese singer Teresa Teng (Teng Li-chün, Deng Lijun, 1953–1995). She was an instant star in China, and during the first years of the Reform Era, Beijing tried to ban her music as "decadent" and "yellow" (which means "pornographic"). She was, after all, from "enemy territory," and her voice was said to be reminiscent of the Nationalist female spies in Communist movies about the civil war. Indeed, among villagers along the coast, it was commonly rumored that the Taiwanese floated balloons with canned food and tapes of Teng's music across the Taiwan Strait. The Chinese weren't allowed to buy her music in stores or hear her on state-run radio or television. It didn't matter. Smuggled onto the mainland, her tapes were copied and recopied at little cost and her music spread from southeastern China across the country.

Teng's songs introduced new themes into Chinese music, such as love, nostalgia, and other long-suppressed emotions. As her popularity grew, she became known by the affectionate Chinese diminutive "Little Teng." Her fame even began to eclipse that of China's reform leader Deng Xiaoping, with whom she shared a surname. (*Teng* is an alternative way to transliterate the Chinese character *Deng*.) Some even joked, "Give me Little Teng over Old Deng any day!" Much like bubble tea and other Taiwanese imports, Little Teng was quickly imitated by Chinese such as Li Guyi, who adopted her gentle, breathy style to record the first pop hit of the post-Mao era, "Hometown Love." Finally, in 1987, Teng's records were officially allowed.

The themes that dominate Taiwanese mandopop are the key to its popularity in China: nostalgia, the disappearance of traditional values, the desire to develop one's own individual lifestyle, and romance— topics rarely discussed, let alone sung about, under Mao. The music also allows consumers to feel more cosmopolitan by tapping into trends within the Chinese diaspora. Gently sung Taiwanese mando-pop, with its predominant themes of loneliness and isolation, stood in stark contrast to Maoist-era music, which demanded a cheerful inten-sity in celebration of the state. Mandopop allows the Chinese to ex-press loneliness, sorrow, and heartbreak, emotions that, according to Moskowitz, are "difficult to express in Chinese and Taiwan's cultures, which idealize stoic endurance and emphasize indirectness as a means to maintaining social harmony."

In the early 1980s, Taiwanese "campus folk music" by singers such as Luo Ta-you (Luo Dayou) captured the student market by reflecting the feelings and problems of ordinary people. The music appealed to students cynical about Chinese politics and attracted to the simple style of songs such as "The Olive Tree" and "Grandma's Penghu Bay." The music also showed a new generation that pop music could be a vehicle for critical thought and not just bourgeois escapism. Inspired, homegrown Chinese rock stars soon emerged, such as Wang Yanjun, Li Haiying, and, the most popular of all, Cui Jian, who in the 1980s recorded the generational anthem of students, "I Have Nothing at All." These new cultural influences were quickly copied by Chinese artists covering Taiwanese music. The industry took off, and in the 1990s China launched the first all-music radio stations dedicated to pop.

At the same time, the spread of Taiwanese-style karaoke bars (known as KTVs) throughout China gave people a new reason to fol-low Taiwanese pop culture. KTVs have been central to the popularization of Taiwanese mandopop and of new private commercialized gathering spaces in China. In the 1970s the Taiwanese created businesses that rented small private rooms with karaoke machines, TVs, and amplification. These rent-a-living-room spaces were used to host parties, impress dates, or allow men to meet women supplied by the businesses. Until the intellectual property rights crackdowns in the late 1990s forced many out of business, Taiwan also offered "MTVs," similarly ubiquitous establishments in which to watch movies. By the end of the 1980s, Beijing had one disco and seventy KTVs. A decade later, KTVs were everywhere, not only in the capital but throughout China, exposing consumers to a much wider array of mandopop tunes and (due to laxer policing of copyrights) movies than those available through state-controlled media.

As is true throughout the world, deliberately or not, musicians were not just selling music. Taiwanese pop stars appealed to Chinese consumers for the lifestyles they represented, coming to play a critical role in reintroducing gender differentiation in contemporary China. After decades of attempting to play down or erase gender differences and create a masculine unisex ideal under Mao—remember those Mao suits—Chinese women eagerly abandoned their masculine short haircuts and frumpy clothing and found in female pop stars role models for an updated though still traditional femininity. These pop stars became vehicles for a revived sense of womanhood emphasizing fragility, softness, and sexuality, and consumer choice—in this case, over which star to listen to and emulate—became a way to create real and imagined distance from state control. It also offered a means to redefine manhood, representing men as a product for female consumption and ensuring a preponderance of ballads celebrating soft males.

Following the Tiananmen Incident of June 4, 1989, many artists fled or assumed a lower profile, temporarily dampening interest in Taiwanese pop music. But Chinese policy makers, eager to counteract the negative international publicity, loosened restrictions on pop culture outlets to redirect anger over increased political controls, thus allowing the spread of pop culture through radio, TV, and publications. Taiwanese and Hong Kong stars remained the trendsetters, selling four fifths of all pop albums and headlining concerts in China. The dominant Taiwanese pop star in China in the 1990s was Chang Hui-mei, known simply as A-Mei. Her popularity reflected many things, not least of which was the sophisticated American-style marketing machine that promoted her, often through her endorsement of products such as Sprite soda. She was the first solo performer to appear at Beijing's Workers' Stadium, a site once used for political rallies, and the tickets for her concerts sold for record prices and triggered a media frenzy. In the feedback loop of popular consumption, the marketing of A-Mei taught the Chinese culture industry the value of public relations in promoting pop culture consumption, and such practices have since become commonplace.

The Chinese can now get their Taiwanese entertainment through concerts, satellite TV, overseas radio broadcasts, pirated music CDs and concert DVDs, and the Internet. Concerts have also become big business. Tickets for a Shanghai concert by the wildly popular Taiwanese boy band F4 sold for a record 2,000 yuan. The market for this sort of entertainment is not limited to big cities and big venues but extends across China.

The Chinese government has periodically tried to limit Taiwan's influence over popular culture, regulating concerts, banning some TV shows, restricting the number of Taiwanese actors allowed to appear in mainland-produced TV dramas, forbidding the inclusion of Taiwanese production company's names in the credits, and setting quotas for the broadcast of Taiwanese TV variety shows. These periods of restriction often accompany the lead-up to major political events such as the Chinese Communist Party's National Congresses (held every five years). In the months preceding the Sixteenth National Congress of the CCP (November 2002), for instance, China Central TV (CCTV) banned Taiwanese TV series and reemphasized "patriotic" programming such as game shows.

But the periodic politicizing of pop cultural icons misses the larger point: as noted earlier with cars, the consumer genie is now out of the bottle. Nothing establishes this more clearly than Chinese officials who, while deploring imported pop culture, have tried to create sanitized substitutes. In 1993, for instance, four hundred music videos with patriotic themes were produced for China's MTV, part of a plan to Sinify imported mandopop in a way to, as officials put it, "reflect China's 5,000 year cultural history." Sinification included videos featuring gratuitous shots of the Chinese flag and the Great Wall and songs praising life in China. It is little wonder that these groups, such as the Heartbeat Boys and Power of China, have failed to match the popularity of Taiwan's F4, Korea's H.O.T., or Japan's V6. As one veteran Chinese music blogger, Massage Milk, recalled, "We believed, we fervently believed and we superstitiously believed" in the superiority of Taiwanese pop music.

The Fad Four and Girls with Needs

The Taiwanese mastery at marketing and the Chinese central government's decreased ability to control the consumption of pop culture are nowhere more evident than in the popularity of the boy band F4. F4 got its start in a nineteen-part Taiwanese TV mini-series, *Meteor Garden*. Producer Angie Chan wanted to create a soap opera featuring good-looking boys and found an appropriate storyline in a Japanese manga called *Boys Are Prettier Than Flowers*. First broadcast in Taiwan in April 2001, it was an immediate hit. Thanks to the highly integrated East Asian youth culture and new communication technologies such as satellite TV, the Internet, and DVDs, the program spread throughout the Chinese-speaking world and into Japan and Korea within months.

Sony capitalized on the show's success by turning its lead actors into a boy band called F4—an abbreviation for Flowers Four. Initially, China's State Administration of Radio, Film, and Television (SARFT) allowed a heavily censored version of the series to be aired, and the Ministry of Culture granted permission for the release of the band's first album, *Meteor Rain*. State-run TV stations throughout China paid handsomely for broadcast rights, expecting large profits from higher advertising fees. By early 2002, some nine hundred small and medium-size cities had shown the program. Shanghai and Beijing telecasters, however, held back, fearing political repercussions, but the extensive and sophisticated black market for pirated TV shows meant there was little the government could do to stop people from watching. As put by Zhang Lulu, a nineteen-year-old Shanghai fan, "When girls like us have needs, there is nothing anyone can do to stop us." She alone bought fifty copies of the program to give as gifts. By that summer, Sony had sold half a million copies of the band's album and estimated that another five million copies had been pirated. Taiwan, once a notorious intellectual property infringer, had now become a victim itself.

Although the state reversed its decision and yanked the show "temporarily" because it could "easily mislead the youth," its failure to suppress its dissemination reveals the near impossibility of containing consumer culture and markets in China. The Chinese now own more than three hundred million TV sets, and TV advertising revenues are in the billions of dollars (witness CCTV's spectacular new headquarters in Beijing). The availability of inexpensive pirated DVDs and VCDs means that the Chinese have grown used to having access to foreign entertainment. As a result, bans invariably backfire. The ban on F4 only heightened demand and redirected consumption to the black market. In the end, a face-saving compromise was reached: the program was banned, but the group was not.

Taiwan's pop cultural invasion of China reveals the cascade of consequences that began with Taiwanese investment. What it demonstrates is that there are few if any effective dikes a government can erect to stop the demands of consumer culture. You cannot sell tape recorders but easily restrict what's heard on them, or market pop music but not the clothing lines that ape pop icon styles. The more China wants the Chinese to consume and bolster its economy, the harder it becomes to dictate what they consume, or to anticipate the direction in which Chinese desires will leap.

Reviving Consumer Culture in Print

While Sony and others have used new technology to break into the Chinese market, a far older technology, books, is selling like never before. Here, too, Taiwan has been a major player in the Chinese publishing revolution as its publishers and writers have sought a share of China's huge market. Just a few decades ago, it was hard to find bookstores selling much more than the collected works of Mao Zedong and a few of his favorite authors. But by 2000, China was adding 140,000 new titles and selling more than 7 billion books a year. Unlike some cultural industries, publishing is not restricted to the major coastal cities; thriving publishing centers have developed in provinces across China, such as Shandong, Liaoning, Hunan, Yunnan, and even impoverished Guangxi. Entire new genres of books have been introduced in the past decade, with books on business and wealth management regularly topping the bestseller lists.

Taiwanese publishers have enviously eyed the China market for decades. Chin Show Publishing was the first to arrive, in 1987, initially focusing on jointly publishing expensive or hard-to-produce oversize volumes such as art books with Chinese publishers. It also took advantage of lower labor costs, hiring Chinese writers, photographers, and translators to publish three massive reference works on Chinese art. As with so many other companies setting up business in China, Chin Show did so to reduce its production costs for products aimed at an export market. But with the emergence of a Chinese middle class, the company is now selling Chinese consumers the more expensive books it publishes in Taiwan. As China lowered trade barriers in anticipation of full membership in the World Trade Organization in 2001, Taiwanese publishers sought to expand farther into its domestic market. Although they encountered non-tariff barriers, such as having to secure a "book number" for each book and a "periodicals number" for every magazine, some managed to find a way around the regulations, often illegally. These restrictions suppressed growth but also inspired invention: Taiwanese publishers have published mainland versions of their titles under different names and have been allowed to publish individual issues of magazines. Multinational publishers have also seen tremendous opportunities in this underdeveloped market to generate advertising revenue, especially in magazines on technology, fashion, leisure, and family issues.

In the 1980s and early 1990s, Taiwanese publishers would buy the rights to international bestsellers and then resell them to Chinese publishers. By 2000, things had changed: mainland publishers had grown in confidence and were beating the Taiwanese at their own game by outbidding them for the rights to Chinese-language editions and reselling the rights themselves. Chinese publishers were then buying the rights to more than seven thousand titles annually, up from fewer than two thousand five years earlier. The Taiwanese, however, still maintain an edge, as they remain better at reading the market than the newcomers and generally pick more profitable titles to buy for resale. As a Taiwanese book industry executive noted, experienced Taiwanese publishers at the Frankfurt Book Fair are shadowed every year by five or six of their less experienced Chinese counterparts, who want to see what the Taiwanese are buying.

Taiwanese authors have had a similar edge, and their books are increasingly popular on the mainland. As early as 1999, Taiwanese author Liu Yung wrote seven of the top ten bestselling works in China. Likewise, Taiwanese Internet author "Slicker" Tsai (Tsai Chih-heng), whose writings launched intense Chinese interest in online literature, was voted the second most important cultural figure of 2001 by a mainland media organization. So why are these books so popular? One reason is that these works of "urban literature," using fictional lives set in more familiar contexts than American and European literary works, provide Chinese consumers with a road map for what Chinese life could be like. This same spirit has made Taiwanese inspirational and self-help books immensely popular in China. One young suburban woman browsing a popular Beijing book market reported that she reads Liu Yung's inspirational essays to help motivate her toward her dream of opening a boutique. Marketing is again crucial, with Taiwanese writers promoting their latest works with book tours and signings, press conferences, and speeches. But although the popularity of literary works is growing fast, the real revolution is in anything to do with pop culture, and the Chinese consumer just can't get enough of things like published photo albums of top stars such as F4. While the influence of books isn't as immediately evident as the influence of a phenomenon such as F4, it reflects the same basic force at work: China's mushrooming growth in desired goods, a process Taiwan has helped lead.

Other Eastern Influences: Korea

Although Taiwan remains a profound influence on Chinese consumer culture, it is not the only one. There is intense competition from other countries in the region. Take Korea, for example, whose influence has become so pervasive that it has spawned in China the term *Korean Wave*. This wave initially washed over the mainland in the form of a TV soap opera, *What Is Love*, which was broadcast in 1999 and became an instant and huge hit. Other soaps quickly followed, and by 2002, China had imported sixty-seven programs from Korea, second only to those coming from Hong Kong. This wave of influence, known as K-pop, has expanded from TV soaps to animation, cosmetics, food, electronics, clothes, hairstyles, music, movies, computer gaming, and even TV ads. Likewise, the Chinese desire for Korean brands such as LG flat-panel TVs, Samsung cell phones, and Hyundai Sonatas has boomed. Learning Korean has become so trendy that Korean stars now regularly appear in big-budget Chinese-language films. And concerts by Korean mega-singers such as Rain sell out Beijing's forty-thousand-seat stadium.

Korea is now the primary purveyor of Asian hip-hop, which it makes more appealing to regional ears by substituting the anger prevalent in U.S. hip-hop lyrics with love stories and more regionally familiar evocations of painful experiences in the education system. A cottage industry of Korean consultants has emerged to advise up-and-coming Chinese pop bands on everything from music and dance moves to fashion. What is cool among Korean trendsetters becomes cool among Chinese trendsetters, whether it's Yankee caps or Japanese Astro Boy dolls. In China, South Korea often acts as an intermediary for Western values and commodities, which are often easier to assimilate in their Korean form than undiluted American culture. As twenty-eight-year-old Wang Ying, a Beijing employee of an American company, put it, "To many young people, 'Korea' stands for fashionable or stylish." At the high end of consumer spending, Chinese brides regularly include traditional Korean robes for their lavish wedding photos. Beijing's trendy Xidan Shopping Center now hosts a store named Korea City on its top floor and smaller shops that sell Korean hip-hop clothes, music, and cosmetics.

The infusion of other pop cultures into Chinese consumerism has given a much broader portion of the Chinese population new reasons to travel. Record numbers of Chinese are now traveling as leisure tourists rather than simply in search of employment or on behalf of their employer. Not surprisingly, the Korean Wave has created an ever-increasing interest in visiting Korea. At the more extreme end of such tourism, young Chinese women and men go to Seoul to get plastic surgery to lengthen and accentuate their noses to look more like Korean pop stars. Such medical tourism has become so popular that some Korean plastic surgeons have opened clinics in China. But more often the desire to consume an imagined "Korea" is stoked by determined marketing efforts. Korea has styled itself as the "Italy of Asia," a peninsular country focused on food, family, song, and romance. This image, broadcast via pop culture throughout East Asia, has inspired more than a million Japanese and Chinese tourists a year to visit TV-linked theme parks in Korea, where visitors may wear royal Korean robes and explore the set of their favorite soap opera. These "set-jetters," tourists who travel to see the original sets and locations of their favorite movies and TV dramas, accounted for 1.2 million of the 6 million foreign tourists who visited Korea in 2005. The Korean government promotes set-jetting to more than fifty locations and production companies, and TV stations now purposely pick set locations with future tourism in mind.

Chinese pop culture has also been directly influenced since the 1990s by the increasing number of Koreans who have relocated to China, which has become the top travel destination for Koreans. Economic ties between the two nations have strengthened, and in 2005, China replaced the United States as Korea's top trading partner. Like their Taiwanese counterparts, Koreans often arrive for two- to five-year stints with established companies but grow accustomed to their increased purchasing power and opt to remain after their contracts run out, often to start their own small businesses. Like the Taiwanese before them, Koreans have created "Korea Towns" in Chinese cities such as Beijing, Qingdao, and Shanghai.

The types of Korean companies launching operations in China have also changed, in line with the Taiwan model, from primarily manufacturing to service industries and brand management. And, as with the Taiwanese-owned brands and retailers, the commodities they are hawking are not necessarily "Korean." In Shanghai, for example, you can pick up a cake at the Korean bakery chain Paris Baguette, then spend some time at the bar franchise Wa Bar, perhaps grab some fried chicken at BBQ, and upon arriving home change out of the clothes you bought at the casual apparel chain Eigenpost before spending a few hours shopping on Korea's leading home-shopping network, CJ. It is not too much to say that Korea has come to China.

One measure of the Korean Wave's success is the backlash it has inspired in China and Taiwan. Officials in both countries fear Korean domination of lucrative new culture industries and have sought to limit airtime for popular Korean dramas. After the widely popular *Jewel in the Palace* aired in 2005, Chinese officials, celebrities, and the media openly expressed such concerns. China's State Administration for Radio, Film, and Television (SARFT) and CCTV floated plans to limit airtime. TV actor and director Zhang Guoli went so far as to say that watching Korean TV dramas was equal to "selling out the nation" and "a waste of national resources." The Chinese film magazine *Star* accused the Korean government of obstructing Chinese food and cultural imports. But other observers, such as Beijing University sociologist Xia Xueluan, blame China itself: "The fact is, Chinese directors and producers aren't making good enough stuff to attract that audience, and it's embarrassing for them."

Nearly every chapter in this book demonstrates in some way the influence of other East Asian countries, particularly Taiwan, on Chinese consumerism. Taiwan, for instance, has been essential to the development of the beauty industry, and Japan to the car culture and consumer electronic industry in China. It's unlikely that the Korean Wave has crested or Taiwanese influence is over as long as both countries remain eager to replace a manufacturing base that is, as in so many other developed economies, uncompetitive with China. Service and leisure industries such as tourism and animation have become serious matters of state. In Korea in 2001, for instance, Kim Dae-jung, the South Korean president, named the entertainment industry one of the nation's key economic areas and committed government funds to a multibillion-dollar media center in Seoul to house production facilities for movies, music, television shows, and animation. Ten years after the Korean Wave began, it has become a multibillion-dollar industry. Culture industries, the fastest-growing area of Korean exports, are now essential to modern economies. The global animation industry alone generates more revenue than shipbuilding. In short, Korea, like Taiwan, will continue to capitalize on Chinese consumerism by promoting a commercialized interest in Korean culture.

One cannot simply blame or credit Taiwan for the explosive growth of Chinese consumerism any more than one can blame the United States or the WTO. This boom primarily reflects a long-suppressed desire for what Taiwan and other developed nations had to offer—hence all those families bringing over TVs and washer-dryers. The moment China encouraged Taiwanese investment and the Taiwanese leapt at the opportunities provided by the Chinese market, the process could not be stopped. China, like Taiwan and other developed nations before it, is discovering that there is no natural limit to the spread of consumer culture. Bubble tea leads to coffee, pop music to KTV. It is tempting to think about this in terms of who conquered whom, but that would overlook the power of the Chinese consumer. As much as either gov-

ernment would like to believe otherwise, Chinese needs are easier to
meet than to direct or, even harder still, to keep in check.

The fall of the Berlin wall was celebrated as the triumph of capitalism over communism, with clear winners and losers. But in East Asia
the struggle between these two ideologies has not had such a clear or
dramatic resolution. Rather, the introduction and spread of markets
and consumerism into China has occurred in countless small ways, with
effects that are still unfolding. True, Taiwan has facilitated the creation
of the contemporary industrial and consumer economy in China, and in
that sense perhaps Taiwan did retake the Ancestral Land (*zuguo*), as
the motherland is called in China. But the success of Taiwan in China
also hasn't been one-sided. Just as the United States and other developed economies look to China to save the world economy by consuming much more, the Taiwanese now do the same, even as some Taiwanese
mourn the diminished prospects for Taiwanese independence now that
their economy is so economically dependent on the mainland. For better or worse, a seamless and expanding chain of consumer resources
and demands now links China and Taiwan, as new desires have led to
new channels and new channels have created new desires. These
Taiwan-China flows are now so ubiquitous that they appear almost a
natural part of China's urban consumer landscape, so much so that neither a Western businesswoman in Shanghai or Ningbo nor her Chinese
counterpart is likely to recognize that she has the Taiwanese to thank
for the opportunity to dine at an American-style steakhouse, a French
bistro, or a "traditional" Chinese vegetarian restaurant.

4 ★ STANDARDIZING ABUNDANCE

Before you can have a consumer culture, of course, there must be something to buy. When I first visited China in the mid-1980s, my Chinese friends would tell me there were only two words I needed to know when it came to shopping: *mei you*, or "we don't have any," the most common response one heard from store clerks. Worse than having little choice was having nothing to choose from at all. When I arrived in China to study, things had improved a good deal, but shortages remained a fact of everyday life. At the time, most Chinese undoubtedly would have viewed the fare available at our student cafeteria as sumptuous, but I certainly didn't. Although the food cost almost nothing, I would gladly have paid extra for something more edible than the stringy chicken and adulterated rice we were served. Though my Chinese fellow students were accustomed to it, they were also aware of the extremely low quality of the food, especially as vegetables grew scarcer by spring. My Chinese roommate back then developed a theory: the student protests that broke out across college campuses each spring were inspired not by the students' stated high-minded reasons (that year, a desire to elect their own student representatives) but by the quality of the available food.

This, too, changed rapidly with the coming of economic reforms. A decade later, urban Chinese were beginning to have access to supermarkets, twenty-four-hour convenience stores selling foods and snacks, and (perhaps the most revolutionary change in a country formerly plagued with famines) all-you-can-eat buffets. Since the mid-1990s, this plenty has spread outward to smaller Chinese cities and downward to the less affluent.

While a few decades ago there was little to buy and even fewer places to buy it in China, the country's urban areas have since undergone not only a transition from scarcity to abundance but also a revolution in how things are sold. At Walmart supercenters, 7-Eleven convenience stores, traveling peddler carts parked outside high-rises, and even among the permanent shops lining the lanes up to Buddhist and Confucian temples, the Chinese today are never far from opportunities to shop. They have seen a stunning increase in the number of products available to buy and of places to buy them; exercising consumer choice among an abundance of items is now an everyday activity for the Chinese, just as it is for consumers in the United States and other developed nations. And urban Chinese love to shop. According to a 2008 survey, they have come to spend on average nearly ten hours a week doing it (while Americans spend slightly under four), and two in five called shopping their favorite leisure activity. Such retailing opportunities are the primary mechanism by which market economies expand consumption and translate consumer desires into economic realities.

Although this retail revolution has taken place across the full range of consumer goods and services, perhaps in no area of Chinese life has the transformation been more obvious and dramatic than in how the country now meets the most essential of human needs, food. As late as the 1980s, grocery shopping was a time-consuming and grim experience as customers faced long lines and uncertain supplies. What little was available to buy was unattractively packaged and sold by unmotivated and unhelpful workers ever ready to respond to inquires with *mei you*. At the advent of the Reform Era in 1978, city dwellers spent 58 percent of their income on food, most of it on staples such as rice and locally available vegetables. Today they spend only about a third of their income on food, and have many more varieties of food-stuffs to select from, including frozen foods, snacks, wines, carbon-ated drinks, and imported fruits and vegetables, all of them attractively marketed, packaged, and displayed. Consumers are no longer limited to shopping for food in state-run stores and mom-and-pop shops, but can choose from a variety of superstores, supermarkets, discount stores, and convenience stores. Such retail options, almost nonexis-tent until the early 1990s, now represent a third of urban food mar-kets, and they are spreading. According to the China Chain Store and Franchise Association, the number of supermarkets in China expanded from just one outlet in 1990 to approximately sixty thousand just ten years later, an expansion that only accelerated after China formally joined the WTO in 2001. By 2003, these supermarkets were generat-ing an estimated $71 billion in sales. This metamorphosis from dingy state-run stores to brightly lit international chain stores staffed by po-lite and helpful uniformed attendants at computerized checkouts is a particularly telling and vivid example of the retail revolution (or "Wal-Marting") transforming the everyday consumer experience in China. Its history also provides a vivid example of China's larger shift from a centralized to a consumerist economic model and the lifestyles it made possible.

From Shortages to Abundance

China's decision to allow consumers to decide where, when, and how much to buy and to eat marked a dramatic reversal of the Maoist-era model. After the Communist Revolution in 1949, the new government at first permitted the existing private, family-run shops to continue, but within a few years its socialist reforms begin to centralize retailing by creating a system of unified administration and monopoly supply—that is, a state-owned distribution system. All urban staple food shops fell under the control of the Staple Food Bureau, which supplied all state-owned stores with nearly identical items at identical prices. To purchase food in these stores required not only cash but also, as I discovered when I tried to buy that bicycle at the Nanjing Friendship Store, local ration coupons. Even when supplies were available, a purchaser could buy only a limited amount. Prices and supplies were set from above and fixed. The lack of competition showed, and these stores quickly became notorious for their lack of service, variety, innovation, and respect for local preferences. Packaging served only the functional purpose of separating and protecting products—and did even this poorly, as damage rates exceeded 10 percent. Clerks often applied labels haphazardly and even incorrectly before placing goods on shelves. Consumers, separated from the merchandise by a wall of salespeople and counters, had to request products from inattentive clerks, who rarely let buyers examine goods before purchasing them. Indeed, clerks often were responsible for maintaining their stocks and therefore had a *disincentive* to take items out of their protective cases and packaging for customers to inspect.

But starting with the economic reforms in 1978, the state began a rapid withdrawal from managing the retail sector, ending its monopoly over the procurement of commodities and relaxing state control over prices. In effect, China began moving away from a command economy, where the government decides how much of what is produced, and reintroduced markets, where consumer demand determines production. The first to benefit were farmers, who began growing and selling their surplus produce. But as private ownership, country fairs, and urban marketplaces reappeared, other small retail entrepreneurs also emerged, the very ones who became China's first post-Mao newly well-off. In towns and cities across China, such small-scale businesses became critical participants in the reintroduction of mass retailing and therefore of consumerism. Of course, these budding entrepreneurs also needed to have something to sell, and in December 1978, the Communist Party leadership restored "private plots" (though not private ownership of the land) and permitted the reestablishment of markets, both in the abstract economic sense and in literal marketplaces. The state now allowed producers to sell their privately grown produce directly to consumers or private middlemen and not exclusively to the state, let alone at state-set prices. Motivated by the opportunity to make a profit, farmers began to grow more. And as agricultural production boomed, so did rural incomes.

Markets tend to beget more markets and consumption more consumption, so retail offerings quickly spread beyond agricultural produce. Between 1980 and 1985, the number of individually owned mini-stores, stalls, and booths selling goods rose from one million to six million, and by 1986, sixty thousand local marketplaces had opened across China. To give but one example, during this period Shenyang, the capital of Liaoning province in northeast China, established ten large open-air marketplaces and thirty-four smaller ones throughout the city, which together served three million urban residents and another two million in the surrounding area. The largest of these, the Bei Hang Agricultural Market, was as large as an American football field.

The story of the Bei Hang Agricultural Market encapsulates the tumultuous twentieth-century history of selling things in China. First established in the 1920s, after 1949, Bei Hang's fate was tied to the CCP's on-again-off-again policy of using market mechanisms in general and marketplaces in particular. It was allowed to operate until 1957, when it was abolished as part of the collectivization of farming, the creation of giant communal farms. But after the dramatic failure of the Great Leap Forward and after the subsequent Great Famine, China's leaders reversed their position toward small-scale market-places, making it legal for those living on communes to have small private plots and to grow some extra vegetables for sale, and reestablishing Bei Hang in 1960. Six years later, however, the market was outlawed again as the Cultural Revolution re-vilified material incentives, calling the use of money and personal profit to motivate people "capitalistic." With the advent of economic reforms, Bei Hang was officially re-reopened at the start of 1979, and within two years became one of forty-four large marketplaces hosting more than five thousand peddlers across the city. Dan Dejun, a longtime Bei Hang vendor, remembered the policy shift as it appeared in newspaper political cartoons. In late 1978, the newspaper printed a cartoon with someone riding a bicycle with two basketfuls of produce. Over the cyclist's head was the caption "Speculator." A month later, the identical cartoon was run, but "Speculator" was replaced with a large red flower, signaling the Communist Party's endorsement of such commercial activity.

Because few Chinese had refrigerators and all had a tradition of buying fresh meat and produce, more than half a million began shopping at Shenyang's forty-four marketplaces every day, immediately reintroducing choice and consumer control. Within a few years, every resident of Shenyang, and those in cities like it across China, had access to similar open-air marketplaces. Even state-owned enterprises such as hotels and restaurants began going to such markets to buy at least part of their supplies. Indeed, this reemergent market culture spread so quickly and widely that state-owned shops and agricultural communes began selling their own surplus produce in such market-places, although the latter still had to meet their hefty state quotas before they were allowed to sell anything and keep the profits. During the early years of the reforms, the contrasts between state-owned and private retailing were quickly and easily visible.

This reintroduction of mass retailing, beginning with these local produce marketplaces, signaled the restoration of choice, an end to chronic shortages, and a shift toward the perception of plenty. It also signaled a change in everyday influences on one's purchasing decisions. In state stores, the Chinese had had to rely on employees to select the particular items they could buy. As one woman recalled, "I could only buy my favorite candies at a state-owned food store in Tianjin. I could not choose the flavor and wrappings of candies I wanted. My favorite flavor was lemon, but shop assistants only grabbed random candies in a big jar. I was very disappointed that in the large pile of candies there were only a few lemon ones." But at marketplaces, buyers could choose which piece of fruit or clothing item they wished to buy. The reestablishment of private buying and selling, then, also restored the power of choice to the consumer (and, as we shall see, explains the simultaneous reemergence of branding and advertising to coach consumers on what to buy). But although marketplaces usually supplied much higher quality items than the state stores, they did so at higher prices. True, Shenyang's inspectors joked that they could identify goods originally obtained at state stores rather than private marketplaces by their dirty appearance, poor presentation, and low quality. But along with improved quality came steady price rises, sowing discontent among those earning fixed salaries. I vividly recall, for instance, the anger of my Chinese roommate who in 1986 declared it an abomination that many of these new entrepreneurs, including the guys running the noodle stands that ringed the campus, earned more than he would as a university professor.

I don't recall, however, my roommate's complaining about his newfound ability to buy hot noodle soup at all hours or to enjoy the newly available fruits, vegetables, and other products from faraway provinces now available in Chinese cities such as Nanjing. Where products were absent or in short supply, peddlers now had an economic incentive to meet demand, and soon goods were moving across the country to wherever they would fetch the highest price. Perhaps it's not surprising that many of his classmates decided that if they couldn't out-earn these peddlers, they'd join them. The original vendors at marketplaces such as Bei Hang were mostly migrant laborers, former prisoners, and farmers from the surrounding area—that is, those with low social and economic standing. But a decade or so later, such vendors included college graduates.

The ongoing creation of integrated markets for products spanning the country also helped transform China from a country of shared scarcity and immobility under Mao to one with circulating people and products. The Bei Hang market, for instance, within a couple of years of its reopening, hosted peddlers from nearly all of China's provinces and regions, and the variety of goods sold there expanded rapidly; the development of national markets for regional products soon ensured that fresh produce from southern China, which enjoyed later harvests, was being transported north. Dual-track prices (that is, one price dictated by the state and the other determined by the private market) further undermined state provisioning, as suppliers now had an incentive to hold back their best products from the state to sell on the market, hastening the end of state-run shops.

The experience of shopping changed in other ways as well. While state stores had sold products at prices fixed by the state, the advent of markets brought a gradual return to bargaining. At first both sellers and buyers were reluctant to haggle, behavior that had been discouraged as "capitalistic" and, given fixed prices, had been unnecessary during the previous decades. But within a few years nearly every customer at markets such as Bei Hang tried to bargain for lower prices. The end of fixed prices and the new diversity of goods also made comparison shopping important again, although state-owned stores continued to provide a reference point for what was a legitimate price. Likewise, choice made every consumer his or her own quality-control expert, requiring heightened vigilance—particularly in a retailing environment awash in fakes. Not surprisingly, the uneven quality of goods led to the careful inspection of products by potential buyers. Few consumers now buy goods without the opportunity to inspect them; every piece of fruit and every seam is checked.

The end of fixed prices also saw the return of the image of the "cunning merchant" (*jianshang*). In traditional Chinese culture, merchants were generally viewed as making money not, like most Chinese, through hard agricultural labor in the hot sun or even making things by hand, but rather by manipulating prices and information. Even before the Communist Revolution, in the early twentieth century merchants were often portrayed in popular culture as treasonous, helping to sell imported products from the imperialist powers, especially Japan, who then dominated China. Then, as now, not everyone sold the same product at the same price. Now price has again become, like so much else in China, relational, with premiums demanded from foreigners and anyone unfamiliar with the market or the seller. In this environment, no wonder bargaining quickly reemerged as the quintessential marketplace experience. Although the subsequent standardization of shopping and prices in large retail stores doesn't leave much opportunity for haggling, in smaller shops and even in mid-tier department stores one might still ask for and perhaps get a discount. What something should cost has once again become the source of endless conversation in China: "What did you pay for that?" has become—after the traditional greeting, "Have you eaten?"—the second most frequently asked question in the country.

One way to measure this initial stage of China's expanding commitment to consumerism is that between 1981 and 1991, the number of retail outlets more than quadrupled, from 2.02 million to 9.24 million, and the number of people working in the retail sector doubled, from 7.63 million to 21.99 million. Consumerism, in short, has grown more entrenched on both sides of the counter. The experience of expanding consumer choice necessarily means that millions of Chinese are also experiencing the seller side of sales, especially as the Chinese government pushes its economy toward developing a service sector to match its manufacturing prowess.

The Retail Revolution

In 1992 the Chinese leadership under Deng Xiaoping recommitted their country to pursuing a market- and consumer-driven model of economic development, including gaining full membership in the WTO. The latter meant meeting the demand of foreign governments and multinationals for greater access to Chinese consumers, which would also require the expansion of retailing opportunities and strategies. And just as they had with cars, Chinese leaders recognized that one way to finance rapid reform and create domestic demand for goods and services was to invite foreign investment without surrendering complete control. Where shortages had been a way of life, now the issue was clearly consumerist: how to entice people to buy and consume more, shifting control from suppliers to consumers. This new era of mass marketing in China began with formerly dreary state-owned stores experimenting with marketing techniques they were learning from the Taiwanese and others. Even such seemingly small changes as Beijing's Number One Department Store on Wangfujing handing out free samples belied a fundamental shift: rather than dampening desire in an environment of scarcities, stimulate it. Likewise, signs, billboards, and other public advertisements informing and enticing potential buyers appeared in urban centers. Overnight, Chinese cities began to glow with neon lights advertising Beck's beer and

Oreo cookies. Major shopping streets such as Nanjing Road in Shanghai, once drab and dull, again began to resemble Hong Kong's Golden Mile at night, with families and couples strolling the streets window-shopping and responding to street vendors. Across the country, central planners introduced nearly identical pedestrian shopping malls modeled on Wangfujing in Beijing, Binjiang Avenue in Tianjin, and Shangxia Jiu Pedestrian Street in Guangzhou.

During the late 1990s, Chinese retailing underwent intensified expansion and consolidation. Although the central government tried to limit foreign investment, local governments began to ignore central controls and encourage such investment. Soon international retail giants such as Carrefour, Metro, and Walmart began to aggressively expand across the country, further transforming the retail environment. This process continued to accelerate after 2004, the end of the three-year transition period following China's entry into the WTO, as remaining restrictions on the ownership, location, and number of branches of chain stores were abolished. Chinese retailers such as Wumart and Lianhua have countered this spread of these international companies with their own mergers and acquisitions and become increasingly like their competitors: larger chains of bigger stores using advertising to promote established brands promised at lower prices. Several of the largest Chinese-owned chains are still state-owned, including Beijing Hualian Group and Dalian Dashang Group, further ensuring that China will not simply surrender its retailing industry to foreign companies. And these outlets are no longer limited to big coastal cities. To achieve economies of scale, first-mover advantage, and lower labor and land costs, both international and domestic retail chains are rapidly pushing beyond the major coastal cities and into interior second- and third-tier cities.

As with the spread of cars, the expansion of supermarket and convenience store chains has benefited from political decisions at both the local and national levels. Some local governments, for instance, have facilitated the transition to supermarkets by closing down traditional street markets, often with the pretext that they were unhygienic. In some cases, local officials have converted traditional large, indoor "wet" markets selling produce and meat into supermarkets. At the national level, China's Ministry of Commerce launched a five-year plan in 2004 to develop a retail network of chain supermarkets and convenience stores in small towns, pushing the supermarket format into the country's vast rural hinterland. And all of this urban-rural national integration is aided by the massive road-building under way in China— the same roads carrying those millions of new automobiles also have trucks supplying new regional and national distribution networks.

With them has come the demise of many medium- and small-size retail establishments and family-operated shops across the country. Supermarkets are rapidly gaining a competitive edge over these traditional retailers, as they offer a cleaner, more comfortable, convenient, and predictably standardized shopping environment, places where the experience of buying bananas or canned yams is nearly identical whether the items are purchased in the northeastern city of Dalian or the southwestern town of Dali. Likewise, a younger generation is increasingly unfamiliar and uncomfortable with unbranded commodity consumption; China's youngest consumers want to shop in Walmart and Wumart. As a young man told me, "China's wet markets are generally very dirty, so I don't like to go to them. The things for sale at supermarkets are much more trustworthy, though more expensive." Of course, Walmart and other retailers have responded to this perception by using techniques such as loss leaders, selling some common items at cost or below to stimulate sales, and the perception of "everyday fair prices," to quote the catchphrase Walmart uses in China. When Walmart first arrived in Nanjing, for instance, the store became synonymous with "eggs" and "rice" for selling those two items even more cheaply than a nearby wet market.

Beyond cheaper staples, imported foods, until recently a rarity in China, are also now widely available, where everything from Washington apples to California wines and from Thai lychees to New Zealand butter are stocked on Chinese supermarket shelves. The same applies to many international food brands, such as Kellogg's cereals, Hormel sausages and hot dogs, Nestlé and Danone milk products, and Skippy peanut butter, many of which are manufactured locally, sometimes with imported ingredients. Following China's entry into the WTO, the fragmented domestic marketing system still hindered the transfer of products to consumers, but supermarket chains have begun to change this situation by introducing modern procurement systems into China, thereby providing consumers with a larger and more unified market. These chains have created their own massive distribution centers that draw products from across China and around the world and move them to individual stores around the country, from which the Chinese are quickly learning.

Chewing with Confidence and Convenience

The recent history of rice, that quintessential Chinese commodity, offers a striking example of the transformation of the experience of buying and consuming in China. Before the price reforms of the early 1990s, consumers bought generic rice at government-set prices from state-run grain shops. Local farmers, who were forced to "sell" their grain at set prices, unsurprisingly tended to sell their worst rice to the state, which also practiced little quality control. This rice was often broken and unevenly colored and unpolished and, worse still, often contained stones or bugs. During my own earliest experiences as a student in China, the first time I discovered a black bug in my unpolished white rice, I lost my appetite for rice for the next couple of meals. As I gradually assimilated to eating state-procured rice, I began to simply pick out the bugs and continue eating. But I still had to chew gingerly, as I often bit into tiny rock granules. Chewing rice with confidence is a relatively new experience for the Chinese and visitors alike.

Within a decade of my first encounter with a black bug, however, the country had established a very competitive rice industry built around brands, types, quality, origins, and prices. This competitive environment allowed consumers across China access to varieties of rice and catered to regional preferences. Beijing supermarkets, for instance, now supplied local buyers with the most widely preferred japonica variety (short- to medium-grain) and brands of rice grown and transported from distant counties in the country's northeastern provinces. Indeed, the current availability of japonica rice throughout China illustrates how food markets and brands are becoming national, sometimes even eroding regional differences in tastes and preferences. Southern Chinese, who traditionally preferred long-grain indica rice, now often eat japonica rice, particularly in wealthy areas such as Shanghai and Zhejiang province. The rise of branded rice has also addressed growing concerns about food safety. Rice brands often seek and advertise government-designated "green food" seals, which certify the reduced use of chemicals during production and a relatively pollution-free factory environment. Since 2001, new labeling regulations for foods containing genetically modified organisms have also been in place.

Today more young Chinese live away from their family home, work long hours, and need to manage two-career families. In short, like their counterparts worldwide, Chinese consumers increasingly demand convenience and predictability. And, as elsewhere around the globe, these expectations have fueled the rise of convenience store chains. Chinese today are rarely far from places to buy something to eat. These stores were first introduced into China in the mid-1990s by one of Japan's largest chains, Lawson. By 2004, there were nearly five thousand identical Lawson convenience stores in China, over half of those in Shanghai, where convenience stores now so blanket the city that many blocks host several. As elsewhere, convenience stores carry all the basics that people run out of or need more of at the last minute: bottled water and juices, alcohol, magazines, salty snacks, prepared lunch boxes, newspapers, and cigarettes. And, following the Japanese model, they have expanded to offering many other time-saving services such as photocopying and accepting payment for telephone, gas, and electrical bills. By 2004, the Japanese-owned 7-Eleven chain, the world's largest convenience store operator, also had stores in south China and had formed a joint venture with two Chinese companies to open the first twenty-four-hour outlet in Beijing. Five years later, the company had nearly six hundred stores in China.

To gain the economies of scale that make them profitable, convenience store chains like Lawson and its Chinese equivalents such as Wumart have opened as many outlets as manageable, thereby dramatically altering urban China's nightscape. The former darkness of most city streets is being replaced with bright fluorescent lights, and more people are out late picking up milk or a snack, browsing the magazines and newspapers as they do so. Nonetheless, these retailers are finding that convenience is not always enough to draw shoppers. During Beijing's long winters, for instance, 7-Eleven finds its stores largely empty and unprofitable; what they offer is not inducement enough to brave the cold. And despite national efforts of mass retailers to lure customers away from traditional wet markets, many Chinese cling to the perception that these carry fresher, cheaper goods, especially fruits and vegetables. Thus wet markets, though greatly reduced in number, have not disappeared, even in cities such as Shanghai and Beijing. Indeed, many shoppers continue to purchase fresh produce from these markets, supplementing them with weekend trips to the supermarket for other items.

But such traditional preferences are not the most likely check on the seemingly endless expansion of retailing in China. Rather, as Chinese and multinational chains compete over smaller and smaller markets, some economists and observers worry that China hasn't yet a sufficiently large middle class with enough disposable income to justify this expansion and consolidation. But even if many of these stores end up like some of China's spectacular shopping malls—huge, empty spaces, monuments to misplaced hopes for demand that never materialized—they will, for better and for worse, have transformed the everyday experience of shopping for hundreds of millions of Chinese. For the average shopper, the shift from simply not having enough to having a bewildering range of choices is captured in the transition in common Chinese expressions regarding food from *chibaole* to *chihaole* to *chiqiaole*: from the simple objective of "eating to fill your belly" to the pleasures of "eating plenty of rich food" to the present situation requiring consumers to "eat skillfully." For as we shall see later, navigating the now dense markets overflowing with new products while avoiding food scandals, fakes, and misinformation is indeed a learned skill.

Just as it would be difficult for most Chinese to go back to using a public toilet, it would be similarly difficult for them to return to shopping in a poorly lit neighborhood wet market after becoming accustomed to driving a car to a Walmart and never worrying about availability or the need to haggle over prices. Retailing, then, is transforming the ways Chinese see the world. The idea that one would walk into a Walmart to find it was out of toilet paper or into a McDonald's to find it had sold out of hamburgers becomes unthinkable. In short, modern retailing turns the population into consumers who are independent (they get to choose), rational (they must comparison-shop), and individualistic (they have access to a variety of items and stores to suit every consumer taste).

Famine to Feast

Perhaps no irony better highlights the changed world for the Chinese consumer than the fact that increasing numbers of them are using this new abundance of choices to overeat, perhaps even to an early grave. Food has always defined differences among Chinese in at least two ways: who could afford to eat meat divided China by economic class, and rice-eating distinguished southern Chinese from their wheat noodle–eating northern compatriots. As noted, national chains have accelerated the integration of national and even international markets, bringing not only a wider variety of traditional foods but more meat and processed food to consumers across China. Similarly, when fast-food restaurants first arrived in Chinese major cities, they were novelties visited infrequently; now, as the thousands of KFCs, McDonald'ses, and their Chinese equivalents popping up across urban China confirm, they play a wider role in urban lifestyles. The result: Chinese eat much more oily, fatty, salty, and sugary foods. City dwellers, for instance, eat twice as much meat as they did in the 1980s. Accompanying the increase in calories are expanding waistlines, a problem compounded by sedentary office work and the displacement of the bicycle as the primary means of transportation. Twenty years ago one rarely saw fat Chinese teenagers; now they're commonplace. While twenty years ago the idea of fat camps for overweight children would have been considered absurd, now they are widely advertised. It doesn't help that pudgy babies have traditionally been viewed as healthy and that anyone born in the 1960s or earlier is old enough to remember famine. The new food options, along with economic inequality, have expanded the traditional distinctions made through food to include who can afford to contract "lifestyle diseases" such as cancer and diabetes, which the World Health Organization estimates could kill as many as eighty million Chinese in the next decade.

The effects that economic inequality has had on the Chinese diet are clearly written on Chinese bodies. For instance, urban residents eat twice as much protein as their less affluent rural counterparts, mostly from poultry, eggs, and shrimp, which translates into height differences. Urban residents stand, on average, 4.6 centimeters higher, becoming a symbol of the inequality between urban and rural consumers and even a source of discrimination. But these diet changes have also included increased consumption of fats. Over the past ten years the number of Chinese suffering from high blood pressure increased by a third, and hypertension now afflicts a fifth of those over eighteen. In major cities, where the shift toward Western-style diets has been most marked, nearly a third of adults are overweight, and one in ten is obese. The trends for urban children are even more alarming. By the end of the 1990s, childhood obesity in the country as a whole had increased from 4 to 6 percent; but in urban areas, the percentage of overweight urban children had risen from 15 to 29 percent.

Overconsumption is visible in other ways. In the Mao era, extravagant banquets and other opportunities to overeat were for most Chinese nonexistent or exclusively for special occasions such as New Year's festivals and weddings. The notion of "leftovers," even less of "doggie bags," had not yet arrived. Now doggie bags are common, and discarding leftovers is even more routine. Shanghai alone throws away two thousand tons of food every day, and Beijing discards sixteen hundred tons. Despite water shortages across the country, water, too, is wasted in new ways. In one egregious and widely publicized example, a Harbin brewery—in a bit of poorly considered consumer outreach—used ninety tons of beer to create a fountain in a downtown square; the stunt required not only eighteen tons of barley and rice but also eighteen hundred tons of clean water.

Food waste is also embedded in Chinese customs. The difference now is that what was once an affectation of a very select wealthy and powerful few has become a status-gaining gesture for the ever more numerous aspiring middle classes. Wu Mingzheng, a manager of a Hangzhou export company, explaining why he ordered sixteen dishes at a four-star restaurant for a table of business contacts, few of whom touched much of the food, said that "if there aren't enough dishes or the guests don't have enough to drink to their heart's content, everyone will think I am cheap and it may affect our business dealings." This scene is repeated hundreds of thousands of times a day across China. According to a survey conducted in Zhejiang province, 70 percent of those taking guests out to dine decline to take away leftovers.

Officials make periodic attempts to discourage overconsumption. In 2008, Zhang Xinshi, a city official in Jiangsu province, for instance, charged in his blog that "China was the most wasteful consumer of food and beverages," adding that Chinese should emulate other countries and have fewer but better dishes. His conclusion was backed by stories of waste from around China. In the northeast city of Harbin, one reporter estimated that the city's twenty thousand restaurants discarded at least four hundred tons of food a day. Although she found waste in all restaurants, she also discovered that the more expensive the restaurant, the more the waste. In many cases, more than half the food went to waste, particularly by those dining at public expense. But in all cases at least a fifth of the food was left behind. In response, Zhejiang provincial authorities launched a campaign to urge consumers to avoid "unscientific and uncivilized" consumer practices such as deliberately wasting food and hosting extravagant wedding celebrations. But platitudes and a few specific policies have done little to counter an ancient cultural practice suddenly put within reach of millions more Chinese.

Obesity and waste are just two of the clearly unexpected and undesired consequences of the increasingly unleashed and prodded Chinese consumer. And as has proven true elsewhere in the world, the new consumer culture is more likely to produce market reactions—from increased sales of diabetes medication to food delivery services—than it is ever to be reformed. Thanks to the introduction of modern retailing practices, though, one thing we know for sure is that the Chinese are unlikely ever again to be far away from opportunities to consume as much and as frequently as they can afford—for better or for worse.

5 ★ BRANDING CONSUMER CONSCIOUSNESS

Because the Chinese certainly have more money than they did twenty years ago, there is no shortage of people ready to instruct them on how to spend it, including the Chinese state itself. When David Ogilvy, dubbed the Father of Advertising, visited China in the early 1980s, he was struck by the near-absence of advertising. Print advertisements looked like specification sheets, containing little more than detailed, technical information about a product, and no evocative images. The few commercials on Chinese television mostly featured industrial products such as electric motors rather than consumer goods. The rare big billboard proclaimed the latest in Communist propaganda. Ogilvy noted that the most important advertising medium in China was radio, "the communal speaker system reaching 75% of the population" that would broadcast ads, one right after another, twice a day. There were fewer than seventy ad agencies in all of China, with a quarter of those producing advertisements for Chinese goods overseas.

Today it is a very different story. With market reforms came advertising, and suddenly in every corner of China a wide spectrum of bright colors has replaced the unofficial colors of Maoist state socialism, the navy blue of workers' clothing and green of soldiers' uniforms.

The transformation has been both dramatic and rapid. China's ad market has grown by 40 percent a year over the past two decades and may become the second largest in the world in 2010; some reports expect China to replace the United States as the world's largest ad market as soon as 2020. In 2008, bolstered by the Beijing Olympics, advertising spending in China grew to nearly $70 billion, still under half of what the United States spends but up 17 percent over 2007. China now has more than two thousand newspapers with a total circulation above a billion, the world's ten largest general-circulation magazines, and more than a thousand satellite, cable, and broadcast television channels and three hundred radio stations. Nearly all Chinese have access to TVs and the advertising that comes with it. As China shifts its economy to a heavy reliance on markets, it is forcing these media outlets, which once relied on state subsidies, to support themselves via advertising. The results of this policy shift are visible everywhere.

It began with outdoor advertising, now a billion-dollar industry, which was the only sector to allow foreign investment before China joined the World Trade Organization in 2001. Large media companies quickly stepped in and took over, including the world's largest outdoor advertising company, Clear Media, which now manages a network of twenty-seven thousand bus stop panels in China. Clear Media introduced international "best practices," such as the use of vivid color, celebrity endorsements, catchy slogans, the frequent rotation of advertisements, and other established eye-catching techniques. China may even outdo the ad-saturated United States in finding new public places to put advertising. In addition to all the usual places—buses, bus stops, along roads, on buildings—ads have also popped up on little TV screens in taxis and on the backs of airplane seats. Even elevators now sport flat-panel screens broadcasting ads. As one woman I interviewed exclaimed, "Ads are now ubiquitous! And sometimes they don't even appear as ads but as product placements in movies and TV series."

Advertising in China is now a huge industry, including more than eighty thousand ad companies that employ over a million people, making the industry a larger employer than its counterpart in the United States. A lot of energy and money is facilitating the introduction of global advertising techniques, all designed to make Chinese consumers think about brand-specific products and identify with brand-specific lifestyles. In 2004, one cosmetics brand alone, Oil of Olay, spent 4.7 billion yuan in advertising in China. Joining the WTO required China to open its advertising industry to foreign investors and to allow wholly owned foreign firms in by 2005, accelerating the introduction of the latest advertising practices and bringing with them a globally standardized visual culture. To compete, Chinese ad agencies embraced this standard as Chinese companies such as Haier, Huawei Technologies, Lenovo, and Li Ning sportswear spend billions of dollars on advertising to build their brands against those of foreign competitors.

The purpose of such advertising, of course, is not simply to provide information about available goods and services but to help create *brands*, the fundamental building blocks of modern consumer cultures, and thereby to shape the way people develop their individual and collective identities. As expressed by one thirtysomething professional woman in Beijing, "Brand names are social status and quality of life. For example, when I was in the United States, I didn't pay much attention to brand names. Here it's a culture. Look at me now; I'm equipped with nothing but brand names, say, Gucci, Fendi, Armani, Versace, and the like." Brands are symbolic embodiments of all the associations, real or imagined, connected with a product or service—such as thinking that driving an expensive Toyota Prius makes you an environmentalist. They incorporate not only information but expectations: "Coke adds life," they would have us believe, rather than, say, an increased chance of childhood obesity and diabetes. Branding, then, of which advertising is a key component, includes not only the creation, management, and delivery of a product or service but also the formation of expectations connected with it.

And the psychic and social power of brands cannot be denied. A year or so ago, I traveled to a number of remote areas of China that I had not visited for twenty years, curious to learn if the consumer culture so visible in China's cities had also reached its hinterlands. In a remote region of southwest China, I quizzed the man running the guesthouse about whether he had heard of McDonald's and french fries and whether he desired them. He found my questions ridiculous—thanks to television, everyone knew about McDonald's and french fries. Although he expressed little interest in the food himself, his daughter was another story. Not only had she heard of every brand for which I could remember the Chinese name, but the promise of Kentucky Fried Chicken had helped her father persuade her to relocate to the provincial capital, an eight-hour bus ride away, to attend a much better school. Years of being bombarded with ads about the wondrous food and lifestyle available at KFC made his bribe effective.

Brand China

In China, branding is more overtly an issue of economic nationalism than in the United States. Most Americans associate the work of branding with companies and the marketplace, not with government officials and the state. Americans think it is Apple's job to make the iPod brand a household name, not the U.S. government's. But in China, consumerism is not simply a product of "the free market," something that developed naturally once the Chinese state got out of the way. Rather, it is a consequence of ongoing policy decisions by China's leaders, most notably the decision to join the WTO. But another decision has been to encourage the rapid development of internationally competitive Chinese-based brands even while allowing multinational companies much greater access to Chinese consumers. As Chinese marketing expert Leng Zhen-xing has argued, "Banknotes are just like votes. The more the foreign brands get, the less will be left for domestic products."

A useful measure of the shift from a few to a plethora of branded products in China is visible in trademark registrations. In 1980 the Chinese government received 20,000 trademark applications, a number that by 1993 had reached 132,000. By 2004, more than half of all the 2,240,000 registered trademarks had been registered since 2000, a quarter of them just that year. Although the number of foreign applications has also expanded dramatically during the Reform Era, from only 20 countries with 5,130 trademarks to 129 countries with more than 400,000 trademarks, more than 80 percent of those applications have been made by Chinese companies.

Most consumers outside China, despite being surrounded by goods made there, would probably find it difficult to name a famous Chinese brand. But if China has its way, this will soon change dramatically. It is hard to exaggerate China's current level of national anxiety over the competitiveness of Chinese brands. Its historical analog might be the urgency in the United States to win the space race after the Soviet Union launched Sputnik in 1957. Similarly, Chinese leaders believe they need to launch national brands or gain ownership of international ones before it's too late, and survival is seen as much too important to leave to "the market." Rather, building or buying brands is considered a matter of national economic security and, of course, of national pride—China wants its *own* international brands to reflect its commercial success and its status as a first-rate power.

The success of Chinese brands depends first of all on persuading Chinese consumers to buy them, which is no easy task. The country can no longer ensure consumer loyalty by protecting its markets, banning imports, limiting access to the foreign currency needed to buy imports, or levying tariffs so high that foreign goods become prohibitively expensive. Chinese brands also have to overcome an unreliable marketplace saturated with fakes. No wonder a 2005 survey of 1,200 students in Shanghai and Beijing found that all of their favorite brands were foreign, led by Nike, Sony, Adidas, and BMW. Chinese policy makers fear that if such trends continue, China will become permanently stuck at the low end of the brand chain, doing the hard manual labor and collecting low wages but owning precious little of a brand's "value added," the difference between the cost of making and the value added through marketing, distribution, and retail sales. Moreover, foreign owners of favored brands, such as Nike, could always decide to shift production from China to countries with even lower labor costs and weaker environmental protections. This provides the logic of China's economic development strategy of urging state and private companies to spend billions building brands.

Beginning in the 1980s, Chinese government officials, business leaders, and academics began to urge domestic companies to climb the value-added chain—from simply manufacturing products for multinationals to developing technology and managing and owning globally competitive brands. These experts contend that China's massive trade surplus is misleading: Chinese exports have primarily low value added, meaning that the real value is collected not by China, which provides the physical labor, but by foreign multinationals, which manage and own the technology and brands. For example, a 30-gigabyte iPod has an export value of $150, but the value added and collected by Chinese labor amounts to only $4. According to China's Ministry of Commerce, less than 20 percent of Chinese enterprises participating in foreign trade have their own brands, and less than half of those export them abroad.

Going forward, Chinese officials hope to emulate the Japanese model of moving up the value-added chain, routinely pointing out that while products "Made in Japan" were considered inferior forty years ago, they are now viewed as standards of excellence. According to Li Guangdou, a Chinese marketing expert, domestic enterprises can also learn from the success of South Korean firms: "South Korean products used to be synonymous with low-grade products. But when we look at the current situation, Samsung has become one of the world's 100 most valuable brands." For the Chinese, matching these countries' success is a matter not only of national economic well-being but of national pride.

That this government-directed movement has had some success in weaning Chinese consumers from a preference for international brands can be seen in the growing popular indignation of Chinese consumers toward foreign companies. China's aspiring and middle-class consumers increasingly declare that multinationals selling in China take market access for granted, cut corners on safety and quality, ignore Chinese laws, and dump their low-end products there. A sentiment popularly held about Japanese companies, for instance, is that they sell their highest-quality products in European and American markets, their second best domestically, and their lowest grade in developing markets such as China. One woman I interviewed, for instance, insisted that Japan "sends us mobile phones that couldn't make it in Japan, and their cosmetics often contain different ingredients."

The Chinese media, sensitive to such slights and feelings, inevitably highlight the foreignness of a company when any consumer scandal related to imported goods breaks out. In 2005, quality problems and recalls undermined the reputation of several major international brands: KFC and Heinz were exposed for including the banned carcinogenic dye Sudan 1 in their food, Nikon had to recall defective batteries, Sony had to suspend distribution of six digital camera models with defects, and the level of iodine in Nestlé's Golden Growing 3 Plus Baby Formula was found to exceed national standards. In 2005, General Mills's high-end ice-cream brand Häagen-Dazs (widely known for its Chinese advertising slogan, "If you love her, treat her to Häagen-Dazs") was castigated for operating an "underground" ice-cream-cake factory in Shenzhen without proper permits. In contrast, powerful domestic brands are sometimes protected from similar consumer scandals. For instance, in 1997, the head of the *Beijing Youth Daily* was fired after publishing a report claiming that yogurt drinks manufactured by the state-owned Hangzhou Wahaha Group had fatally poisoned several children.

For their part, Chinese consumers demonstrate a deep ambivalence toward domestic brands, as reflected in consumers' demands that the government protect Chinese brands against international rivals even as those consumers simultaneously buy foreign products. Photographs of anti-Japanese protests in the spring of 2005, for instance, ironically show many protesters holding Japanese cell phones and cameras. That same year China's biggest private pollster found that despite popular anti-Japanese sentiments and protests, almost half of those surveyed said they would buy a Japanese car. Such mixed feelings were expressed by Lin Li, a thirty-five-year-old woman shopping in Beijing's Japanese-owned Ito Yokado Shopping Center, who, while putting a tube of Korean conglomerate LG's toothpaste into her basket, observed that "I like foreign brands because they ensure stable quality and good service. Of course, I hope there will be a day when I can no longer tell the difference between domestic and foreign brands."

This ongoing tension over the seductive power of foreign names has led to some official policies to resist it. Paris of the East Plaza, French Gardens, and the Ginza Office Tower are a few of the real estate developments forced to change their names by authorities in the southwestern city of Kunming. The city decided that the trend of attracting China's new middle class by giving new developments foreign-sounding names served to debase traditional culture and "is a loss to native culture and reflects poor taste." Officials sometimes also take action against advertising that they find disrespectful. In 2004, the government banned a Nike commercial featuring U.S. basketball superstar LeBron James outwitting a kung fu master, citing the ad campaign's disrespectful use of the traditional symbol of dragons. Likewise, in 2003, Toyota created a controversy with an ad for a new Land Cruiser by showing stone lions, traditional symbols of authority, bowing to the vehicle. According to one ad industry executive, "The government sees itself as a guardian of people's dignity and, every so often, it picks a victim to attack in the interests of nationalism."

Chinese companies sometimes take advantage of these sentiments to boost business, killing two birds with one stone as they build bigger businesses and create nationalistic-minded consumers at the same time. The Beijing-based company Huaqi markets a line of domestically developed and manufactured digital cameras by naming them after significant events in China's war against Japan. The Patriot V (Aigo V) series included models such as the V815, named after the date of the end of World War II (August 15). The company's president, Feng Jun, while claiming his products were selling well, took the next obvious step and suggested that business competition with Japan was simply war by other means: "We're determined to take the offensive against Japan until its digital cameras, which the country considers Japanese brands' last stronghold in the electronic products market, fall to the ground."

Economic Nationalism in China since 1900

China's aspirations to create competitive brands have reintroduced a central theme in Chinese consumerism that traces back to the arrival of mass-produced branded imports in the late nineteenth century. By the early twentieth century, the rapid increase in imports and the desires they stimulated threatened powerful domestic interest groups. Chinese politicians worried about trade deficits and the new consumer lifestyles; educated elites feared the loss of sovereignty implicit in the growing foreign dominance of the economy; domestic manufacturers struggled to compete against new imports. No one believed that the average Chinese housewife would, for patriotic reasons, choose what were called Chinese "national products"; indeed, it was assumed she would intentionally choose foreign products, whether for price, perceived quality, or simple fashion. These anxieties over consumers choosing price and quality over patriotism ultimately produced a multifaceted "Buy Chinese" campaign in which advocates developed countless ways to exhort fellow Chinese to consume China-made products.

The formation of the People's Republic of China in 1949 soon ended the ease with which consumers could choose foreign products. Mao Zedong's regime aimed to turn cities known for their consumption into centers of production instead, emulating the Soviet Union's economic model with its emphasis on state-owned heavy industry over consumer goods. Foreign multinationals were gradually forced to leave China, and most foreign products were eliminated from store shelves. After some initial hesitation, which allowed consumer lifestyles to persist into the mid-1950s, the state appropriated all private enterprises and consumer culture was virtually outlawed. Thirty years later, after the death of Chairman Mao in 1976, China dramatically changed course. With the start of Deng Xiaoping's economic reforms and the policy known as "opening to the outside world," or simply the Open Door Policy, China slowly began to permit the import of consumer goods. Policy makers reckoned that allowing imports was a small price to pay to gain access to foreign consumer markets for their own products. But over the past three decades, as the range and volume of imports has grown, the tension between "Chinese products" and "foreign products" has periodically reemerged. One reason for this is that China's WTO commitments have rendered countless village-owned and state-owned enterprises uncompetitive and created millions of unemployed and angry workers. Chinese students continue to invoke the language of economic nationalism when calling for boycotts of foreign goods, as in the widespread boycott of the French retailing giant Carrefour in retaliation for the disruption of the 2008 Olympic torch relay in Paris.

A hundred years ago, China struggled to catch up as a global *manufacturing* superpower. Mission accomplished. Now the Chinese recognize that in the "post-industrial" reign of service economies, their country needs to become a *branding* superpower. Chinese government and business leaders view domestic ownership of global brands and intellectual property as symbolic of national wealth and power, the economic equivalent of hosting the Olympics, but much more permanent. China wants its own domestic companies to join the list of prominent global brands associated with powerful countries such as the United States (McDonald's, Microsoft, Boeing, Google), Germany (BMW), Japan (Honda, Nintendo, Sony), and Korea (LG, Samsung). Moreover, the government wants to develop competitive brands across the spectrum of consumer products and services, including high-tech consumer electronics (such as Midea, headquartered in Shunde, near Hong Kong), and to revive "established brands" such as Tongrentang, the traditional medicine company. This push to create Chinese-owned brands also applies to the service sector, where the Ministry of Commerce has set ambitious targets that include developing one hundred restaurant brands, fifty hotel brands, and prominent brands in the beauty industry. To help reach these goals, state policies have promoted the creation of large-scale, horizontally integrated multinational corporations to compete against foreign multinationals. In the 1990s, the state selected a "national team" of 120 industrial groups to receive state assistance, and it promoted 925 top domestic brands.

In 2002 the Chinese state further strengthened its control over large companies by creating the very powerful if infelicitously named State-owned Assets Supervision and Administration Commission (SASAC) (pronounced *sah-sack*). This acronym is worth remembering; it may prove to be the most important one in China after PLA (People's Liberation Army). SASAC owns and runs more than 150 enormous corporations, including 8 of the 14 mainland Chinese enterprises listed on the Fortune 500. Where China's Open Door Policy once invited foreign investors in, since the early 1990s the government has also been laying the groundwork for these new Chinese conglomerates to take their products out that door. For instance, the Chinese government has used SASAC to entice the conglomerates to "go global" with favorable policies, including the abolition of foreign currency restrictions for overseas investment. China intends to remake the perception of Chinese brands, and hence of China itself, around the globe through these new, internationally prominent brands.

The effects of the Chinese government's pressure on the nation's biggest companies to sell more branded products abroad is most visible in developing markets, where the Chinese already sell branded appliances, consumer electronics, and even automobiles. One can find Chinese-made Geely cars even on the streets of Havana, where there are reports that Cuban Communist Party officials have switched their allegiance from their old, solidly built Russian Ladas to new-model Geelys.

These initiatives are simply a dry run for entering developed markets. China's biggest appliance maker, Haier, already sells small refrigerators under its own name in the United States and plans to popularize its full-size refrigerators next. It's also aggressively trying to acquire established brands, including a failed attempt to buy Maytag in 2005 and a subsequent effort to buy GE's electric home appliances division. In a country where after-sales service had disappeared under Mao, Haier has attempted to brand itself as a leader in customer service, differentiating itself from its rivals with its slogan "Phone up for immediate repairs, twenty-four hours a day," and has tried to extend this branding abroad.

Although international pressure and its entry into the WTO forced China to remove formal barriers to foreign products, this hasn't stopped China's leaders from playing both a direct and an indirect role in promoting brand nationalism. For instance, in 2003 the former chief negotiator in China's efforts to join the WTO, Long Yongtu, claimed that encouraging Chinese consumers to purchase Chinese products "will violate neither the WTO rules nor the market economic rules." Chinese entrepreneurs routinely express a similar sentiment. According to underwear manufacturer Zhou Xiaoning of the Zhongke Group, domestic brand consciousness is critical to Chinese economic development: "Without the recognition of domestic consumers, how can China brands grow and mature?" In the summer of 2008 the national government even incorporated the establishment, protection, and management of national brands into its National Strategy.

Although accepting WTO restrictions ostensibly promises a level playing field for foreign products in China, Chinese leaders continue to use government policies to create non-tariff barriers to foreign trade. For example, the China National Tobacco Corporation (CNTC), a government monopoly, still controls 90 percent of the domestic cigarette market, helped by non-tariff barriers such as the regulations governing new cigarette factories, limits on the number of sales offices, and provincial-level quotas to preserve its market share. Successful foreign brands, most notably Philip Morris's Marlboro, are allowed to enter the market only by producing their branded cigarettes at

CNTC-affiliated factories. These "partnerships" allow CNTC to limit competition, acquire new technology, leverage a high-profile international brand, and gain access to overseas markets. And these barriers can be erected at the local and provincial level, too. One county in China made international news for trying to raise revenue by requiring its officials to smoke only local brands or face fines.

Government-sponsored promotion of Chinese brand consciousness has included setting up new mechanisms to help domestic consumers identify Chinese products among the torrent of brands now available. In anticipation of stiff foreign competition after entry to the WTO, the State General Administration of Quality Supervision, Inspection, and Quarantine, China's watchdog for product quality, set up a "China Brand Name Strategy Promotion Commission" and awarded fifty-seven brands from forty-five enterprises the title of "China's Top Brand," in an effort to alert Chinese consumers to high-quality domestic brands. In a move reminiscent of China's anti-imperialist economic nationalist campaigns of the early twentieth century, the government now organizes exhibitions for "established brands" to increase national brand awareness.

Another advantage Chinese companies have over their international competitors is that China's highly competitive domestic market forces multinationals to adapt international brands to local tastes— what some have called "glocalization." This has become ever more essential as Chinese consumers, now confronting choice rather than scarcity, become pickier about what they buy. For international brands, one of the earliest and most basic localization efforts has been selecting a Chinese-language brand name that sounds felicitous and invokes the right image. Unlike alphabets based solely on sounds, most Chinese characters also have evocative meanings, making essentially meaningless brand names such as Xerox or Intel impossible in Chinese. Laurent Philippe, the head of Procter & Gamble in China, recognized the importance of selecting Chinese names that "trigger meaningful visuals or associations with benefits," and thus it is no accident that the Chinese characters used for Pampers, the disposable baby diaper brand, carry much the same meaning as the English name: "helping baby's comfort." The product's phenomenal success in China has become international marketing history.

Companies have learned that they cannot target "the Chinese" as a homogenous market of largely identical consumers. The resulting move toward market segmentation—the recognition that subgroups within a market share common characteristics that set them apart—is forcing companies to expand their product offerings to accommodate regional, generational, class, and other preferences. To meet regional taste preferences, for instance, KFC sells "Old Peking Style Chicken Rolls" with sweet bean sauce and mushroom chicken porridge. At the same time, the consumption of branded products makes those segmentations possible. Consuming segment-specific branded products has become a way for Chinese consumers to manifest differences in wealth, education, and regional identity. If you are what you consume (say, a BMW), you are also what you do not consume (a Red Flag, Brilliance, or other Chinese-brand car).

Now that China's biggest cities have become major markets for both Chinese and international brands, marketers are increasingly turning their attention to capturing the brand loyalties and purchasing power of Chinese consumers outside the 100 million-plus Chinese living in a handful of big cities. After all, China has more than 150 cities with populations of more than 1 million (compared to the United States, which has around 10 such cities). On the one hand, by creating nationally recognized chains and brands, companies are standardizing the shopping experience so that the majority of the population now recognizes hundreds, even thousands of brands. But while producing brands intended for mass or even universal consumption, companies are also segmenting the market and expanding product offerings to accommodate varying preferences. For instance, in 2000, GM offered a limited number of car models in China, primarily large, high-end Buicks costing around $40,000. Private ownership of cars had just begun, and GM's primary customers were government officials and entrepreneurs who wanted large sedans to transport top cadres. Just five years later, GM was marketing $75,000-plus Cadillac SRX SUVs to the very rich; the popular $30,000 Buick Regal to cost-conscious entrepreneurs looking for a high-status car; the $15,000 to $20,000 Buick Excelle to mid-level managers; the $19,000 Chevrolet Epica sedan, the $10,000 to $12,000 Aveo hatchback, and the $5,700 Spark minicar to younger urbanites buying their first cars; and $4,000 to $6,500 minivans, designed to carry seven passengers and their cargo, to buyers in the countryside. To reach this broader market, it also expanded its distribution network to more than a thousand outlets, up from just nine in 1998.

If You Can't Build Them, Buy Them

A century ago, Chinese leaders and media conducted a nationalist economic campaign that urged the Chinese to buy Chinese products. Today Lenovo offers the Chinese a story of a homegrown company that's so successful it could buy the most famous international computer brand, a corporate rags-to-riches tale. Founded in 1984 with $24,000, Lenovo, a state-owned enterprise (SOE) that originated in the Chinese Academy of Sciences, began as a distributor of other computer brands, including IBM. In 1990 it began manufacturing its own computers, profiting from state commissions and little competition. By 1997 it controlled over a quarter of the Chinese market, making it the country's largest-selling brand of PCs. In 2000 it followed the government edict to "go global" and began selling overseas. In April 2003, because of copyright conflicts in other countries where the company's original English name, Legend, was already registered, the company renamed itself Lenovo. (In Chinese, it's still called Lianxiang.) It became the world's third largest producer of computers in December 2004 by spending $1.25 billion to acquire the PC arm of IBM, which was then three times its size and, with its Thinkpad brand, much more recognizable. Now Lenovo sells billions of dollars' worth of computers worldwide under its own global brand. Even so evident a success story, however, carries ambiguities: nearly all of the Chinese people with whom I have discussed the takeover think, as one friend put it, "that Lenovo hurt IBM's brand value" rather than helping Lenovo's.

No matter. This purchase proved a harbinger of what was to come, as a stronger yuan made it possible, and even strategically necessary, for Chinese companies to buy iconic foreign assets. The decade and a half since has brought many such acquisitions, particularly of established but struggling international brands, such as Nanjing Auto's purchase of MG Rover and Dongxiang's acquisition and successful marketing of the Kappa brand, most closely associated with British football hooligans but now a leading fashion brand in China. Li Ning, China's top domestic sports brand, entered into an alliance with Lotto Sport Italia, and Peace Mark, Asia's biggest watch retailer, bought Swiss watch brand Milus. Within Chinese pop culture, fueled by endless media coverage of these acquisitions, these branding efforts represent heroic David-versus-Goliath sagas for the era of global capitalism, tales driven by nationalism that reinforce Chinese national identity.

China's Branding Challenges

Despite government investments and policies that favor China's own products, Chinese companies face a number of challenges as they make the transition from the country's earlier fragmented, state-run, and production-oriented economy to one driven by creating consumer desires and meeting consumer demands. The first of these is one China initially faced a century ago, when Japan surpassed it as the world's largest exporter of silk and the British in India took a commanding share of the global tea trade: the mass production of consistency. Chinese products have real and perceived problems with consistency—that is, with producing large quantities of identical high-quality goods. This is especially true in the food industry, where foreign brands provide nearly identical products regardless of time or place. Consumers at a McDonald's or KFC anywhere in the world can expect their food to look and taste the same wherever they buy it. In contrast, the well-known Chinese fast food Yangzhou Fried Rice tastes different from restaurant to restaurant and even from chef to chef.

Under the productivist paradigm of the Maoist era, consistency was much less important than supply. Demand was assumed and, thanks to shortages, ensured. But with the country's reintegration into global capitalist markets, China's political and business leaders want to consolidate and standardize domestic products before foreign companies do. Take the tea industry, where one would assume China had a competitive advantage. China has more than a thousand varieties of tea, many of which are renowned throughout the world. However, there are no national tea brands, not to mention international ones. Thanks to climate and soil conditions as well as traditional preferences, most Chinese tea brands are regional. Southern Chinese tend to prefer green tea and northerners prefer jasmine-flavored tea. Moreover, many teas are still produced by families, making it nearly impossible to ensure their quality. These problems, combined with a growing Chinese appetite for trustworthy branded products, have confirmed government fears: aggressive foreign expansion. The Anglo-Dutch Unilever Group has bought out a Chinese tea brand, Jinghua tea, and expanded its offerings from Lipton black tea to Lipton green and jasmine tea. If Chinese companies can't create competitive tea brands, what hope is there for other products?

As noted, Chinese companies and officials trying to build Chinese brands also battle a legacy of the socialist economy's emphasis on managing shortages on the supply side rather than appealing to consumers on the demand side. That is, the Mao regime emphasized quantity, not quality, much less the product differentiation that is the foundation of branding. Another legacy of the socialist era is the near absence of prominent domestic brands. Before the reforms, watches were one of the "three luxuries" for most Chinese, and China had several prominent domestic watch brands, such as Shanghai, Seagull, and Five Star. In the early 1970s, when there were almost no imported rivals, the Chinese willingly waited in long lines whenever supplies of watches such as the Shanghai appeared, despite their costing the equivalent of four or five months' salary for most people. But this began to change in the early 1980s, when domestic brands began to lose the mid-level and high-end watch market first to Citizen and Seiko and then to Rolex, Omega, and Cartier. Chinese watchmakers have attempted but failed to develop luxury watch brands and seem unable to overcome the public perception that domestic watches are inexpensive but inferior.

Other Chinese companies have had similar difficulties. Take Maotai, the famous Chinese liquor distilled from fermented sorghum and manufactured exclusively in the southwest province of Guizhou. (Like Champagne, Maotai is trademarked by place.) Maotai was a favorite liquor of Chinese leaders Deng Xiaoping, Zhou Enlai, and Mao Zedong and was used for toasts at important state occasions, including ceremonies marking major events from the founding of the People's Republic of China to its entry into the WTO. With its high profile and paucity of competition, Maotai never needed to advertise. Although it is now affordable, available, and heavily advertised, intense competition in the liquor industry has undermined its status and therefore the value of the brand. Cognac is the liquor of choice today, thanks to its position as a status symbol among China's newly rich. Savvy producers have reinforced this image. In 1994, Seagram introduced a mid-priced cognac, Martell Noblige, aimed at middle-class Chinese consumers anxious to emulate elite lifestyles. At home and abroad, the Chinese now consume a fourth of the global cognac supply.

Despite government efforts to help established Chinese brands compete, the companies behind these brands still often make basic mistakes of brand management based on socialist-era assumptions. In 1990 the former Ministry of Commerce awarded the title "old and famous brands" to sixteen hundred shops and enterprises in the clothing, medicine, and food and beverage industries. It hasn't helped. Twenty percent of these designated famous brands have been operating at a loss for years and are nearly bankrupt, while another 70 percent are barely profitable. Thus these former pillars of Chinese consumer consciousness have begun to disappear. In January 2003, for instance, Wangmazi Scissors, a Beijing institution founded in 1651, sparked a national debate on traditional brands by announcing its bankruptcy.

Beyond the problem of profitability, established companies sometimes lost out to opportunistic newcomers in the race to register established brand names. The names of a famous Hunan provincial stuffed steamed bun, Deyuan Baozi, and the famous Jinhua ham, for instance, were both registered by new companies. (Imagine if a Pittsburgh-based company owned the rights to Philly cheesesteak.) It took the original company nearly twenty years to recover the rights. In other cases, foreign companies have registered the names of long-established Chinese brands in their own countries. By 2005, 180 Chinese brands were registered by foreign companies in Australia and at least 100 Chinese brands in Japan; a full 15 percent of Chinese brands that applied for registration abroad were embarrassed to learn that others had already beaten them to it.

But perhaps the biggest hurdle for Chinese brand development is the fact that China often resembles a collection of diverse markets rather than a single, integrated one. There are, for instance, four hundred brands of cigarettes in China, the world's largest consumer, where about 60 percent of men smoke. Given regional tastes, China more closely resembles the historically fragmented European market than the relatively homogeneous North American market. Because of a lack of distribution infrastructure, national brands must rely on local partnerships or acquisitions. In the 1990s, Tsingtao Brewery, for example, successfully built a national network by acquiring twenty-two local breweries stretching from Shenzhen in the far south to Beijing in the north, as did the less expensive Beijing-based Yanjing Beer Company, China's largest brewer. In contrast, foreign breweries such as Anheuser-Busch, after an expensive misstep with enormous centralized production facilities, ultimately had to buy a fourth of Tsingtao to gain access to the Chinese beer market, now the world's largest.

China's leaders, along with many throughout the developed world, have wanted China to embrace consumerism, which has meant embracing branded products. In the world created by the WTO, Chinese brand loyalty cannot be easily ensured, and consumption cannot be controlled the way it was in the Mao era. What the world has gotten, then, is a Chinese government obsessed with shaping consumption not only within China but also globally by creating global brands that will challenge the rest of the world's, or at the very least give multinationals within China a run for their money. For China, this is part of a longer and larger project. Since the late nineteenth century, China's leadership (if not necessarily its on-the-street consumers) has developed a strong sense of economic nationalism and demonstrated a willingness to make any sacrifice to develop world-class industries in the name of "national survival," including sacrificing the well-being of the country's workers and the health of its environment. In the current postindustrial world, Chinese leaders see ownership and control over world-class brands as the key to continued economic development. As a result, Chinese consumers may have less power to consume whatever brands they want.

6 ★ LIVING IN A WORLD OF FAKES

Even as retailing and branding have been encouraging much more consumption in China, consumer confidence (both nationally and internationally) has been undermined by the massive production of Chinese counterfeits. I have firsthand experience. In preparation for a recent research trip to China, I bought a sleek new netbook, reassuring myself that I needed an ultra-portable computer because my two-year-old laptop was too heavy to lug around the world. Shortly after the purchase, I decided to double the machine's memory but opted to wait until I got to China, where I assumed I'd find a lower price. On my arrival, I went to the electronic district in Shanghai and found a vendor who sold and installed the new memory card. The price was not as good as I'd hoped, in part because the vendor assured me the card was authentic. When the computer crashed for the first time a few days later, even though I'm no stranger to such crashes and have no idea what causes them (nor, apparently, does Microsoft), I instantly suspected the new memory card: Had I been cheated?

My experience captures a reality of everyday life in China, a country rife with low-quality and counterfeit products, so much so that consumers there have learned to live in a world of uncertainty. Many

Chinese have shared horror stories of trying to be vigilant when shopping to avoid inadvertently buying substandard or fake products and of failing time and again. Even supposedly reliable brands often provide unreliable performance. Exhausted by the confusion, one cabdriver told me he had simply surrendered and learned to live with uncertainty, saying, "Who knows what's real and what's fake?" China's rapid shift to a deregulated market economy, where price and profits are paramount without a parallel commitment to consumer protection, has created a consumer culture permeated with omnipresent consumer anxiety.

At the heart of the problem is the integrity of brands. Brands, as we've seen, are the building blocks of consumerism. A brand is a name, an idea, and, above all, a monopoly on manufacturing an easily imitated product. Most of all, brands are a promise to consumers that they are buying what they think they are. Protecting as well as creating brand identities is critical to modern consumer culture. If consumers regularly got sick after drinking Evian water, an imported premium brand in China, few would continue to buy that brand. If there were frequent stories of brakes malfunctioning on $80,000 BMW sports cars, nobody would want one. Likewise, if your friends couldn't tell the difference between your real Rolex watch and a fake, would you be willing to pay thousands of dollars more to own the genuine article? In China, however, weak protections and a massive manufacturing capacity create an unusually unstable brand environment. But the history and role of counterfeits in China raise not just arcane issues of business practices in a faraway country but concern for consumers everywhere.

Over the course of the last three decades of economic reforms, China has become both the largest producer and the largest consumer of fake products. By 2001, for instance, the government estimated that the country was flooded with $19 to $24 billion in counterfeit goods. Brand owners in China estimate that 15 to 20 percent of all prominent branded goods in China are actually counterfeit, with much higher rates for expensive but easily reproduced products such as computer software and movies, whose piracy rates are over 90 percent. DVDs loaded with software or movies usually sell for a dollar or two, anywhere from a hundredth to a fourth of the legitimate product's price.

The counterfeit market pulls in consumers by offering them not only better prices but also better selection. American hit movies are available within days of their theatrical release, which allows Chinese consumers to buy them on DVD even before they appear in domestic theaters, and months before their counterparts in America can. It also allows Chinese movie fans to view movies, such as *Memoirs of a Geisha*, that the government has banned. Even banned books are pirated. After *A Survey of Chinese Peasants*, a heartbreaking exposé of the plight of China's farmers, became a bestseller, it was banned in 2004. But some thirty book pirates kept it in print, selling an estimated eight million copies. High profits motivate pirates, who don't pay licensing fees or royalties to the book's publisher or author. The pirating of music and computer software similarly allows consumers access to technology that might otherwise be prohibitively expensive, with many sellers minimizing the risk to consumers by allowing them to try out or swap defective DVDs on the spot with no questions asked.

The variety of fakes for sale in China has long moved beyond the stereotypical Gucci handbags and Rolex watches. Along with Hollywood movies and Microsoft software, every imaginable product in China is counterfeited, including such top-selling products as Oral-B toothbrushes, Gillette razor blades, Zippo lighters, and Duracell batteries. Unilever Group claims that knockoffs of its shampoos, soaps, and teas are growing by 30 percent annually. A fake battery or cheaply constructed knockoff lighter poses one sort of risk; of far greater concern, given the scale of possible consequences, are counterfeit versions of products such as powdered milk, alcohol, fertilizer, pesticides, and even aircraft components that don't contain the ingredients or parts promised.

Conventional wisdom holds that as China's manufacturers move up the value-added chain and China has brands of its own to protect, it will do a better job of protecting intellectual property. So far, however, what is clear is that as China moves from inexpensive and easy-to-manufacture goods to producing more complex things such as electronics, its counterfeiters do the same. Very few consumables prove immune, from technologically sophisticated products such as DVD players to, more alarmingly, pharmaceuticals made from inert or dangerous compounds. Bogus antibiotics and toxic fake drugs have been known to kill hundreds of thousands in China in a single year and to contribute to a worldwide epidemic of fakes estimated by the World Health Organization at 8 percent of all manufactured drugs. Chinese counterfeits of lifesaving drugs for illnesses such as malaria are increasingly showing up around the developing world, discovered only after they fail to work.

The quality of Chinese counterfeits ranges broadly. Gone are the days when imitations were comically imprecise and easy to spot with misspelled names such as "Reebek" shoes. Now counterfeits may be so accurately reproduced that they are indistinguishable from the originals. Given increased efficiencies on the part of counterfeiters, fakes can also appear nearly simultaneously with the launch of an original. Knockoffs of new models of golf clubs, for instance, appear within a week. According to Stu Herrington, who supervises brand protection for Callaway Golf, "back-engineering a golf club is a piece of cake." Not surprisingly, then, as much as 5 to 7 percent of all global trade, or about $500 billion a year, is estimated to involve counterfeit goods, a total expected to reach $2 trillion by 2025. This suggests, among other things, that there are going to be a lot more people uncertain about why their computer just crashed or wondering whether their medicine might kill them.

Becoming the World's Biggest Faker

The incentives for anyone anywhere to produce fake products are obvious, chief among them the promise of huge profits. Fake Marlboros that are sold for more than seven dollars a pack in Manhattan cost only a few pennies to make in China. No wonder, then, to give but one example, that in 2003 six men were arrested in New York for importing thirty-five million counterfeit cigarettes from China. Similarly, while it costs between $11 and $24 to make a pair of genuine New Balance shoes that retail for $120, the fakes cost around just $8 a pair to make and can fetch ten times that much in Australia.

Producers of fakes can reap such huge profit margins because they avoid costs that the manufacturers of the genuine article cannot. Reverse engineering is much less expensive than original research and development, particularly if the goal is imitating appearance rather than performance. Counterfeiters also profit from free marketing: by aping established brands, they have a preexisting market for their products and benefit from someone else's brand building. They may also avoid paying taxes, an especially large incentive for manufacturers of knockoff cigarettes and alcohol and other heavily taxed luxury goods. They are also subject to few or no environmental restrictions; manufacturers of counterfeits by definition are eluding regulation and needn't worry about consumer backlash if they are caught dumping toxic waste. Nor are they bound by labor laws and government oversight. And because they are not concerned with the maintenance of a brand, they can cut corners by using low-grade raw materials and equipment.

China has become the global leader in both the production and the consumption of counterfeits simply because it can: unlike many developing countries, it has the manufacturing and technological ability. Ironically, foreign companies seeking cheaper labor costs have inadvertently contributed to the counterfeit problem. Hundreds of billions of dollars have been poured into China to build countless factories, transfer innumerable production lines, and import all levels of manufacturing technology. In some cases, making knockoffs is as simple as keeping a factory running even after it has fulfilled its licensed orders. During these "ghost shifts," a factory runs extra shifts using cheaper material, unofficial labor, and safety shortcuts.

Perhaps the most significant reason for China's emergence as a global superpower in the production and consumption of fakes is an ongoing and irresolvable tension between national and local interests. Simply put, despite international pressures on the national government to enforce intellectual property rights, localities have a greater interest in producing fakes than the national government has in stopping them. (The same conflict between local and national interests, incidentally, calls into question assumptions about Beijing's power to enforce limits on greenhouse gases.) Even as economic reforms provided greater local autonomy, the national government decreased subsidies for state-owned enterprises, forcing local officials to find new ways to finance local industries and in effect offering them new ways to support and enrich themselves through illicit payoffs. But money isn't the only consideration. Local officials are often more frightened by the prospect of large numbers of dislocated, unemployed workers than they are by the specter of multinational companies and their lawyers, chastisement from Beijing, or even lost tax revenue. For local officials, looking the other way or even promoting the production of counterfeit goods often solves very real and immediate problems. Indeed, at times desperate local authorities have actually sanctioned counterfeiting as a valuable source of cash to help keep legitimate state-owned enterprises from going under. Entire cities and counties have become regional counterfeiting centers and are now completely dependent on their expertise in producing fakes. Wenzhou specializes in fake car parts, Yuxiao County in cigarettes, and Jintan in pesticides.

Until the relatively recent development of Chinese brands, enforcing intellectual property rights (IPR) meant protecting the interests of multinational companies. This made the problem a national rather than local issue, and one that few leaders worked to change. Even at the national level, Chinese officials have tended to view IPR infringement as a victimless crime, especially when the victim is a company and even more so when it's a foreign company. Even with recent new laws, fines and conviction rates remain low, especially in areas where official complicity is at play. The national government can get tough when people get hurt or killed—a man found guilty of selling adulterated baby formula, for example, was sentenced to eight years in prison. But compare this with the Guangdong businessman convicted of producing fifteen different brands of fake windshields, some falsely labeled as manufactured by GM and Mitsubishi Motors, who was only fined $97,000 and given a suspended sentence.

Even national officials appear complicit in some trademark violations. For instance, the manufacturers of the BlackBerry email device sought entry into the Chinese market for years, struggling to overcome one hurdle after another thrown in their way by the government. On the very eve of its eventual entry into the Chinese market, a competing "RedBerry" was rolled out by two different Chinese companies selling a BlackBerry-like service on a non-BlackBerry mobile device. One of the companies was a private start-up, but the other, China Unicom, is largely owned by the Chinese government. It is hard not to conclude that BlackBerry was excluded from the potentially lucrative domestic market until a domestic equivalent backed by powerful Chinese interests could be produced, which also neatly exploited BlackBerry's brand recognition by using a very similar name.

With the counterfeit industry accounting for approximately 8 percent of China's GDP and employing three to five million people, Chinese authorities have a difficult time investigating and correcting lax enforcement practices in places notorious for protecting their counterfeiters. That is, except when local officials have their own reasons for working to prevent the sale of fakes. Local governments with manufacturers of the original products in their jurisdictions often work hard to crack down on fakes, but the legal system makes intraregional police and judicial cooperation time-consuming and ineffective, and sometimes even dangerous. On August 3, 2005, for instance, hundreds of employees of a clothing company, Yanglaoda, who objected to a ruling on its disputed trademark, surrounded the local court in the northern city of Yulin and beat up a dozen judges. Conflicts of interest don't help. Wholesale markets throughout China, in which many counterfeits are distributed, are regulated by the local Administration for Industry and Commerce (AIC). This branch of local government is also responsible for enforcing IPR, thereby policing the same markets in which their local governments have extensive investments and financial interests. Even further down the supply chain, local officials themselves sometimes make money operating stores selling counterfeits; in more than one case, police were found profiting from counterfeit shops located in or adjacent to their headquarters.

Chinese legal culture also plays a role in lax enforcement. For thirty years following the Communist Revolution, the state had sole ownership of all property, so personal, much less intellectual, property is still a relatively novel concept in China. The government has gradually introduced a legal system that protects property rights, though the earliest patent and trademark laws were not enacted until the start of the 1980s, and not until 2001, and under foreign pressure, did China began revising these laws in preparation to join the World Trade Organization. But tension between the national interest in complying with WTO obligations and local interests remain: closing a factory changes a national problem (WTO compliance) into a local one (unemployment and lost revenue). And because China's three thousand county courts are under the control of local governments, half-hearted enforcement, prosecution, and punishment continue to ensure the production of counterfeits.

Ironically, Chinese companies have begun to use international law to harass foreign brand owners. Nowadays, Chinese companies rush to file patents and claim trademarks for products that copy foreign patents or make only minor changes to them, thereby becoming the legal owners of a specific type of product within China. Rather than hiding from the law by moving a factory from village to village, in other words, such companies protect themselves with a Great Wall of patents, sometimes even turning the tables and suing foreign companies for infringing upon their rights. In IPR legal culture, "first to file" patents and trademarks are more important than claims of invention, so if Chinese companies can gain possession of the IPR first, they can even stop the original brands from entering China or can sue the foreign manufacturer once it arrives. When foreign companies countersue, the Chinese companies simply outlast them in China's notoriously lengthy legal appeals process. And even if the foreign companies prevail, local officials usually pressure the courts to award only compensatory and not punitive damages.

Complicity of Foreign Consumers

Although there is a booming domestic market for faked goods in China, it could not flourish without the greed and complicity of foreign businesses and consumers. In fact, the initial impetus for the counterfeit market was to cater to the foreign visitors—businesspeople, students, tourists, and even government representatives—who traveled to China in ever-increasing numbers following the country's reopening to the world. Since the late 1980s, major tourist cities in China have offered marketplaces specializing in selling fakes to foreign tourists. The history of these "must visit" places reflects the history of China's response first to foreign demand for bargain versions of luxury goods and then to foreign pressure to respect the intellectual property rights and brands of international companies.

The first of these counterfeit markets was Beijing's Silk Alley, a market of open-air stalls conveniently near the district in which most of the foreign embassies are located. The market was installed there in 1982, when economic reforms made it legal for local Beijingers to sell clothes, fruit, and vegetables from tricycle carts, mostly to fellow Chinese. Suddenly, fashion was in, Maoist-era clothing was out, and in Beijing and across the country, small-scale shops and streets with stalls emerged that specialized in selling fashionable clothing made in backroom factories. But in 1985, vendors began to focus on foreigners interested in buying higher-quality traditional Chinese silk products and crafts. By 1987, the hundreds of stalls crammed into the Alley were attracting foreign tourist groups on package tours and wholesalers from foreign countries.

The market shifted again in the mid-1990s, as Chinese clothing production techniques improved and international brand manufacturers themselves relocated to China. In response, Alley vendors began instead to meet foreign demand for high-quality fake international brands by buying factory seconds and unlicensed surplus goods from manufacturers licensed to make them. By specializing in higher-quality counterfeit apparel, Silk Alley set the standard for marketplaces popular with foreign tourists. As a shop clerk selling bogus Louis Vuitton bags at a similar market noted, "Even fakes have many grades of quality, and these fakes are really, really good." Rather than selling a clunky replica Rolex that broke quickly (like the one I bought in the early 1990s), the Silk Alley sold fakes that were virtually indistinguishable from the genuine articles. Indeed, actual and fake often came from the same factory, meaning that foreign tourists could return home to boast of buying a quality fake for less or simply of owning, say, five Gucci bags.

Because of the Silk Alley's notoriety, foreign business and governments attempting to pressure China to enforce IPR would cite it as a prime example of lax enforcement and rampant piracy, even though most of its millions of customers came from those countries doing the complaining, the United States and EU member states. By 2005 the pressure to crack down on Silk Alley merchants led to periodic high-profile raids. In the spring of that year, for instance, plainclothes inspectors posing as consumers seized more than three hundred items with Prada, Gucci, Chanel, and other luxury brand logos. International luxury brands also began using China's legal system to try to protect their intellectual property. Five luxury brand owners filed lawsuits against the owner of the shopping emporium, demanding 2.5 million yuan in damages for permitting vendors to infringe upon their trademarks. A year later the courts agreed and ordered the operators of the Alley to pay each company 20,000 yuan, considerably less than the 500,000 each had sought.

Although city officials wanted to demolish the market, it was, after the Great Wall and Forbidden City, the best-known tourist attraction in the city, drawing 100,000 shoppers a day and generating over 100 million yuan in sales and 10 million yuan in taxes annually. Finally, at the end of 2004, stall owners were given two weeks' notice that the Alley was closing, and in March 2005, the New Silk Alley Market opened in a new five-floor mall with 1,500 stalls selling clothes, shoes, bags, and other goods. Opening day attracted 50,000 shoppers. Although vendors were required to take an oath not to sell fakes, and a huge red banner over the main entrance proclaimed, "Protect Intellectual Property Rights and Promote Innovation and Development," visitors can still find counterfeits for sale there (and elsewhere) without much difficulty. Perhaps it's a fitting tribute to the history of Silk Alley that its name remains so popular that some enterprising Chinese entrepreneurs even came out with a Silk Alley clothing line in time to take advantage of the millions of Olympic visitors. It would be supremely ironic if the brand became successful enough for others to counterfeit its products.

Although open-air marketplaces overtly selling fakes to foreign tourists are now gone from cities such as Beijing and Shanghai, closing them simply forced merchants to relocate and wholesalers to find new ways to distribute their products. In Shanghai, for instance, some moved to Qipu Road, and the city government arranged for others to move to a cavernous subway station in Pudong, although a merchant told me during a 2009 visit that the move from the main tourist area had hurt his business. Major tourist thoroughfares such as Nanjing Road in Shanghai and Wangfujing in Beijing are crawling with young women stopping foreigners to show them photo album catalogs of pirated goods. Interested shoppers will have products brought to them or are led to nearby safe houses. In Shanghai in 2006, I followed one hawker from Nanjing Road down back alleyways to a living room piled high with handbags. Finally, Internet sites such as eBay and Taobao allow customers from around the world to shop, knowingly or not, for fakes from the comfort of their own homes.

The Market in Substandard Goods

A lack of regulation and enforcement has allowed Chinese suppliers to produce products much more cheaply than in developed market economies, contributing to China's remarkable economic boom. Yet the consequences are now making themselves felt worldwide, and nowhere with as tragic results as in China itself. A substandard computer part is more likely to be a hassle than a life-or-death issue. But Chinese markets buy and sell fakes of every conceivable type, even life-threatening ones. In the spring of 2004, China faced what became its biggest consumer scandal of the new millennium. The "big-head baby" scandal broke with revelations that nationwide sales of substandard milk powder had contributed to disproportionately swollen heads and severe malnutrition in Chinese babies. The scandal centered around the city of Fuyang and the surrounding countryside in the eastern province of Anhui, where thirteen infants, mostly between three and five months old, died after consuming poor-quality milk powder purchased in rural markets. But the scandal was not limited to a single province. An investigative team identified fifty-five low-quality milk powder brands sold in ten provinces and Beijing and Shanghai. More than two hundred infants across China suffered some of the symptoms, including high fever, diarrhea, and nutritional deficiencies.

The scandal shocked the nation, and not just the families of babies who receive breast milk substitutes. At over a billion tons a year, China is the world's largest consumer of powdered (dehydrated) milk. Chinese desire for milk, cheese, yogurt, and ice cream is propelling skyrocketing global demand for dairy products. Milk, not a part of traditional diets in East Asia, was introduced by Westerners in the early twentieth century. At the founding of the PRC, China had only 120,000 dairy cows, a herd that increased to only half a million by 1978. But dairy consumption has exploded since the mid-1990s, despite periodic tainted-milk scandals, becoming one of the fastest developing industries in China. The country now has 12 million dairy cows producing billions of dollars' worth of fresh milk each year.

In recent decades, the consumption of milk and milk products (like so many other consumer products) has spread quickly across the entire social hierarchy. Middle-class consumers associate milk with healthy and tall children, while poor female migrant laborers, forced to leave millions of children behind with grandparents, turn to powdered milk out of necessity. And the dairy industry expects continued rapid expansion. China raised its consumption of milk from under 5 kilograms per person daily in the mid-1990s to 11 kilograms per person in a decade, still well below the rate in leading economies of 258 kilograms and the global average of 93 kilograms. With government support, the Chinese are rapidly catching up.

The big-head-baby formula scandal hurt the credibility and sales of domestic baby milk powder manufacturers and reinforced a bias for foreign brands, which Chinese presume to be of better, more reliable quality. A sales assistant at Beijing's Wumart Supermarket estimated that sales of leading international brands such as U.S.-based Abbott Similac, Denmark-based Dumex, and the Swiss brand Nestlé have more than doubled since the scandal. As one anxious father buying Similac infant milk powder explained, "My five-month-old son drinks four to five jars of milk powder a month, which costs at least six hundred yuan, and that is a lot of money for me. But I have to buy it because my wife doesn't trust any domestic brands after the fake milk powder scandal." It is a measure of Chinese consumers' mistrust of domestic regulations that although both domestic and international brands are subject to the same state standards, Chinese believe that the imports, which cost two to five times more, are somehow more nutritious. In reaction, domestic companies often select names such as "Australian Excellence" to suggest the brand is in fact imported.

The Chinese government responded to consumer outrage with a high-profile crackdown, emphasizing the state's role as the consumer protector of last resort. During a rash of well-publicized raids, police confiscated one hundred thousand bags of milk powder and arrested nearly fifty people for manufacturing or retailing the adulterated powder. In Beijing, officials launched a ten-day campaign to eliminate low-quality and fake dairy products from store shelves, seizing more than six thousand bags in just a few days, some of which contained less than a tenth of the required protein. A store owner in Fuyang, Li Xindao, was sentenced to eight years' imprisonment for peddling shoddy powder, the court concluding that its unusually low price should have alerted him that something was not right. Sha Changban, an unlicensed milk producer, was fined 50,000 yuan and sentenced to seven years for producing and selling unhygienic food, and his distributors got sentences ranging from four to eight years. Two hundred officials were punished for dereliction of duty.

Such dramatic crackdowns, however, miss larger forces at work. As Chinese society pushes people to rely on commercial products to fill new needs, consumer anxiety has increased. In this case, powdered milk fills a need created by women working outside the home for longer hours and farther away. Many of the new for-profit hospitals in big cities such as Beijing, Shanghai, and Guangzhou allow formula milk producers to market directly to new mothers. High-pressure marketing even occurs in what the Ministry of Health has designated as "baby-friendly hospitals," which are supposed to provide better service but are also increasingly financially dependent on baby food companies. A reporter for the Nanjing-based *Jiangnan Times* who posed as a would-be mother reported that doctors and nurses gave her leaflets and advised her on what brand of milk to use and found that doctors promoting a particular brand earned as much as ten to thirty yuan for each tin of milk powder sold. All this even though China is a signatory to the World Health Organization's international code banning all advertising and promotion of breast milk substitutes, and despite a 1995 regulation mandating that doctors promote breast-feeding. In other words, sensible laws are in place but not enforced, except after a scandal breaks, and then only publicly and briefly.

In the end, the number of children affected by the big-head-baby scandal is inestimable. In addition to those who died, many will suffer from deformities and other health problems that may not manifest themselves for years or decades. Perhaps even sadder, it is unclear whether anything has actually changed. Many of the precipitating problems are deeply woven into China's new society. Formula advertisements continue to undermine breast-feeding, migrant women workers continue to cut short their breast-feeding and leave their babies in the care of grandmothers, pseudoscience continues to promote the health benefits of milk substitutes, poor rural families continue to dilute costly formula with unclean water and remain reluctant to take sick babies to hospitals they cannot afford, and greedy companies and merchants continue to try to make a quick buck by taking advantage of a weak regulatory structure staffed with corrupt local officials.

Shortly after the scandal, a CCTV network investigation found thirty-three of the blacklisted brands still available in the local markets, as there is no mechanism in place to enforce a recall or ensure quality standards. Not surprisingly, within a year another outbreak of big-head babies occurred in Hunan province. And in 2008, an even bigger milk and milk formula scandal occurred. This time the culprit was not the absence of protein but the presence of a dangerous chemical, melamine, which was added to poor-quality milk to make it appear to have more protein. The adulterated products poisoned an estimated three hundred thousand Chinese, hospitalized nearly a thousand infants, and killed six.

Response to Poorly Made Products and Counterfeits

To restore domestic and international confidence in Chinese goods, the government has engaged in a number of high-profile reforms and crackdowns. In response to U.S. and EU pressure, it periodically gets tough on counterfeiters by seizing millions of CDs, DVDs, and VCDs—often theatrically steamrolling the massive piles of contraband. Between 2001 and 2005, for example, the national government claims to have seized 500 million pirated discs and to have dispatched thousands of agents to check CD and software dealers nationwide. In the summer of 2004 alone, Chinese authorities made 555,000 inspections of audio-video businesses, confiscating 154 million DVDs and VCDs and impounding some 6.5 million fake foreign trademark labels and 10,000 machines for counterfeiting such labels. The government also established a hotline number—12315—for the public to report trademark violations.

In the mid-1990s, with its WTO application hanging in the balance, China adopted another way to demonstrate that it was aggressively countering counterfeits and cracking down on intellectual property rights violations: officially encouraging consumers to defend their "rights" through a quasi-governmental organization, the China Consumers' Association (CCA). Founded in 1984, CCA was viewed by the Communist Party as an opportunity to align itself and its image as "the defender of consumers" even as it sought to help Chinese companies survive foreign competition at home and maintain markets abroad by ensuring quality. In the 1990s important consumer protection laws were adopted by individual provinces—with penalties imposed for consumer fraud, contracts provided to renters, and exchange and refund policies ensured for consumers—followed by national laws regarding product quality (1993), unfair competition (1993), consumer protection (1994), and advertising (1995). *Consumer* is now a term that permeates the Chinese political vocabulary.

The banner of consumer activism has allowed disgruntled Chinese to voice a much wider variety of social complaints as aggrieved "consumers" than they can as aggrieved "citizens." State-sponsored organizations such as CCA work to direct consumer interest away from politics and into learning about products. In consumer cultures such as the one emerging in China, a country is populated by "consumers" focused on their own private choices and individual gains, such as what car to buy, rather than "citizens" concerned about the public good, such as whether creating a car culture and economy is better than investing in trains and public transportation. In this way, China is creating not only a consumer culture but consumer politics similar to America's.

The CCA began modestly—just fifteen people and a tiny office without its own labs, lawyers, or large budget—but it quickly emerged as a national consumer protection organization of more than 3,000 county-level consumer associations and 156,000 branches in villages, small towns, and cities, with some 27,000 full-time employees, 102,000 council members, and 93,000 volunteers. CCA members come from government departments, social organizations, press circles, local and regional affiliates, and consumer representatives. Its responsibilities include providing consumer information, mediating consumer complaints, helping consumers file suits, and exposing and publicizing consumer fraud.

In its first few years alone, the organization received some twenty thousand letters from angry consumers, which were often resolved by confronting manufacturers. Nearly two thirds of these complaints concerned electrical appliances, not surprising given the huge demand but uneven availability of television sets, refrigerators, and washing machines in the 1980s. By the end of 1996, the CCA had investigated nearly three million cases in a variety of areas, including poor quality goods, dishonest advertising, false labeling, overcharging, food poisoning, wrongful body searches by store guards, and breaches of contract, and had recovered 1.29 billion yuan for consumers. The number of cases has grown exponentially; according to CCA statistics, by the end of 2004, the CCA had accepted more than eight million cases, settling 96 percent and recovering over 6 billion yuan.

The CCA has promoted numerous activities to inculcate the notions of both consumer rights and responsibilities. Every March 15 since 1986, the CCA has organized China's annual participation in World

Consumer Rights Day with street performances, exhibitions, and symposia. Like the mass mobilizations of earlier decades, these annual events are organized at national, regional, and local levels. For example, the CCA organizes educational events at companies and schools, setting up workshops to educate consumers on consumption-related issues. Each year, the CCA selects a consumer-related theme, such as the use of credit, rural consumption, consumer safety, or green consumerism. In 1991, consumer rights organizations in two thousand Chinese cities held activities designed to encourage consumers to join in efforts to improve product quality. As a result of these yearly campaigns, the date March 15 has been incorporated into the organization's emblem and is now a symbol for consumer protection; since 2000, it appears on product packaging as a guarantee of product and service quality. The CCA also has other outreach activities, such as *China Consumer Reports* magazine, which began as a monthly in 1994; modeled on the U.S. *Consumer Reports* and the UK *Which?*, it does not accept advertising and it conducts comparative product testing and investigations and issues consumer warnings. The organization also fields hundreds of thousands of calls on a consumer hotline established in 1999.

Government efforts to protect consumers have been joined by similar efforts by private individuals and groups. Perhaps the most notable of these is Wang Hai, whose crusade against counterfeits has earned him considerable media attention and accolades as a "fake-fighting hero." In 1995, Wang, a high school dropout and salesman who had taken a legal correspondence course, used a little-known section of China's new consumer protection law, Clause 49, to demand compensation for fake products. The clause stated that businesses committing fraud must compensate consumers with double the purchase price. Buying a pair of Sony earphones at a local department store that he knew were fakes, Wang sued and won. For the next two years, he traveled the country buying fakes in bulk from retailers and manufacturers. Rarely seen or photographed without his trademark dark sunglasses, which he claimed were to mask his identity from vindictive merchants, in 1997 he formed Beijing Dahai Consultants, which included a network of some two hundred undercover investigators across China. Wang's much-publicized exploits have proven useful to Chinese and foreigners alike. The Chinese government and the official media, keen to demonstrate China's efforts to crack down on piracy, honored Wang as emblematic of its own periodic campaigns. Foreign governments, including the United States, have found applauding the efforts of Wang Hai and other activists a convenient means of urging greater protection of IPR throughout China; in 1998, Wang even met the visiting president Bill Clinton in Shanghai.

Wang is, of course, the best brand for Dahai Consultants, which is just one of an increasing number of similar firms. Frustrated international and Chinese brand owners unwilling to wait for local authorities to get around to enforcing their rights have turned to private investigators. At least twenty counterfeit-busting detective companies now comb the Shanghai streets looking for pirated products. After identifying culprits and collecting evidence, they call the Administration for Industry and Commerce to shut the business down. International owners of IPR have also formed a trade association to promote their common interests and help the Chinese government enforce the law. The first was the Anti-Counterfeiting Coalition (ACC), founded in 1998 and reorganized and expanded to more than 120 companies in 2000 as the Quality Brand Protection Committee (QBPC), which is a unit of the China Association of Enterprises with Foreign Investment (CAEFI).

Shanzhai Culture

A recent manifestation of this hybrid consumer culture permeated with fakes is a cultural phenomenon known as *shanzhai*, from a term originally referring to a remote mountain stronghold beyond the reach of the government, where bandits (or, in this case, underground factories) could hide from the authorities. First applied to counterfeit consumer electronics such as cell phones and laptops with names nearly identical to their originals (Sumsung for Samsung and Nckia or Nokir for Nokia), the term has become a popular way to describe anything that is unofficial and unregulated, even celebrity look-alikes. There are, for instance, professional imitators for nearly every Chinese pop star, including three shanzhai Jackie Chans, and instant parodies of successful TV series, including *Ugly Wudi* (for *Ugly Betty*) and *Number One Prison of the Orient* (for *Prison Break*).

Although shanzhai products resemble their well-known counterparts in appearance and name, they are not passed off as fakes but offered as imitations of famous brands that provide significantly lower prices and sometimes more features. In many cases, shanzhai products are sold openly, even through late-night television ads promising equivalent quality at a third to a tenth of the original's cost. Some ads go a step further and suggest that buying Chinese shanzhai products is patriotic—consumers may gain the benefits and pleasures of foreign brands without providing profits to foreign companies. Take cell phones, perhaps the most commonly sold shanzhai product. The Apple King brand shanzhai cell phone imitates the appearance and performance of the Apple iPhone but costs 499 yuan rather than 4,000. Although shanzhai cell phones have been around for only a few years, they have already captured an estimated fifth of the Chinese market and are quickly spreading abroad. Such products therefore are providing the growing consumer base of less affluent Chinese with access to otherwise unattainable luxury products. As a twenty-five-year-old salesman from Shanghai said of his purchases of a shanzhai phone, MP3 player, and watch, "They were usable and cheap. They look exactly like real ones and make me cool. That's enough for me."

The shanzhai phenomenon also enables smaller Chinese manufacturers to experiment with branding products higher up the value-added chain without having to pay value-added taxes or comply with costly regulations, thereby creating an intermediary zone between simply producing licensed products for a brand owner (such as a Chinese manufacturer making Nokia phones) and developing their own brands (as with the regulated Chinese cell phone maker Bird). In the case of cell phones, a Taiwanese chip manufacturer, MediaTek, made the small-scale production of customized phones easier, allowing nimble underground factories to imitate stylish brands and even respond to the market by adding features, blurring the line between imitating and originating. They have also benefited from policy changes such as the deregulation of phone manufacturing by discontinuing requiring a license to manufacture them. In any case, these products are eating into the profitability of established brands and forcing them to lower their prices and profits, especially the mid-tier Chinese brands aimed at those who cannot afford the more expensive foreign brands.

Considering these benefits for many Chinese producers and consumers, it is little wonder that shanzhai culture has gained a level of social acceptance not accorded outright counterfeits. Many see it as a creative appropriation of technology in response to "grassroots culture," especially when it involves tinkering with the original to add features demanded by Chinese consumers, such as dual-mode SIM cards to allow two phone numbers, firewalls to block incoming calls from anyone on your blacklist, analog TV-watching capabilities, theft deterrent, and solar batteries. Such localization, and the fact that shanzhai products sometimes outperform the originals, makes civic-minded consumers more comfortable with violating the intellectual property rights of multinationals. As in English, the Chinese terms for "pirated" (*daoban*) and "counterfeited" (*jiahuo*) have negative connotations, implying stealing and inauthenticity. As one twentysomething female friend explained to me, "I feel 'counterfeit' is a negative word and so buying 'counterfeits' is shameful. But shanzhai to me sounds cute, creative, and interesting." Some go so far as to see shanzhai products as a form of popular consumer resistance to elite culture and elite monopolization of expensive brands enjoyed by a small fraction of the population.

At the same time, many things about shanzhai make the government, business leaders, and consumers nervous. According to a survey by the Shenzhen Mobile Communication Association, by 2008 there were at least ten thousand shanzhai companies in China churning out more than ninety million electronic products. As with the counterfeit industry, shanzhai manufacturers have become a huge vested interest of their own, employing 2 to 3 million people. There are also safety concerns with shanzhai products, which the Chinese Consumers' Association calls "three withouts" because they lack a production date, certification, or named manufacturer, making it impossible to monitor or enforce compliance with safety regulations. In the case of cell phones, the CCA warns of dangers such as inferior batteries that may fail or even explode and the difficulty of identifying the responsible defect or culprit. But judging by market share, clearly many consumers are willing to take such risks to have access to more stylish products.

If global consumers are concerned about the safety of such Chinese imports as toys, paint, and drywall, imagine what it's like to be a consumer in China, where the authenticity and quality of everything in your life is suspect: the food you eat, the water you drink, the pills you put in your body, the building you live in, the computer you use, the airplane you fly in—right down to the "Mont Blanc" pen you may use, say, to write a book manuscript. The uncertainty created by Chinese counterfeits is making consumer life in China unpredictable and tainting the "Made in China" label or "Brand China," even for international brands manufactured in China. At the same time, counterfeits and imitations are allowing more Chinese consumers to enjoy the fruits of industrialization without the expense of high-end brands, further consolidating the creation and spread of a consumer culture in the world's most populous nation. The standard line among international interests with the most to gain from access to that burgeoning market is that as China comes to own more IPR of its own, it will have a greater vested interest in protecting everyone's IPR. That explanation, however, assumes a massive state capacity to protect IPR that China may not have, doubly so if production technology is sufficiently diffused and if local governments have an economic and therefore political stake in unregulated production. In the end, consumer desire and local unemployment may pose a more serious threat to Chinese leaders than New York lawyers.

7 ★ EXTREME MARKETS

Before the Communist Revolution of 1949, rich Chinese families—like their counterparts in the West—had for centuries hired poorer women to breast-feed their babies. During the Maoist era, however, the Communists declared the buying and selling of lactation exploitative, and it largely disappeared. Thus it created quite a stir in 2006 when twenty-four-year-old Xiong Baoxia agreed to stop nursing her own five-month-old son and became the first openly marketed wet nurse in Shenzhen, across the border from Hong Kong. (A company in the eastern city of Yangzhou had previously tried to market such services, but had backed down after intensive media criticism for selling an immoral practice.) As Xiong saw it, "There is nothing wrong with getting paid by offering a service; it is just the same as other jobs." Her husband supported her decision, saying she was doing it for their son. Xiong was a migrant worker from the poorer province of Jiangxi, where jobs were in short supply. The company training and marketing her as a wet nurse, Shenzhen Zhongjia Household Services, reported that she would earn more than 2,000 yuan a month, significantly higher than the average of 800 yuan earned by conventional nannies in Shenzhen. In Beijing, wet nurses may earn four times as much. After yet another baby formula scandal in the summer of 2008, one that seriously undermined public confidence in the reliability of infant formula, prices for wet-nurse milk skyrocketed, and lactation entrepreneurs popped up throughout the country.

This is only one example of the ways in which what Chinese have seen as fit to market has changed dramatically over the past century. During the Mao era, Chinese leaders attempted to eliminate markets in general, and extremely exploitative markets in particular, making it difficult or impossible, for example, to hire the services of a wet nurse, buy a bride, or sell a child. But as the state withdrew from most areas of private life and started creating new market incentives following the rise of Deng Xiaoping in 1978, China soon witnessed the return of pre-Communist markets for seemingly anything that one could buy and sell. What this chapter refers to as China's extreme markets prove the universal and uncomfortable truth that there is no pale beyond which unchecked or unenforceable markets will not go, including the sale of infants, wives, sex slaves, human hearts, and endangered species. These extreme markets also illustrate once again how, once unleashed and prodded into action, Chinese consumers and consumer markets have unintended consequences that resist control, by China or other nations that benefit from them. For as this chapter will show, although such markets have deep roots in Chinese culture, they could not thrive without the complicity of international markets and consumers.

The Market Value of Girls

Cultural and economic forces in China have long made sons far more valuable to families than daughters. In the traditional Chinese household, when a daughter "married out" of her birth family, she became part of her husband's. This represented a real transfer of wealth: a daughter ceased being her father's property, becoming instead her husband's. Consequently, daughters were liabilities for the families that raised them, while sons were assets. Sons and their wives were expected not only to share the work of the family but to care for elderly parents. For several thousand years, Confucianism thus promulgated the idea that failing to have a male heir was the most unfilial act. The resulting preference for male children was further heightened by China's One Child Policy, introduced in 1979 to counteract the economic pressures of uncontrolled population growth. Under this policy the Chinese government began penalizing families for having more than one child, a policy that, when enforced, gave couples only a single chance to secure a male heir and thereby a caretaker in their old age, which took on renewed importance with the collapse of state-provided health care and retirement benefits. As boys became even more desirable and girls less so, female infanticide, long a way to dispose of unwanted girls, rose precipitously. When ultrasound scanning became more widely available in the 1980s and provided parents with a reliable and inexpensive way to determine the sex of fetuses, tens of millions of Asian parents elected to abort female fetuses. Even though China banned ultrasound testing in an effort to stop sex-selective abortion in 2004, the market soon provided a growing number of for-profit "maternity clinics" and back-alley stalls performing the tests for only a few dollars and offering abortions for $15 to $120. The result has been an alarming gender imbalance in China, which now has about 120 boys for every 100 girls, rising to 144 to 100 in some areas. Moreover, there are 152 male second children for every 100 females. And of the girls who are born, across the country a disturbing number are being abandoned, becoming wards of the state in Chinese orphanages.

Since the early 1980s, however, thanks to the desire for babies elsewhere, Chinese baby girls have become a valuable international product. In the 1990s, the increasing availability of contraceptives and abortion and an increasing acceptance of single mothers in the United States meant that millions of American couples with infertility problems were confronted with a declining number of American babies available for adoption. Even when available, an American baby could easily cost more than $30,000 in adoption fees. Thus American couples increasingly began to look abroad for children to adopt, and by 2000, American couples were importing 20,000 children per year from Asia and Central and Eastern Europe. Between 1991, when China began to liberalize its adoption laws to address the growing number of abandoned girls, and 2005, China became the world's primary supplier of adopted children, sending more than 62,000 to the United States and another 10,000 to other countries. Between 1991 and 1992, the number of Chinese children adopted by Americans rose from a mere 61 to 206, and by 2005 the United States granted nearly 8,000 orphan visas for Chinese children, who made up a third of all foreign adoptions. Of these, 95 percent were girls. Assuming that each adopting family paid a rough average of about $15,000 to $20,000 for the entire process, Americans paid Chinese orphanages $24 million in 2005 alone.

The baby adoption market has also spawned an entire consumer industry in China. Travel agencies shuttle adopting foreign families to sightseeing spots in Beijing, then on to the provinces handling international adoptions. Five-star hotels in cities across China have become hubs for foreigners with new Chinese babies. The best known of these is the White Swan Hotel in Guangzhou, whose rooms, lobbies, and elevators are regularly filled with multiethnic families waiting to obtain U.S. visas for their new babies. The surrounding streets are lined with shops selling silk infant clothing and renting strollers. Each family staying at the hotel receives a special "Going Home Barbie Doll," the iconic blond-haired and blue-eyed plastic figure holding a Chinese baby.

The surplus of mostly girl babies in China has served multiple American markets, including career women, affluent single people, and homosexual couples. (A fifth of all adopted Chinese babies go to New York State, and the highest concentration of these to New York City's Upper West Side, which has a high percentage of people in all three categories.) In 2006, however, waiting lists of up to two years, bad press, and abuse led Chinese authorities to introduce new rules that excluded homosexual couples, older couples, the obese, those medicated for depression, and families with a net worth of under $80,000. Since then, the number of imported Chinese babies has been halved to under four thousand a year. But China is not the only supplier. Americans have returned to South Korea, which remains a leader in international adoptions, and are also adopting babies from Guatemala, which in 2008 replaced China as the number one exporter, not to mention Russia, Ethiopia, the Ukraine, Kazakhstan, and India. The baby export industry may soon follow the example of shoe manufacturers and shift to less expensive, less regulated labor markets in places such as Vietnam.

This legal international market is partially an outgrowth of a domestic black market in babies serving Chinese customers. Because orphanages impose age and residency restrictions on domestic adoptions, buying a baby and legalizing the adoption process with bribes is often more convenient and less expensive than facing fines imposed under the One Child Policy. The international adoption programs have skewed the domestic market, however, especially after 2001, when the China Center of Adoption Affairs (CCAA, established 1996) ended its restrictions on the number of international adoptions and when orphanage directors began to recognize the high international market value of each adoptee. A few orphanages began to make hundreds of thousands of dollars through mandatory $3,000 "donations" from adoptive parents. To generate more supply, some orphanages began to buy babies from surrounding orphanages that were not engaged in international sales. The market value even tempted a few orphanage directors to pay for abducted infants.

Stolen babies are worth enough for some to risk the penalties. According to the confessions of baby abductors, one can earn $36 to $60 per child, in a country with an average income of approximately $100 a month. Middlemen sell children to orphanages for $400 or more. The baby market is carefully calibrated: the end purchaser pays some $1,200 for "substandard goods" (girls) and over $2,000 for "quality goods" (boys). Likewise, healthy babies fetch more than unhealthy ones. (This is true even in legal adoptions; one American friend jokingly referred to her Chinese adoptee as a "half-price" baby because he was older and had special needs.) In another sign of a maturing market, organized gangs are replacing family rings and freelancers in the child theft business. In 2006, for instance, Liang Guihong, a fifty-six-year-old woman who claimed to find homes for abandoned infants, was sentenced to fifteen years in prison for leading a gang that had sold seventy-eight infants in 2005 alone. As with other markets, those engaged in adoptions and baby trafficking have begun utilizing the Internet. Babies have even been offered for auction on eBay's Chinese website, EachNet, with an asking price of 28,000 yuan ($3,450) for boys and 13,000 yuan ($1,603) for girls.

The exact size of this illegal market is unclear. From 1980 to 1999, Chinese police reported that more than 10,000 children were abducted and sold for illegal adoption, an estimate that is probably low. In 2004 alone, authorities rescued 3,488 abducted babies, considered only a small fraction of those stolen. Chinese media routinely include news stories on the arrests of child traffickers. In 2005, police busted a ring of 27 traffickers who since 2002 had abducted or bought some 1,000 children and sold them to orphanages in Hunan province for $400 to $538 each. Unsuspecting American families then made mandatory contributions of $3,000 per baby, the highest of the many fees involved to adopt these children. As with other illegal market activities, local officials were often complicit, and defense attorneys argued that the babies were abandoned. Heads of orphanages have tried to cover their tracks with forged reports confirming abandonment, as China has strict regulations to avoid baby selling and Western countries refuse to permit adoptions through baby selling. Given the lucrative market incentives, however, the practice is all but impossible to stop. For example, in 2005 the Hengyang orphanage in Hunan province, a major provider of children for Americans, was caught buying babies, leaving adoptive parents uncertain if they had adopted a stolen baby rather than rescued an impoverished orphan.

As with its other extreme markets, China often gets bad international press about its adoption market, which puts pressure on officials to impose restrictions, make arrests, and pass laws prohibiting baby buying and forbidding the resale of purchased babies on international markets. Parents of the missing say the state should also work to eliminate the market by severely punishing those who buy children. But lack of enforcement is a consistent problem with the regulation of all Chinese markets. While baby buyers, for instance, are subject to a three-year jail sentence, few ever see the inside of a cell.

Another illegal domestic market is in children who are abducted or even sold by their parents and forced to become beggars, thieves, child brides, caregivers for the elderly, or sex workers. The mass migration of several hundred million Chinese from the countryside to cities since the start of the Reform Era, the largest migration in human history, makes estimates of such "missing" children difficult. But the international charity Save the Children estimates that in China's Xinjiang region alone, tens of thousands of boys have been bought or kidnapped by gangs and forced to work as pickpockets in China's eastern cities, with the Chinese authorities rescuing three thousand between 2006 and 2008. The children of desperately poor migrant workers in big cities are easy targets, with urban police often ignoring the complaints of parents with missing children. Perhaps the most shameful new entrepreneurs in this new domestic market are con artists who, claiming to have seen a lost child, offer to track him down for an advance fee.

The unintended gender imbalance partially caused by China's One Child Policy has led to the creation of another extreme market in China: brides for all those favored sons wanting to produce their own male heirs. Until the 1940s, marriage by abduction or "seizing the bride" (*qiangqin*) was common in parts of China. The buying and selling of women in pre-Communist China was sometimes a socially accepted way for the rural poor to sidestep the expensive dowry/bride price system, often after secret negotiations with the girls' parents. It was also considered more acceptable to abduct certain women than others, such as widows of reproductive age. Likewise, pre-Communist times also saw sophisticated kidnapping gangs that would steal girls from impoverished families and sell them as concubines and slaves in other provinces. And desperate families might sell their own daughters and even wives as brides and maids.

This illegal practice is again on the rise, judging from widespread stories of young women being bribed into marriage or even kidnapped, including women from surrounding less prosperous countries such as North Korea or Vietnam. While it is difficult to assess the size of this market, according to Chinese police statistics, some 360,000 women and children were sold in the bridal trade from 1995 to 2000. According to their own statistics, in 1990–91 Chinese police apprehended 65,236 persons for participating in female trafficking. The scale of this practice continues to rise, even as the average age of the trafficked girls has fallen into the teens. Periodic high-profile cases confirm that the problem remains acute. In 2002, for instance, a Guangxi farmer was executed for abducting and selling more than 100 women for $120 to $360 each. And in the province of Inner Mongolia, another sold 112 women for prices ranging from 3,000 to 8,000 yuan.

The market in brides, like so many other markets that had been suppressed under Mao, has now reached new extremes with international and regional dimensions. Other Asian countries are facing similar demographic problems. For every 100 girls, Taiwanese give birth to 119 boys; Singaporeans, 118 boys; and South Koreans, 112 boys. Wealthier countries such as Japan have turned to China to resolve their bride shortage, buying Chinese wives and creating entire industries. The *New York Times* reporter Seth Faison found dozens of agencies brokering marriages between Japanese men and Chinese wives. These marriages are overtly commercial transactions, such as the case of one Osaka-based Japanese customer, Hitoro, who selected his wife from photo albums and paid $20,000. When he arrived in Shanghai, the potential bride demanded an extra $5,000, which Hitoro refused to pay. The brokers, anxious to seal the deal, scrambled and, within a day, found another woman willing to marry a stranger with whom she could not even converse. Although Hitoro had hoped they might use English as a lingua franca, the new bride, a retired prostitute, claimed that she knew only two English phrases: "I love you" and "I am a virgin."

This demand for wives has also led to the development of a submarket in virgin brides, who can draw a premium. In the past few years, Chinese newspapers have carried hundreds of advertisements placed by wealthy bachelors seeking virgin brides. In one case, an advertisement by a supposed billionaire (in yuan) drew six hundred applications. The phenomenon got the attention of the highly regarded Chinese newspaper *Nanfang Weekend*, which published a report on billionaires seeking brides that sparked a heated online discussion, especially over one woman's comment that "Isn't the purpose of saving our virginity to get a good price?" Many readers labeled her a prostitute, while others mocked the billionaire for thinking he'd find an honest bride this way.

The irony is that cultural preferences and, indirectly, political policies have created a shortage of brides to marry the next generation of baby boys. There are at least some initial indications that this shortage may provide its own solution by raising the market value—and correspondingly the social value—of baby girls. One wonders, however, about the fate of the forty million (and counting) frustrated bachelors who won't benefit in time from the "market correction."

The Sex Trade

The lack of brides, combined with China's hundreds of millions of men of all ages with increased disposable income, has, perhaps not surprisingly, created a huge market incentive for organized criminal networks to build a massive brothel industry. Again we can see that while impersonal market forces can create new opportunities for some consumers, they can also lead to sharpened inequalities. In China these inequalities have both class and regional dimensions, as men in rich coastal regions, where the gender imbalance is often the worst, are more likely to be able to afford to pay for sex, wives, children, and mistresses. Nonetheless, markets can also provide opportunities for those at the bottom of the socioeconomic ladder. While migrant male laborers in cities may not be able to afford girlfriends, much less wives, the market allows them to buy sex. Nevertheless, the inability of China's market economy to supply wives and progeny to this new underclass of frustrated bachelors, which Beijing estimates will reach thirty million by 2020, may come to pose a serious political threat to its leaders.

The shortage of women and the demand for paid sex underscores the difficulty China's government faces when cracking down on socially dubious markets. After all, how willing (or even able) would the Chinese government be to restrict male access to sex by enforcing a ban on prostitution? Indeed, one convicted trafficker of women claimed that he was doing the Chinese government a favor by balancing "the yin and yang" (feminine and masculine) by moving women from Sichuan province to points north, where there are too many bachelors chasing too few brides. He argued that he was "just trying to supply what the market needs" with an activity that "helps dissolve young guys' sexual tension."

The market for various types of sexual services would probably not be possible without the sexual revolution that has been under way in China over the past couple of decades. As perhaps best symbolized by the shift in young urban Chinese women's clothing from baggy Mao suits to revealing designer dresses, sex has gone from being invisible to being ubiquitous. Before the Reform Era, there were few private, unmonitored spaces such as hotels or MTV bars for couples to meet, and public spaces were open and crowded. (When I studied at Beijing University, on any given evening lovers occupied every available cluster of bushes surrounding the lake at the center of the campus.) In short, it was difficult to have sex outside of marriage. And given the shortage of housing, and the fact that couples needed official permission to marry, even married sex wasn't much more available. As with so many other changes during the Reform Era, the shift from suppressed to widespread sexual activity has been rapid. In the 1980s, the vast majority of Beijing residents who got married were virgins, but by 2005, researchers had found that 70 percent reported having sex before tying the knot, often with more than one partner. Over the same period, the average age of the first sexual experience of people in China's seven largest cities dropped from twenty-four to seventeen. The abortion business is up for single women, who over the past ten years have surpassed married women as the primary customers at health clinics. Popular attitudes affirm these changes: a Chinese magazine poll found that one third of Chinese under the age of twenty-six did not object to extramarital affairs, and the vast majority thought premarital sex was not immoral.

And sex, of course, sells. So it is no surprise that the sexual references central to the marketing of products in modern consumer cultures have now pervaded China. Rare in the Maoist era, they are now omnipresent on Chinese billboards, magazines, and movies and in women's fashion, especially in urban settings. Indeed, such references appear to have become iconic of what it means to live in modern times, a way of contrasting up-to-date urban life with a sexually puritanical, old-fashioned, and backward past of the countryside. New industries popularizing and catering to sex have spread across the country, and lingerie boutiques are now common sights in big cities. After decades of supplying the globe's adult sex toys, China now has its own domestic market, including Guangzhou's hugely popular annual Sex Culture Festival, which was launched in 2003. Sixty thousand mostly middle-aged men attended the opening day of the 2009 festival, which included guest appearances by Japanese porn stars. Likewise, the southwest city of Chongqing is home to Love Land, the country's first theme park devoted to sex (inspired by a similar park in South Korea), which includes displays of giant genitalia and naked humans.

The new acceptance and popularity of sex has not entirely erased traditional attitudes toward premarital sex, however, which has created a market premium for women who are virgins and a corresponding industry for manufacturing what we might term "fake virgins," created with hymen repair surgery. For-profit hospitals and clinics do a brisk business, and because the procedure is simple, even cosmeticians and underground doctors perform it in under an hour for a few thousand yuan. In 2005, one doctor who had been performing the service since 1997 estimated he had made at least one thousand "repairs" to women, some as young as sixteen. This "re-created virgin" industry began in Beijing and Shanghai and has spread to cities across China. Huge profits are being made, and some entrepreneurs have tried to undercut the surgery business by manufacturing "artificial virginal hymen" inserts. Many Chinese women visiting public restrooms in cities today can expect to find advertisements reading "Get your Virginity Back for 260 RMB!" and "Your unspeakable secret will be erased!" In Shanghai, I visited a high-end sex shop that was selling (for 136 yuan) a pair of fake hymen implants imported from Japan that released a red liquid upon penetration. According to the proprietor, the product was especially popular among sex workers, who charged clients extra for the experience.

In addition to making representations of sex ubiquitous in Chinese cities, markets have also created opportunities for paid sex in all manner of locations. There are opportunities to buy sexual services at hostess bars, from escorts, in massage parlors, at "barbershops," in karaoke clubs, and, most notoriously, in hotels. (Ask any experienced male traveler to China about the late-night calls inquiring if he needs any "assistance.") Indeed, China now has the largest commercial sex workforce in the world. It is estimated that some ten million women and men work in the industry—three hundred thousand of these in Beijing alone. Rather than trying to shut it down, some local governments have moved to legalize it. When the northeastern city of Shenyang began laying off tens of thousands of workers from state-owned enterprises in the late 1990s, for instance, the city legalized prostitution to offset some of the layoffs and levied a 30 percent tax on the sex trade's five thousand "places of entertainment." The policy was so successful that other cities soon followed suit. And like so many Reform Era markets that have spread and evolved in unpredictable ways, once consumer demands are both met and legitimated, and the state's endless need for new revenue sources identified, the market is hard to eliminate. Once you can buy a Polo shirt, eat fast food with disposable chopsticks, knock back a couple of cognacs, and then buy a real or fake virgin for an hour—taxes included at each step—it's very hard to take the choice away.

Like the marriage market, the prostitution market also reflects a preference for virgins. A recent scandal broke in the Henan provincial city of Nanyang, for instance, when the parents of two teenage school girls noticed that their daughters were wearing new dresses and had more spending money. When the girls confessed that they had obtained the money by selling their virginity to a middle-aged man, Deng Jun, investigators found ten other girls who had done the same and detained another three girls who, after selling their own virginity, had made more money recruiting other virgins for Deng. The incidents had gone undiscovered for so long because most of the girls' parents were off working as migrant laborers in big cities.

Although sex workers are overwhelmingly female, young men known as *yazi*, or "ducks," also sell themselves to bored housewives whose husbands often have mistresses and to female sex workers. Recognizable by their tight-fitting clothing, designer sunglasses, and, originally, red socks that made their legs resemble those of ducks, they congregate in bars where their work is similar to that of hostesses: chat, pour drinks, play dice, flirt, and maybe more. In Beijing, many of these young men come from China's rust belt in Manchuria, where unemployment is high and men are often taller—a trait many Chinese consider attractive. In Shenzhen, the city with the most male sex workers and where male prostitution as a profession first emerged in the mid-1990s, four-fifths of the customers were found to be lower-middle-class women visiting on holidays from Hong Kong or Taiwan.

One twenty-six-year-old woman described a same-aged friend's attitude toward hiring prostitutes: "She's bored of sex with her husband, so she spends his money sleeping with *yazi*. It's very normal. It's not cheating, because it has nothing to do with love; I can easily separate sex and love. I just do it for the sex."

Of course, sex work has nothing to do with love on the part of the sex workers, either; overwhelmingly, they are driven into the trade by economic desperation or coercion. Although "ducks" may experience less direct physical threat or violence than their female counterparts, they also report the common feeling of objectification and the assumption by their customers that once a fee is paid, a customer has unhindered access to a worker's body. As one duck put it, any demur from him draws a common refrain from women: "What sort of object are you? I've given you money and want you to do something, so you had better do it." Beijing police have now begun to take notice of places peddling male prostitutes. On their first raid of a male escort nightclub in the spring of 2006, they found ninety-eight escorts entertaining several dozen female "guests."

The Chinese sex trade has also expanded beyond domestic consumption and supply and become part of an international market. China now both exports women and girls to work as sex slaves and imports them from Mongolia, Nepal, North Korea, and Vietnam. Indeed, China appears to be on the verge of replacing Thailand as the regional human trafficking hub. According to the U.S. State Department's Office to Monitor and Combat Trafficking in Persons, hundreds of thousands of North Korean refugees fleeing famine are ending up in China, sold either as prostitutes or as brides to poor farmers.

Girls are trafficked out of China primarily to Malaysia, Singapore, Taiwan, and Thailand. In Malaysia, rich married businessmen, as individuals or as members of clubs, visit Chinese women, often held against their will, in luxury condominiums in the afternoon to drink, eat, and have sex. In other cases, these women are escorted to homes. Known as "noon brides," the Chinese women are lured from the countryside with promises of office work. In Malaysia, the male consumers' shift in preference from Thai to Chinese girls is partially the result of changing consumer preferences and the mistaken assumption that Chinese women are less likely to carry HIV. The market is also facilitated by a growing Malaysian interest in all things Chinese and the massive increase in other forms of contact between the two countries, including business, education, and tourism. Crime syndicates import thousands of young Chinese women on student visas, register them at schools, and then farm them out to work in the sex and service industries.

Organ Sales and Medical Tourism

The extreme market most often decried in the West is that for body parts, such as kidneys, livers, corneas, and pancreases. Although an estimated two million Chinese patients are in need of organ transplants, the majority of the twenty thousand or so performed each year in China involve foreign patients. Over the past decade, China has become a popular destination for medical tourists seeking treatments either unavailable or unaffordable in their own countries. While Koreans, Japanese, and Taiwanese flock to China for such treatments, customers also come from Europe and the United States. A salesperson for China International Transplantation Network Assistance Center, or CITNAC, a Shenyang-based subsidiary of a Japanese firm that matches Japanese customers with Chinese organs, acknowledged that "there are so many Japanese people coming to China to get transplants we cannot keep up. Please do not encourage the French to come here!" Such transplants are pricey: $30,000 for a cornea, $62,000 for a kidney, $100,000 for a liver, between $150,000 and $160,000 for a heart, and $170,000 for a pancreas. Foreigners are not the only customers: high demand within China and a shortage of donors has also created a black market that allows wealthy Chinese to buy organs. In 2004, for instance, the popular comedian Fu Biao bought an executed prisoner's liver for 300,000 yuan.

After the United States, China has become the world's second largest provider of organ transplants. This raises the question of how a country that did not introduce a system of voluntary donor cards until 2009, and in which many Chinese hold traditional religious beliefs that require an intact body in the afterlife, manages to find sufficient organs to offer them to foreign buyers. One source long rumored and finally confirmed by the government was executed prisoners, who account for at least 65 percent of organ donors. China does not disclose the number of executions, but estimates by international observers range from a few thousand to ten thousand yearly. (By contrast, the United States has executed a total of 1,188 prisoners since the death penalty was reinstituted in 1976.) Whatever the number, China harvests an estimated 3,200 organs annually from executed prisoners.

Until recently, officials routinely denied that such a market in prisoner organs existed, despite an availability that seemingly paralleled execution schedules. For instance, Chinese customs require the government to show mercy at Lunar New Year, a time of renewal, by limiting executions, making organ supplies greater in the weeks that precede it than during the rest of the year. In 2006, an official at the Number One Central Hospital in Tianjin admitted to an undercover BBC reporter that the liver for sale came from a prisoner, but reassured him that it was donated voluntarily as a "present to society."

As China became more sensitive to its international image in the several years preceding the Beijing Olympics, the Chinese government changed its official line about prisoner donors and tried to better regulate the market. In 2006, it finally acknowledged the use of prisoner donors and cracked down on organ trafficking, issuing new rules to ensure that written consent was obtained from donors and requiring the licensing of hospitals permitted to perform transplants. Authorities also banned the sale of organs from corpses donated for medical research, limited the types of institutions allowed to accept corpses, and regulated the international transport of corpses. That year they also banned exports and stopped giving preference to foreigners on organ lists.

Since then, fewer executions and the new regulations on harvesting organs from executed prisoners have created acute market shortages for organs inside China and abroad. Consequently, demand has pushed up prices everywhere. The price for a kidney in South Korea, where more than ten thousand people are waiting for transplants, shot up from $27,000 to $37,000 immediately after the Chinese ban. In wealthy countries, there's only one kidney for every ten people on the waiting list, which fuels international demand. With prices high and supplies increasingly regulated, the black market of individuals willing to sell a kidney continues to develop.

Areas in and around hospitals in China openly advertise organ purchases and sales. Those advertising this controversial service have to strike a delicate balance, claiming to sell fresh organs free of communicable diseases such as HIV while simultaneously reassuring consumers that such organs were ethically obtained. In short, they need to make such consumption palatable. So while one website reassured potential clients that organs came from prisoners awaiting execution, it simultaneously reassured customers that prisoners' families received a donation and that advanced screening and blood tests would be used to avoid communicable diseases and ensure excellent matches. As with traded commodities in most extreme markets, however, consumers of organs tend not to be overly concerned about where they originated. Perhaps reflecting a widespread attitude among such buyers, an American who paid $40,000 for a Chinese kidney, although she suspected her new kidney had come from a prisoner, admitted to a *Los Angeles Times* reporter that she "didn't want to know."

Sale of Endangered Species

Another "number one" distinction for Chinese consumers is that China is now the world's largest consumer of wild plants and animals, many of which are endangered species. Once again, the growth of these markets has been an unanticipated result of China's economic reforms. The collapse of the central provisioning of health care, for instance, has led to renewed interest in traditional Chinese medicine (and heterodox religious organizations claiming to have the secret to good health), while the mass media have contributed to the demand for such products by popularizing interest in folk medicine. High-end pharmacies and restaurants are expected to sell popular treatments such as golden turtle's blood to cure cancer; sea horse for asthma, heart disease, and impotence; pickled turtle flippers to promote longer life; and owl meat for improved eyesight.

Rising incomes and international trade networks have made rare wildlife more available and affordable at the same time that popular culture, particularly but not exclusively in southern China, holds that eating rare meat can bestow bravery or sexual prowess. Wildlife delicacies are often featured in lavish banquets intended for conspicuous consumption. Although the government has made efforts to limit consumption—in 1989, the Wildlife Protection Law banned the consumption of internationally protected species—once again the law remains difficult to enforce. Media reports of police seizures reveal the extent of the problem. One smuggling ring in the southwestern province of Yunnan, for example, was caught red-handed with 278 bear paws and 416 dead pangolins (anteaters that resemble armadillos). But the biggest bust occurred in 2004, when Chinese customs officials seized the skins of 31 Bengal tigers, 581 Asian leopards, 778 otters, and 2 lynx—a haul worth well over $1 million.

Chinese consumers have used their newfound purchasing power to buy both items not previously available and items long cherished in Chinese culture. Bear's paw, pangolin meat, camel's hump, monkey's brain, tiger bones dipped in liquor, and tiger penis, though long sought after, were usually expensive because of short supply, and thus beyond the means of most Chinese. That market has grown with the means of Chinese consumers, even though many of these items are derived from animals in short supply nationally or internationally, further endangering already endangered species. And Chinese consumers are eating not only their own rare wildlife but the world's, creating smuggling networks that stretch from China to the jungles of Southeast Asia and the coasts of Latin America. The range of exotic animals bought and consumed in China is illustrated by a recent story of 5,000 rare animals found drifting in an abandoned smuggler's boat off the South China coast. The 200 crates on board included 31 pangolins, 44 leatherback turtles, 2,720 monitor lizards, 1,130 Brazilian turtles, and 21 bear paws—all endangered species banned from international trade but openly sold in Guangdong.

Among these products, practitioners of traditional Chinese medicine, including in Korea and Japan, consider bear bile an extraordinary health elixir and a key ingredient in more than a hundred medicines. The bile, which is abundant in ursodeoxycholic acid, is converted into powder as remedies for arthritis, impotence, kidney and liver ailments, and fevers and even to rejuvenate brain cells. Demand has led to the creation of a "bear farming" industry, where caged bears are milked for their bile with catheters. Just as factory-farmed milk cows in the United States are worked to premature deaths, since the 1980s on these Chinese farms the bears have been subjected to nightmarish conditions and have seen their life expectancy shortened from twenty-five to four years. By 2005, China had nearly five hundred such "farms," but international pressure from animal rights organizations and the European Parliament has forced them to crack down, reducing the number to sixty-eight. The consolidated farms, though, are massive, each housing some seven thousand bears. That their paws are prized culinary delicacies doesn't help. As with so many other natural resources, demand in China has led to poaching around the world. In Russia, for instance, endangered Himalayan black bears are illegally hunted and sold to Chinese middlemen.

The Chinese have also consumed tigers to near extinction. Their numbers in the wild are down to 2,500 worldwide and only a few dozen roam freely in China. In 1993, again under international pressure, the Chinese government outlawed the trade in tiger parts, but demand remains strong, and there is a flourishing black market for tiger skin, used for clothing; bones, used in Chinese medicine for joint ailments such as arthritis; and tiger meat and health tonics. Neighboring states such as India are big providers of illegally poached animals, and entrepreneurs have found legal ways around the ban within China, setting up more than a hundred private tiger breeding "farms" housing five thousand tigers. These farms, which are also tourist sites, legally supply parts from tigers that die from natural causes. The World Wildlife Fund, however, says they are merely fronts for illegal traders. Breeders counter that legalizing the trade would lead to less poaching and the preservation of tigers; preservationists answer that breeders have no program for reintroducing tigers into the wild.

Shark fin soup is perhaps the best-known Chinese delicacy, found more often on international Chinese menus than, say, braised bear paws. The soup is favored for its medicinal and aphrodisiac qualities and, above all, as a status symbol at Chinese banquets. It is often the most expensive soup on lengthy Chinese menus and, as soup is served last, considered a nice final touch to a meal. Less widely known to consumers everywhere is the international impact of the increasing Chinese demand, extending all the way to Latin America, where local fishermen hunt sharks just for their valuable fins, which end up in Chinese soups. In Ecuador a set of dorsal and pectoral fins fetches $100, then sells for thousands of dollars in East Asia, and retails for up to hundreds of dollars for the tiny quantities served in soup. Hong Kong was the largest market for shark fins in the 1980s, but by the 1990s that distinction had shifted to mainland China, where shark fin soup had become trendy. In cities such as Shanghai and Beijing, it is sold in all the fine restaurants, and even by some street vendors. Between the mid-1990s and mid-2000, Ecuador's exports of shark fins to China and Hong Kong had doubled to 279,000 pounds, provided by roughly 300,000 sharks.

The impact of this particular Chinese desire on the world's shark populations has been profound. In only fifteen years, 70 percent of shark species such as the great white and hammerhead have been killed, and other species have disappeared altogether. Countries such as Ecuador have tried unsuccessfully to ban shark fishing and finning, the practice of slicing off fins at sea and dumping the carcass. But lax enforcement and lucrative demand make the prospects for shark survival grim.

In addition to official attempts to curtail such consumption in China, efforts have been made to reduce demand by changing public perceptions toward wildlife. The international kung fu movie star Jackie Chan, for instance, made a public service advertisement in Mandarin for the NGO WildAid, attacking the consumption of shark fins and other endangered species with graphic images. He closed with an appeal to consumers: "When the buying stops, the killing can too." Other prominent Chinese figures such as NBA basketball star Yao Ming,

Hong Kong actress Michelle Yeoh, and the Olympic gold gymnast and footwear entrepreneur Li Ning have made similar spots. International NGOs such as the WWF have called for stepped-up campaigns to dissuade the public from buying products derived from endangered species. Animal-borne illness, though, has done more than such appeals to change public perception. The consumption of civet cats (which resemble mongooses and otters), another delicacy and traditional medicinal ingredient, was blamed by some scientists for the outbreak of SARS in 2002–2003, which killed 774 people. Guangdong province responded by banning their sale, and the United States placed an embargo on them. There is some evidence that the negative association of these delicacies with disease is having an effect: a recent survey suggested that the number of restaurants serving some exotic wildlife was dropping.

Of course, China is not the only country with extreme markets. Consider, for instance, that every year in the United States nearly four hundred thousand women, mostly under the age of twenty-one, get breast implants exclusively for cosmetic reasons, many as high school graduation gifts. Nor are extreme markets somehow inherent to Chinese culture: all of the markets described in this chapter were in fact declared unacceptable, and were not legally or commonly found in China for at least a quarter century during the Mao era. That attempts to rein them in by China's current leaders have been only modestly successful reveals just how far China's consumer culture has moved from one in which consumption was highly regulated under communism to a freewheeling market society in which it has become extremely difficult to place checks on consumer demand. A consequence of China's rapidly expanding market behavior is, at its extremes, more Chinese adoptees on the Upper West Side, more Chinese prostitutes in

Thailand, and more Chinese corneas in the eyeballs of Californians. Although mainstream economists and policy makers want China to rescue the global economy by consuming more, neither they nor the Chinese government have proven capable of controlling either what the Chinese consume or the effects of their consumption. What extreme markets put in a particularly harsh light is the simple truth that it is difficult to have it both ways: to create a consumer culture that celebrates individual choice and also maintain control over what is desired, bought, and sold.

8 ★ ENVIRONMENTAL IMPLICATIONS

Often seemingly insignificant changes best highlight a global phenomenon. For me it was chopsticks. Few objects more immediately evoke China to the wider world. When I first studied in China in the mid-1980s, we were encouraged to carry our own chopsticks whenever we went out to eat. Forget them and you were forced to use dirty, cracked bamboo chopsticks supplied by the restaurant and used by who knows how many people before you. Then the world changed, and ubiquitous disposable wooden chopsticks—like the no-longer-heard bicycle bells—became a potent sign of the growing prosperity that followed. They also neatly encapsulate the often overlooked environmental implications of China's new consumer lifestyles. Even such small changes as disposable chopsticks have huge impacts: every year, millions of Chinese trees are turned into tens of billions of pairs of disposable wooden chopsticks, which add millions of tons to China's waste stream, making the resulting deforestation and increased trash just two of the countless battlegrounds between consumer lifestyles and the environment currently under way in China.

In socialist China, poverty meant that nothing could be wasted; everything was reused, and *recycled* was a euphemism for the way scarcity forced people to repurpose everything. The Mao era promoted frugality, savings, and attacks on personal consumption deemed "wasteful" and "extravagant," to invoke two words in the Maoist-era anti-consumption lexicon. A common Chinese saying in that era held that something was "new for three years, old for three years, and sewed, mended, and repaired for another three years." By the early 1990s, chopsticks, freely given and freely discarded, were an early visible crack in China's anti-consumption stance and a sign of emerging class differentiations. While restaurants frequented by the poor continued to offer reuseable battered bamboo chopsticks, and the growing number of high-end establishments provided fancy reusable lacquered ones, every eating spot in the vast middle was switching to disposables.

To the growing Chinese middle classes, disposable chopsticks became closely associated with convenience—with eating on the go—and, as one Chinese reporter put it, "a civilized lifestyle." The government also promoted their use to check the spread of disease, particularly after the 1988 outbreak of some three hundred thousand cases of acute hepatitis A in Shanghai. Since then, periodic food safety scares have continued to heighten the demand for disposable chopsticks and strengthen the link between them and modern hygiene. Now Beijing residents alone use ten million pairs a day. In its simplicity and ubiquity, the humble chopstick offers a superb window on one of the most disconcerting consequences of the unleashed Chinese consumer: environmental blowback.

Not only chopsticks but the foods that consumers are eating with them present new environmental problems. Growing prosperity allows the Chinese to consume more meat, a source of protein once considered a luxury. Indeed, the purpose of the thousands of KFCs, McDonald'ses, and other fast-food restaurants now spread out across urban China is to make money by persuading Chinese to eat more pork, chicken, and beef. It's working. Fifty years after a famine killed thirty million Chinese, they now consume quadruple the number of calories from animals than they did twenty-five years ago. This transition from famine to feast has its downside, however. In addition to such obvious consequences as the earlier mentioned increase in childhood obesity, the new Chinese diet also produces 2.7 billion tons of animal manure, most of which is left untreated. Also, ever greater numbers of cattle, goats, and sheep graze on ecologically fragile hills and steppes, consuming vast swathes of grassland and loosening topsoil that more readily becomes massive sandstorms or the blinding "yellow wind." Beijing alone is inundated with half a million tons of sand every year. Already deserts have swallowed up thousands of villages, and entire cities have had to be built to house the displaced. Indeed, the country has become the leading exporter of dust, as tens of millions of tons of China's dust and coal pollution enters jet streams annually and makes it to Korea, Japan, and as far as the West Coast of the United States, a literal form of blowback.

With four times the population of America, China eats up resources and consumes more grain, coal, and more than twice as much steel and meat as the United States. Yet the environmental effect of these changes is just the beginning, the result of just a few decades of growth. The Chinese don't even have to "catch up" with the developed world to trigger profound global changes. They just have to keep doing what they are already doing: moving in the American direction. If, as already discussed, China were to have as many cars per person as in the United States—three cars for every four people—it would have 1.1 billion cars (to America's 225 million). China would need to pave nearly the same amount of land as is currently under cultivation and to consume more oil than the world currently produces. This isn't simply hypothetical: as already noted, in 2009, China overtook the United States as the leading market for cars. The environmental implications of the new consumerism in China are immeasurable, the consequences unpredictable, and the possibilities truly frightening.

Consumers versus the Environment

The very speed with which China's consumers are changing their country helps put in sharper relief what elsewhere in the industrial world has already blurred into an unquestioned backdrop: the environmental consequences of consumption. Behind the chopstick is not only a felled tree but a vast machinery of interrelated factors that make it possible for urban Chinese consumers to order fast food and get chopsticks along with their plastic plate and dinner. To cite just one of the most important of these factors, all of these lifestyle changes in China are fueled by the burning of coal, which provides 68.7 percent of the country's total energy consumption (compared with 50 percent in the United States). The 2.74 billion tons consumed in China in 2008 were used not only to generate electricity but also for heating and cooking in millions of homes. The country burns more coal than the United States, the European Union, and Japan *combined*. Furthermore, it is increasing its use of coal by over 10 percent a year, and on average adds another coal-fired power plant each week. (China's several thousand such plants compares with just over six hundred in the United States.) One consequence of this dependence on coal is the production of sulfur dioxide gas, which causes acid rain and leaves China with sixteen of the world's twenty most polluted cities and forces a third of all urban residents to breathe polluted air, contributing to hundreds of thousands of premature deaths a year. The situation got so bad that in 1999 Prime Minister Zhu Rongji told local officials, "If I work[ed] in your Beijing, I would shorten my life [by] at least five years." If this was not awful enough, in 2006, China became the world's leading emitter of carbon dioxide, the primary greenhouse gas contributing to global warming. This still makes it only the eighteenth largest per capita emitter, which means that the fact of China's merely starting to catch up with other major emitters in per capita use is a mounting environmental disaster.

To see how links between consumption and environmental problems build on one another, consider cement. Contemporary China is unimaginable without cement, the binding agent critical to the production of concrete. Without cement and concrete, there would not be the burgeoning forest of buildings at the center of the more than a hundred cities with over a million residents and the thousands of smaller towns, nor the vast network of highways and roads connecting them that are appearing at record rates. Cement production requires energy, and to produce this energy, China burns more coal. When I first visited Shanghai in 1986, the city had only a handful of tall buildings; twenty years later it had four thousand—nearly twice as many as New York. Across the country, many more are on the way: Beijing is currently *adding* the equivalent of three Manhattans of office and residential space. The same growth rates are true of highways and local roads, which also use vast amounts of cement. Even outside the cities, national and local governments see road-building as a way to employ migrant workers during the post-2008 economic crisis and as part of a long-standing program to reduce rural poverty by providing isolated farmers better access to markets and non-farm jobs. While no recent traveler to China would be surprised to learn that the country produces and uses nearly half the world's cement, they probably aren't aware that the chemical reaction at the center of making cement creates vast quantities of carbon dioxide. In fact, cement production accounts for 5 percent of all the world's CO_2 emissions and a fifth of China's. Add to this China's plans to accelerate its urbanization by encouraging hundreds of millions more farmers to relocate to new satellite cities. That's a lot more cement.

The difficulty of changing this situation, as with so many other carbon-intensive industries, is that not simply the government but many individual Chinese (from the rich to the middle class) now have a deeply entrenched interest in seeing countless more buildings constructed. Although nearly all of the richest "developers " (an ironic term given their notorious role in forced removals and the demolition of neighborhoods and communities) in China are children of high officials—including nine of the top ten real estate magnates and thirteen of the richest fifteen construction company owners in Shanghai—demand also comes from below. Even a friend of mine who is a low-level librarian has made more money from property speculation than he'll ever make working at the library. Since the 1990s, it's become a national pastime.

Perhaps nowhere is the mounting environmental cost of the changes under way in China as clear as in its mounting use of another crucial resource: water. Water, in fact, is perhaps the ultimate consumer product. In addition to consuming potable water by cup or bottle, the Chinese, like their counterparts worldwide, consume water indirectly as a critical ingredient in the modern factory farming that produces their new and more water-intensive diets based on meat. It takes approximately 1,000 tons of water to produce a single ton of grain and 7 tons of grain to produce a ton of beef. An upshot, then, of China's switching from their pre-1978 bean-protein-based diet to Kung Pao chicken or McDonald's hamburgers is that it uses much more water. Many Chinese industries also use massive amounts of water; it takes, for instance, 400,000 liters (or 105,000 gallons) of water to manufacture a single car. Increasingly, like their counterparts worldwide, the Chinese are also consuming water in the growing of biofuels to help fuel those cars in the face of dwindling global oil supplies.

All of these changes profoundly impact China's water supplies. The aquifers supplying China's northern wheat belt are dropping 10 feet (3 meters) a year, requiring some farmers to drill down 1,000 feet or more to find water. This has especially ominous implications for China's food supplies, as 85 percent of the farmland in North China relies on irrigation (compared with only 10 percent in the United States). Water shortages have been a major reason for falling grain production in China, which peaked at 123 million tons in 1997. Importing wheat from elsewhere effectively allows China to import water and compensate for shortages, but this, too, is a risky strategy, given the growing global water shortage and rising transportation costs.

All across China, glaciers are shrinking, lakes are vanishing, and rivers are drying up. Over the past twenty years, Qinghai province, on China's northwest plateau, has lost half of its four thousand lakes; Hebei province, which surrounds Beijing, has lost all but a few dozen of its one thousand lakes. Furthermore, at least ninety-six Chinese cities are facing problems relating to sinking land caused by declining water tables. Shanghai, which was built on a low-lying alluvial plain near the mouth of the Yangzi River, has spent over $12 billion to reinforce foundations, fix cracking walls, and repave roads; the problem has become so severe that it now pumps millions of cubic feet of water into the water table beneath the city to slow the sinking. Likewise, by the late 1990s, the Yellow River, which failed to reach the sea for the first time in 1972, was failing to do so two thirds of the year. Already some sixty million people have had difficulty obtaining enough water to meet their daily needs. Furthermore, accessible water sources are often polluted—the Chinese dump billions of tons of untreated sewage into the Yangzi, Asia's longest river, for instance. As a result, as much as half the population—six hundred to seven hundred million people— drink water contaminated with animal and human waste, an even more unappetizing thought than eating with those dirty chopsticks. (As with so much else, China presents a difference of scale rather than kind; some twenty million Americans each year also get sick from drinking contaminated water.)

The market responses to China's water crisis have created additional environmental problems. Gone are those days when visitors to China struggled to find a store that could sell them something to drink. Now water vendors are everywhere, and the waste bins alongside roads are brimming over with discarded plastic bottles. Even more than in Western countries, fewer and fewer consumers appear to trust tap water, or "Tap-ian," to borrow a pun on Evian, the French water brand that has became a fashion statement for the brand-conscious wealthy in China. The habit of buying bottled water is spreading worldwide, with Americans still leading the way, consuming 8.7 billion gallons of bottled water in 2008, almost double what they drank at the start of the decade. But while the U.S. market for bottled water began to decline in 2008, China consumed more than 5.2 billion gallons that year and is now by far the fastest growing market. This is likely to increase, as China drinks only about half the global average of 7.9 gallons of bottled water per person, significantly behind the United States (28.5) and the world leader, Mexico (59.1).

In contrast to locally produced, efficiently delivered Tap-ian, bottled water travels long distances, wasting massive amounts of fossil fuels in packaging and shipping. And once the water is consumed, all those plastic bottles are discarded. Before they begin their thousand-year journey to biodegradation, they are transported once more, to dumps or for recycling. (The United States, for instance, ships roughly 40 percent of the bottles tossed in recycling bins to places as far away as, you guessed it, China.) If Chinese consumers drink even one fourth the per capita rate of bottled water as the average American, China will become the world's largest consumer. As elsewhere, a desire to avoid this wasteful use of water has emerged, but not a solution. As one graduate student from Sichuan put it, "Yes, I think it is wasteful to drink bottled water. But what can I do? I can't drink directly from the tap and I don't like to drink boiled water, as my parents did. Boiled water tastes horrible, and I don't trust the quality, either. I wish there were an efficient way to purify tap water, but so far I don't see any way to solve the problem."

Vanishing Forests, Spreading Deserts

In part due to the increasing grazing of animals being raised for food mentioned earlier, China's deserts are growing at an unprecedented rate, with vast tracts of once-fertile land turning into dust and sand. A quarter of China is already desert, but despite efforts to slow the process, according to China's State Environmental Protection Administration, the deserts are engulfing nearly a million acres of land *annually* (roughly the size of the American state of Rhode Island). The Gobi Desert, in central China, has expanded by about 25,000 square miles since 1994, and soon 40 percent of China will be scrubland. As a result, according to the outspoken deputy minister of the environment, Pan Yue, in the coming decades "China will have more than 150 million ecological migrants, or, if you like, environmental refugees."

If the disappearance of topsoil, the expansion of urban sprawl, and desertification continue to eat away at China's grain yield while the Chinese convert to meat-based diets, China will have to rely even more heavily on international grain markets, further pushing up food prices for the world's 350 million desperately poor. Another possibility, hardly an assurance of future peace and prosperity, is that tens of millions of those hungry Chinese environmental refugees predicted by Pan Yue will pour into Russian Siberia looking for arable land. (Similarly, Chinese may compete with U.S. consumers for the U.S. grain harvest, threatening supplies and costs there.) In fact, Russian officials now estimate that out of a total population of 7 million people living in Siberia, already 350,000 are Chinese, including many there illegally. The Chinese are also moving elsewhere looking for land on which to grow food. One of the most intriguing developments of the last few years has been China's expanding presence in Africa. As of 2008, the Chinese government had earmarked $5 billion to grow food in African countries. Chinese investors have bought over ten thousand square miles (an area roughly the size of Maryland) of African land just since 2006. In addition to farmland, China is also turning to Africa for a wealth of mineral and energy resources to feed its fuel-hungry economy. In southern Africa, for instance, China has set up the Zambian Special Economic Zone, modeled after similar zones instituted in China during the early Reform Era and replete with tax breaks, easy financing, and infrastructure designed to stimulate economic growth and smooth access to the region's copper, diamonds, tin, and uranium.

But China's environmental problems aren't caused solely by the Chinese; global demand for inexpensive Chinese products also contributes to the rapid desertification of China. Take cashmere sweaters, once within the reach of only the rich. Now one can pick up a few cashmere shirts and sweaters from China for $100, with change left over. While Chinese producers have made cashmere clothing inexpensive, they have done so only at a catastrophic cost to the environment. China produces nearly three quarters of the 15,000 tons that make up the yearly global supply of cashmere, and in 2005 alone the United States imported a record 10.5 million cashmere sweaters from China. Each cashmere sweater requires the hair from two or three goats. The image of the millions of goats needed to supply this trade, all quietly munching away, should be more frightening than pastoral. Fragile semi-arid rangeland is too dry, steep, or infertile to sustain food crops, but it can support cattle, sheep, and goats. As family farms have replaced state-run production teams, the number of livestock has grown unchecked. With roughly the same grazing capacity as the United States, China is raising not only ten million more cattle but nearly four hundred million more sheep, mostly in its western and northern provinces. These sheep and goats destroy the land's protective vegetation, the roots of which are essential to securing the topsoil. So begins the transformation from rangeland to desert. Already, residents of some twenty-four thousand villages have been forced to partially or fully abandon their land to sand.

Many other "Made in China" products are creating similar tradeoffs between inexpensively priced goods that stimulate global demand but have worrisome environmental impacts. Also accelerating deforestation is China's consumption of wood, both for domestic use and for the export of manufactured wood products. In the twentieth century, China destroyed more than three fourths of its own forests for such uses. Deforestation along the Yangzi River caused massive erosion and ultimately flooding that, in 1998, killed three thousand Chinese, inundated fifty-two million acres, destroyed five million homes, and caused $20 billion in damage. This led officials to place greater restrictions on domestic logging, which in turn has forced Chinese to seek lumber elsewhere, often including illegally logged timber. Thus Chinese demand is playing a central role in global deforestation: worldwide, forests are being felled at an annual rate of at least thirteen million hectares (thirty-two million acres), or roughly an area the size of Greece. In the past decade, China has also become the leading exporter of furniture, plywood, and flooring, even though about 90 percent of its wood products are consumed domestically as the Chinese build and furnish the increasing stock of individual homes.

Trashing China

Another unintentional environmental effect of increased consumerism can leave one nostalgic for those battered bamboo chopsticks that were washed and reused no matter how worn out they became. For as

China adopts a throwaway consumer lifestyle, it is walking straight into a garbage crisis. It is not just that there is a lot more garbage produced by a growing population increasingly looking to consume goods. The heart of the problem is timing: in comparison with the rest of the world, this explosion in trash happened almost overnight and before "sustainability" became a worldwide concern. If China had waited another twenty years to adopt consumer lifestyles, it is possible it might never have developed a love for disposability. As it is, the country now produces a third of the world's garbage and is having problems burning, composting, and otherwise disposing of all of it. Most goes untreated. The suburbs of Beijing, Tianjin, Shanghai, and Chongqing alone are home to at least seven thousand garbage dumps of fifty square meters or larger.

In addition to its own waste, over the past two decades China has gone from saving and reusing every last scrap to becoming a huge importer of industrial waste. Your last computer probably ended up there, as 70 percent of the world's fifty million metric tons of discarded computers, electronic equipment, and other toxic "e-waste" now winds up in Chinese scavenger dumps. Entire towns such as Guiyu, not far from the Hong Kong border, have become unregulated open dumps for e-waste, employing more than thirty thousand workers in five thousand e-waste mom-and-pop shops. These workers, some of them children, rummage though the parts to salvage over 1 billion yuan worth of metals such as gold and copper, at an incredible risk to their health. What can't be resold is abandoned, left to leach toxic materials into the soil and groundwater. China is also manufacturing a tidal wave of electronic waste on its own. Every year it discards twenty-eight million TV sets, washing machines, and other electronic goods. In 2004, Chinese consumers bought more than eighty million mobile phones, forty million TV sets, forty-three million air-conditioners, nineteen million refrigerators, sixteen million computers, and fifteen million DVD players. And China is already the world's largest discarder, tossing out some seventy million mobile phones a year. As models with newer, must-have features come on the market, the Chinese, like consumers everywhere, want to upgrade; as a result, half of China's three hundred million-plus cell phone subscribers will replace their phone in the next few years.

As noted, the pace of this growth is astonishing. It was only in the mid-1990s that the first six disposable products arrived in China: paper towels, paper cups, paper plates, wooden chopsticks, diapers, and female sanitary napkins. By 2000, one Beijing branch of the supermarket chain Hualian alone was selling a couple hundred thousand yuan worth of disposable products each day. Within a few years of their introduction into the Chinese market, ten billion disposable Styrofoam lunch boxes were being used each year.

Naturally, some Chinese have begun to rethink their country's newfound love of disposability, and the government is desperately trying to deal with this tidal wave of trash. In late 1999, the Chinese State Economic and Trade Commission and State Administration of Light Industry set biodegradability and production standards and, in 2000, also forbade the production, sale, and use of disposable Styrofoam tableware. The Chinese have given such objects a new name, "white garbage," and cities such as Hangzhou, Nanjing, Ningbo, and Shanghai have tried to outlaw their use. The capital of Zhejiang province, Hangzhou, became the first Chinese city to ban plastic packaging. In the capital of Henan province, posters at local markets promote the use of baskets rather than plastic bags, with the mayor even distributing fifty thousand free wicker and straw baskets. In Beijing, residents are encouraged to use cloth bags for shopping, and the municipal government has set up recycling bins throughout the city. Although the Chinese Communist Party is also beginning to see the wisdom in recycling and is taking steps to encourage it, the country's recycling industry is still virtually nonexistent. While recycling is a $3.6 trillion industry in Japan and a $1 trillion industry in the United States, recycling revenues in China are a mere $5.4 billion.

The Price of Breathing

China's attempt to come to grips with its trash is just one of many efforts by its government to place new limits on consumption and products under the guise of a new ideology, environmentalism. Chinese leaders have, for instance, introduced standards and energy-efficiency ratings for air-conditioners, refrigerators, and washing machines, to reduce noise pollution and electricity consumption in large cities. Sales of products that fail to meet these standards are banned. But even such modest regulations have been undermined by hundreds of manufacturers producing low-quality, noisy, and energy-inefficient appliances, which by lowering prices and increasing production to preserve market share have created a glut in the appliance market. Some companies even sell their more environmentally advanced products abroad but their energy-inefficient lines at home. As lower prices lead the Chinese to use more appliances, electricity shortages have become a major headache in newly prosperous cities, especially during the summer. In Shanghai, for instance, air-conditioners account for some 40 percent of all electricity used during the city's sweltering summer.

Chinese leaders have acknowledged that China's energy use has become unsustainable, not only because its environment cannot absorb more pollution but also because the expense of production could render Chinese industries uncompetitive. In essence, the wasteful use of artificially low-priced energy (artificial because it didn't pass on the costs of pollution and other "externalities") that underwrote China's economic ascendancy cannot continue forever. In 2004, official Chinese statistics revealed that each 10,000 yuan ($1,250) in gross domestic product (GDP) required the burning of 2.6 tons of coal or its equivalent, ten times the global average and twenty times that of Japan. Moreover, these same statistics suggest that China is becoming more energy-*inefficient* as its economy grows. As a result, Chinese leaders such as Wen Jiabao routinely call for dramatic energy consumption cuts on a per-unit-GDP basis, and national officials have made gestures such as requiring central government offices to shut off their air-conditioning for a day in the summer to "experience energy shortage." A task force polices offices, hotels, malls, and other large buildings, requiring that they not be cooled below twenty-six degrees Celsius (seventy-nine Fahrenheit) during the summer or heated higher than twenty Celsius (sixty-eight Fahrenheit) during the winter. But such efforts appear weak (there are only twenty compliance officers for all of Beijing) in comparison with decades of evaluating and rewarding officials on the basis of GDP growth fueled by wasteful energy practices.

The Chinese government has made other efforts to address the problem. From 2003 to 2006, it put its support behind the concept of measuring and popularizing a "green GDP" that would include the costs of environmental destruction, eager to have a tool by which to assess the degree to which local officials were sacrificing the environment for economic growth and as a way to stay ahead of the growing environmentally related disasters and protests. But in 2006 the National Bureau of Statistics discontinued the effort, blaming the difficulty of calculating the value of natural resources. The long history of local officials falsifying economic statistics when such measures are used to evaluate their performance undoubtedly eroded the utility of such information. As long as breathable air and drinkable water are considered an externality by policy makers (in China and elsewhere) who place GDP growth above all else, it's hard to imagine a fundamental change in environmental policies. Although Chinese leaders have begun to include the environmental records of local officials in their evaluations, it's still unclear whether such measures will be enough to get them to change their behavior.

The Difficulty of Green Consumerism

On another front, China has seen the rise of a grassroots environmental movement that is trying to change the practices and thinking of Chinese consumers themselves. Linking comfortable new consumer lifestyles with their environmental impacts isn't easy; even in the industrialized world, where we have been trying to do so for much longer, it is an uphill struggle. It's difficult to get individuals who think of themselves primarily as self-interested "consumers" even to consider, not to mention pay more for, such intangibles as their patriotic duty to buy more expensive domestic products, let alone to develop a concern for the environment.

To give one example, in 2003, He Huili, an associate professor at the China Agricultural University, was temporarily assigned as a vice-magistrate to aid the farmers of impoverished Lankao county in Henan province. To fulfill that mandate, she decided to form a cooperative and raise an environmentally friendly strain of rice. Farmers in the co-op shared expenses and trademarked the rice. Things began well enough, and the new strain yielded a bumper harvest. After the fall harvest of 2005, the co-op shipped ten tons to Beijing, marketing their rice as supporting impoverished farmers and grown without environmentally destructive pesticides or fertilizers. But because their rice was more expensive than conventional rice, stores choose not to stock it. In a final act of desperation, Professor He then unsuccessfully tried to sell the rice on her campus. To explain the failure of her efforts, she blamed the lack of awareness of environmental issues among the Chinese, which was undoubtedly true. But another explanation was also at work: China's unstable market is rife with counterfeits that leave consumers rightfully suspicious of many products and their various marketing claims, prompting them to rely primarily on price, established brands, and reputable retail outlets. Chinese stores are saturated with products making bogus claims, and the now near-universal use of "green" labels makes all "green product" environmental claims suspect.

Consider, once more, those disposable chopsticks. Chinese environmentalists have battled since late 1990 to have them banned, efforts that illustrate the larger battle over consumer consciousness. Activists argue that the use of disposable chopsticks is destroying the Chinese environment by deforesting China. One activist, for instance, struggled to make clear that consumers need to contemplate their complicity in destroying China's environment: "That piece of greenery that you have come to deeply love and long for in the end has been destroyed by your own hand." Anti-chopstickers also appeal to nationalistic sentiments, comparing China's dwindling forests to Japan's much higher forest coverage (60 percent). What's Japan's secret? It imports tens of billions of disposable chopsticks, almost entirely from China, rather than destroying its own forests. Adding insult to injury, the Japanese then use discarded chopsticks to manufacture paper pulp that they export back to China. Environmentalists also attack the notion that disposable chopsticks are more hygienic by pointing out that toxic chemicals, including powerful bleaches, are used to process them.

In yet another example of the myriad consequences of the rapid rise of China's consumer marketplace, the country now has its own consumer industry lobbyists, who challenge attempts to make such links as those between disposable chopsticks and deforestation. One food industry newspaper rejected the idea that chopsticks wasted trees, claiming that leftover wood from tree farms is the primary source used by the disposable chopsticks industry, which also creates thousands of jobs in more than a thousand factories in China. However, the chopstick industry's greatest ally is the human inclination, even in as traditional a culture as China, to place individual interest above the collective good. One reporter informally surveying the night market in one central Chinese city, for instance, found that both consumers and restaurateurs thought chopsticks were ecologically destructive but used them anyway. Consumers justified their decision on the grounds of hygiene, and owners cited convenience, low price, and consumer preference.

In 2005, perhaps recognizing the futility of banning disposable chopsticks, the central government issued regulations requiring the use of fast-growing trees and bamboo for chopsticks, but rejected a complete ban on wooden ones. The following year, the Chinese government lumped chopsticks with other luxury items such as yachts, high-end watches, golf clubs, and fuel-inefficient cars on which they imposed luxury taxes (5 percent for chopsticks) and also imposed a whopping 50 percent tax on those exported to Japan, with talk of an export ban. These efforts have been joined by private citizens, such as twenty-six-year-old activist Cao Yu, who in 2008 stormed into the cafeteria in Microsoft's Beijing headquarters and announced to startled diners, "Disposable chopsticks are destroying China's forests!" Such activism has led three hundred Beijing restaurants to vow to use reusable chopsticks and created a burgeoning movement. Greenpeace China has launched a trendy campaign among urban youth urging them to BYOC, "Bring Your Own Chopsticks." The rhetoric of the campaign against disposable chopsticks and deforestation has become widespread enough for the college-age daughter of one chopstick industry executive to accuse him of being an "evildoer."

Another hopeful sign is that even before the national ban on certain types of disposable items was announced, hundreds of small companies in China were already manufacturing more sustainable alternatives, including biodegradable disposable articles such as chopsticks made from yam starch and tableware made from rice husks, starch, and cardboard. Likewise, reports in the media about the dangers of Styrofoam boxes have helped dampen consumer demand for white garbage, despite the weak enforcement of the earlier bans. China now has thousands of local and national environmental nongovernmental organizations (NGOs), most established in the last few years. Organizations such as Friends of Nature work tirelessly to protect and restore China's environment and raise public awareness. But if the history of environmental NGOs in the West offers clues to China's future, there is ample reason to worry that Chinese environmentalism is more likely to be absorbed by the consumer culture and create new markets for ecotourism, sustainable housing, and purportedly green consumer products than to fundamentally challenge a way of life that remains deeply dependent on ecologically destructive and nonrenewable resources.

Like Western nations before them, the more likely expectation is that the Chinese will drag their feet, make token changes, and outsource their industrial pollution to the "next Chinas"—Vietnam, Burma, Indonesia, and India—which have weaker labor laws and environmental protections. Or perhaps they'll follow the European lead with a "cap and trade" market that mostly shuffles the problem around. It's not hard to imagine a day in the near future when Chinese tourists heading for weekend vacations in Paris will have the option to buy carbon offsets, which could become the latter-day equivalent of papal dispensations. But even though it's easy to be pessimistic, the scale and relative suddenness of China's environmental problems linked to changing consumption may also make it easy to imagine how the world's consciousness—reflected in consumer behavior—needs to change. I used to show my students a documentary about China during Mao's Great Leap Forward in the late 1950s that included footage of a doctor setting down his stethoscope and changing from a white medical robe into a heavy smock and protective goggles before going out to his backyard furnace to make steel. Students and teacher would chuckle at the thought—how ridiculous to have a doctor make steel! Perhaps someday a documentary showing people in the West and China driving gas-guzzling, greenhouse-gas-emitting SUVs or tossing out a Styrofoam plate and wooden chopsticks after a single use will strike everyone as similarly ludicrous.

A large part of that hope will depend on the Chinese managing, against the odds, to excel as stewards of the environment with as much enthusiasm as they have learned to become first-rate consumers. Certainly there is evidence that China understands the odds and the consequences. We read in the newspapers nearly daily how China is leading the world in renewable energy, as it must if it is to continue its economic growth. The latest: it's building six gigantic wind farms that will generate the equivalent of one hundred coal-fired power plants' worth of electricity. While China is to be commended for these efforts, whether this commitment to renewable energy will be able to catch up with the speed and size of its emerging consumer demand is still an open question. No other nation in the developed world has yet found a way to reverse the ecologically destructive effects of its way of life faster than any offsetting commitment to correcting, let alone reversing, them. Should we hope and wait for China to take the lead?

CONCLUSION:
THE CHINESE INK BLOT

A few years ago, in the early stages of writing this book, I spoke to an audience of well-dressed southerners at the Palmetto Club in Columbia, South Carolina, on the global challenges posed by China's rapid embrace of lifestyles similar to theirs. All the things middle-class Americans often take for granted, I told them, the Chinese are just starting to desire and have.

After briefly reminding the audience that we shouldn't begrudge the Chinese for having lifestyles similar to our own and that, indeed, many economists see their adoption of our lifestyles as a boon for developed economies, I walked the audience through a few of the many challenges created by Chinese consumerism. As China overtakes the United States as the world's number one market for cars, it also joins the United States in committing its society and economy to a high-polluting mode of transportation and international competition for scarce resources. Likewise, as China's "new aristocracy" learns to enjoy their wealth, they are creating new aspirations (and simmering resentment) in the rest of the country. I also told them that China was far down this path—a consumer culture and economy is already deeply entrenched there. Thanks to Taiwan, the United States, and other developed economies, China now is home to mass retailing that standardizes the shopping experience and to brands created by advertising to teach its consumers what to buy. Millions now owe their livelihoods to jobs dependent on this new economy: from the nearly two million working to produce cars to the millions working on people's hair and nails in salons. And around the world, millions of other jobs are dependent on Chinese consumer appetites.

Of course, I also warned them about the blowback from Chinese consumerism—that China's development of markets is creating unintended negative consequences for China and the world, including the undermining of confidence in brands thanks to counterfeits, the spread of extreme markets for things such as human body parts and endangered wildlife species, and industrial pollution that fouls the air as far away as California. Most alarming of all is China's deepening commitment to a fossil fuel–based economy and society just as those resources are becoming scarcer and our understanding of their impact on global warming and ocean acidification is being confirmed. At the heart of consumerism is a contradiction that neither the Chinese nor the Americans (nor anyone else) has solved: how to enjoy modern consumer lifestyles without exacerbating their many downsides.

At the end of my talk the audience's questions followed a familiar pattern, most of them variations on "What can we do?" One attendee, however, caught me off guard. An elegantly dressed and well-spoken older southern lady told me that while she found my talk convincing, she was *glad* the Chinese were consuming so much and accelerating climate change with ever-increasing carbon emissions. Once the earth's natural resources were all used up, she explained, Jesus would return! Whatever religious beliefs one has, this listener raised a crucial point: how people in China and the world respond to Chinese consumerism and its consequences will depend a great deal on the powers they imagine are controlling what is happening.

One thing is clear: nearly every contemporary problem in China and, indeed, many of the key issues affecting the globe revolve around Chinese consumers. It is clear, for instance, that the Chinese Communist Party is betting its continued existence and legitimacy on raising standards of living, on delivering more goods to more consumers. Indeed, in what we might call *capitalist* realism, the party no longer figuratively and literally paints pictures of a glorious *socialist* future waiting at the horizon. Rather, it promotes the immediate joys of unbridled and ubiquitous consumerism. It would be a gross error, however, to imagine that this is a top-down and managed process. The CCP is riding the same tiger as the rest of the world. After all, can the Chinese government—could any government—stand in the way of the desires of a billion-plus consumers?

My experience in South Carolina confirmed my conclusion that China is for many a sort of Rorschach test. Contemporary Chinese consumerism can be thought of as a complex ink blot, and your interpretation of that ink blot probably says more about you than about China. China is, in the end, a land of staggering contradictions. As discussed earlier, China is both very rich *and* very poor. It's a country with nearly half a *billion* desperately poor living on less than two dollars a day while also the leading creditor nation for the wealthiest country on earth, the United States, which is now the leading international debtor. Likewise, China is black *and* green. As global warming accelerates—and world awareness and concern grow—China will be blamed for its role as the world's worst carbon polluter, even as it's also the biggest green energy producer of wind and solar power and may yet save the planet.

There are, then, many ways to read this book, which contains not one central message but rather an examination of the complexity of the issues involved. On one hand, we can marvel at the country's tremendous accomplishment in lifting hundreds of millions out of poverty in record time, or stand in wonder atop a new Shanghai skyscraper and look down on the thousands of high-rises built within the past decade and a half. On the other hand, though, we can see the inconveniences and downright global challenges created by China's "catching up" with the lifestyles of hundreds of millions of fellow consumers in the most economically advanced countries.

Some who have heard me speak on this topic have accused me of implicitly endorsing the creation of a massive international governmental structure empowered to control every aspect of consumption, or of being yet another millenarian who thinks the sky is falling for one reason or another. But the most common response comes from those with unwavering faith in technological progress combined with capitalist efficiency and motivation to solve any and all problems. Their interpretation runs this way: When enough people demand something, such as breathable clean air or uncontaminated water, the market will work its magic and a solution will appear. Perhaps they are right, or perhaps some unanticipated "solution" caused by war, famine, or disease will check Chinese consumerism and its effects. But given the hundreds of thousands of environment-related deaths, millions of ecological migrants, and hundreds of millions of Chinese already drinking contaminated water daily, it seems only simple prudence to ask when such market solutions will kick in.

I also hear from those who believe democracy and the accompanying transparency and accountability will solve China's problems. Surely, they argue, the Chinese wouldn't vote themselves into extinction. But it's hard to find this answer very convincing, coming as it does from people living in countries that have exported their own pollution to developing economies such as China (and therefore can pretend it doesn't exist) and that haven't done much to end their own reliance on nonrenewable resources. That is, what evidence do we have that democracies in countries such as the United States or the United Kingdom will provide a road map to saving the planet? I admit that the ink blot often looks pretty dark to me.

But just as there is no one "right" interpretation about what the expansion of Chinese consumerism will mean for China or the rest of the world, there undoubtedly will be no single solution, either. As the abundant citation of Chinese newspapers and magazines in these pages confirms, the Chinese government and people are aware of the problems posed by consumerism and have been taking efforts, some of them substantial, to limit them. The rest of the world would do well to do more than just take note and start reining in the worst effects of unbridled consumerism in their own countries. Yes, as China goes, so goes the world. But what happens in China is also deeply influenced by the actions of other countries, particularly the United States, and a similar case could be made that as the American consumer goes, so goes the Chinese consumer and the world. After all, how can we expect China to make tough choices over there when we cannot do so over here? Maybe what we need, then, is a New Golden Rule: consume unto the world as you would have the Chinese consume unto it.

NOTES

FURTHER READINGS
AND RESOURCES

ACKNOWLEDGMENTS

INDEX

NOTES

INTRODUCTION

4   Two decades later: Statistics on the beauty industry differ. See "Beauty Industry Needs Facelift," *China Business Weekly*, Oct. 29, 2004; "Beauty Treatment Heading Up," *China Daily*, Nov. 4, 2004; Mark Godfrey, "World 'Beauty Makers' Knocking China Door," *China Today*, April 6, 2004; Mitzi Swanson, "China Puts on a New Face," *The China Business Review* 22, no. 5 (Sept.–Oct. 1995); "Chinese Women Go 'Crazy' for Cosmetics," *China Daily*, June 7, 2005; Wang Jing, "Beauty Sector Contributes to Chinese Economy," *China Daily*, Feb. 5, 2005; Ma Ruiguang and Jia Bingwei, "2008: China's Cosmetics Market and an Analysis of the Phenomenon of Channel Changes," from www.boraid.com/article/101/101145_1.asp, 2008.12.1; Liu Sheng, "Chinese Cosmetic Companies Reaches 4,316," at www.cyol.net/zqb/content/2008-10/06/content_2378671.htm.

9   At the height: "As China Goes, So Goes . . . ," *New York Times*, Oct. 27, 2008.

9   Then-president George: Peter Harmsen, "Spend Up, Bush Tells Chinese Consumers," *American Free Press*, Sept. 5, 2007.

10   In a speech at: Tim Geithner, "The United States and China, Cooperating for Recovery and Growth." The full text of the speech is available at www.blogs.wsj.com/chinajournal/2009/06/01/full-text-of-geithners-speech-at-peking-university/.

10   In 2008, Li: "China's Vice Premier Urges Demand Boost: State Media," *American Free Press*, Aug. 20, 2008.

10   To provide customers: "The Largest Obstacle to Expanding Domestic Consumption Is the Countryside," *Nanfang ribao*, Feb. 17, 2009; Elaine Kurtenbach, "China Boosts Subsidies for Car, Appliance Buyers," AP, May 19, 2009.

11   Thus, as political scientist: Patricia M. Thornton, "Consumption and Control: Shopping with Mao," presented at "Consumer Revolution or Consuming Revo-

lution: Making Sense of Consumer Culture in China," at Oxford University, Sept. 12–13, 2009.

11 Hundreds of millions: "The Current Policy Has Misjudged the Capacity of Rural Consumption," Zhongguo qiyejia wang, Feb. 2, 2009; on China's admirable attempts, enviable successes, and ongoing challenges to alleviate poverty, see World Bank, "From Poor Areas to Poor People: China's Evolving Poverty Reduction Agenda," 2009, available at the bank's website, www.worldbank.org.

12 China's personal loan market: Hi Lo, "The Rise of Chinese Consumerism," FinanceAsia.com, April 13, 2006, www.financeasia.com/article.aspx?CIID=36661.

12 In late 2009: Sun Lijian, "Culture of Saving Gone as Spendthrifts Reign," *Shanghai Daily*, Dec. 25, 2006.

12 Government and business: Kathy Fong, "China Wants to Boost Consumer Spending," *China Daily*, Jan. 9, 2006.

12 The Chinese government: "Wu Yi: The Positive Development of Leisure and Service, Steadily Improve the Quality of Life," Xinhua, April 23, 2006.

13 The most high profile: During the first National Day Golden Week in 1999, some 28 million Chinese took to the road; eight years later, the number had climbed to more than 120 million.

13 But the fundamental transformations: Karl Gerth, *China Made: Consumer Culture and the Creation of the Nation* (Cambridge, Mass.: Harvard University Press, 2003).

14 By 2000, consumers: Jack Taylor, "Aircons in Hot Demand as Chinese Consumerism Gathers Pace," *American Free Press*, Jan. 30, 2001.

14 By another measure: Jehangir S. Pocha, "China's Hunger for Luxury Goods Grows," *Boston Globe*, March 21, 2006.

15 As a twenty-five-year-old woman: Unless otherwise stated, all direct quotations were gathered by my Chinese friends and me. Although Chinese cities are now associated with better consumer lifestyles than the rest of the country, the inconvenience of using public toilets may have been worse in cities than elsewhere a decade or two ago, as public toilets may have been farther away and led many to create makeshift toilets. For a memoir on living in Shanghai at that time, see Tang Lichun, "A Joke About Toilet Changes," *Guangzhou ribao*, Aug. 19, 2009.

1. NO GOING BACK?

22 Why did China's leaders: So remembers a Shanghai reporter who was a student in the mid-1990s in Shanghai (Shi Jianfeng, interviewed on July 16, 2009).

22 At the same time: Patrick E. Tyler, "China's Transport Gridlock: Cars vs. Mass Transit," *New York Times*, May 4, 1996.

24 In a 2002 survey: "Car Market Hits High Gear," *Asia Times*, Jan. 22, 2002; Ren Shaomin, "Survey of Shanghai Consumer Confidence," *Diyi caijing ribao*, Oct. 13,

2009; Dexter Roberts, "A Buying Spree in the Middle Kingdom?" *BusinessWeek Online*, Dec. 23, 2005.

24 These problems are most: As with every other consumer product, car consumption is unevenly distributed, and now a fifth of all the cars in the vast reaches of China are located in Beijing, Shanghai, Tianjin, and Chongqing. Kelly Sims Gallagher, *China Shifts Gears: Automakers, Oil, Pollution, and Development* (Cambridge, Mass.: The MIT Press, 2006), 8–9.

24 In 2009, Beijing: Cheng Yifeng, "Number of Beijing Autos Approaches 4 Million," Xinhua, Sept. 28, 2009.

25 These cars spew: "Beijing Institutes 'No Car Day' to Clean Up Air Pollution," *American Free Press*, May 16, 2006. In cities such as Beijing and Shanghai, automobiles produce a third to two thirds of the air pollution; the other two causes of air pollution in such cities are dust and coal burning; "Beijing Has the Worst Air in Asia," *Huanqiu shibao*, Dec. 18, 2006.

26 At the start of: Li Yongjun, "Fifty Years of Chinese Cars," *Zhongguo jingji zhoubao* 15 (2008): 14–19.

26 During the cold war: Michael J. Dunne, "The Race Is On," *The China Business Review* 21, no. 2 (March–April 1994).

26 As late as: Eric Thun, *Changing Lanes in China: Foreign Direct Investment, Local Governments, and Auto Sector Development* (Cambridge, UK: Cambridge University Press, 2006), 54.

26 At first, imports: Eric Harwit, *China's Automobile Industry: Policies, Problems and Prospects* (Armonk, N.Y.: M. E. Sharpe, 1995), 29.

26 But by 1984: But rising demand and weakening central controls created ideal conditions for black markets. The most notorious was on Hainan Island in 1984. To promote development on the island, Beijing had granted it tax-exempt status for imports, allowing it to avoid the 260 percent import duties the rest of country paid. Island officials promptly imported almost 90,000 cars, which they resold throughout China at three to five times their cost. Even with the crackdown on the Hainan scheme, imports continued to surge, with more than 100,000 sedans imported in 1985, requiring record amounts of hard currency. Throughout the 1980s, sedans comprised less than 3 percent of total vehicles produced. But from 1989, their numbers rose continually, from 6 percent to 20 percent in four years. "A Retrospective on Thirty Years of Reform in the Chinese Auto Industry," *Xinjing bao*, Nov. 3, 2008.

27 Since then, car production: Harwit, *China's Automobile Industry*, 39; Li Yongjun, "Fifty Years of Chinese Cars."

27 By the early: These vehicles continued to be produced by a very fragmented auto industry, which consisted of some 200 plants producing anywhere from 100 to 150,000 units and an even more fragmented component industry. When Zhu Rongji (later the premier of the PRC) became mayor of Shanghai in 1988, for in-

stance, he promoted the creation of a taxi company that exclusively used Shanghai VWs, sold under the brand name Santana. As a result, these cars became visible on the streets in the 1990s. There were similar "buy local" strategies in other cities, such as Peugeots in Guangzhou and Hyundais in Beijing. Ge Bangning, "An Oral History: Outwardly Soft and Inwardly Hard, Wang Rongjun," *Qiche shangye pinglun*, Aug. 12, 2009.

27   And to boost: Dunne, "The Race Is On"; Huan Lu, "Mergers and Acquisitions in the Auto Industry Creates Uncertainty," *Shanghai zhengquan bao*, Aug. 7, 2009; Wu Qiong, "Local Governments Have Introduced Their Own Plans to Promote Autos," *Shanghai zhengquan bao*, May 22, 2009.

28   The promise of a: Gallagher, *China Shifts Gears*, 39–40.

28   In 2000, the: "An Outline of the Tenth Five-Year Plan of the People's Republic of China's National Economic and Social Development," Xinhua, March 18, 2001.

28   Until the late: Dunne, "The Race Is On."

28   But by 2000: Li Yongjun, "Fifty Years of Chinese Cars."

28   When pressed to: Dexter Roberts, "A Buying Spree in the Middle Kingdom?" *Business Week Online*, Dec. 23, 2005.

29   As one popular saying: "The car has already become a status symbol," *Guoji jinrong bao*, July 6, 2007. A survey of 10,000 wealthy individuals in a dozen Chinese cities reveals a breakdown in types of car ownership by wealth: the wealthiest own much more expensive sedans priced at around 328,000 yuan, the middle own cars at half that price, and the bottom can afford a 77,000-yuan private car.

29   According to a: "Cars in China," *The Economist*, June 2, 2005.

29   And German car manufacturers: Shi Haosheng, "Postcard," *Zhongguo xinwen zhoukan*, Sept. 22, 2008.

30   At the same time: "Cars in China."

30   Raising the complaint: Tong Yinbin, "The Majority of People Cross Road Correctly but a Small Fraction Crosses by Looking at Cars Rather Than Traffic Lights," *Jiujiang ribao*, Dec. 18, 2006.

30   This is not unique: I am grateful to Hyung Gu Lynn for bringing this Korean-Japanese case to my attention.

31   Chinese pedestrians, the: "Chinese Take Longer Time to Cross Streets," Xinhua, June 6, 2006.

31   In 2007, it: "Cars in China"; Philip Bowring, "Getting Rich and Fat," *International Herald Tribune*, Oct. 26, 2004.

31   The effects are also: An estimated 12 percent of auto-related deaths, or roughly 13,200 a year, are caused by defective vehicle parts or poor workmanship. Li Yongyan, "China's New Auto Recall Regulation May be a Lemon," *Asia Times*, March 26, 2004.

31   Shanghai, in addition: "Cars in China"; "Jiading Automobile City," *Xinwen wubao*, Aug. 3, 2009.

32   Chinese consumer culture: Yu Liang, "Autos Drink Gas and People Eat Food," *Zhongguo zhengquan bao*, June 21, 2006; Hui Zhdengyi, "KFC and McDonald's Compete over Drive-throughs," *Diyi caijing ribao*, Jan. 12, 2009.

32   Another odd import: Jim Yardley, "First Comes the Car, Then the $10,000 License Plate," *New York Times*, July 5, 2006; "A Portion of Families with Students Sitting Exams Rent Taxis Long-term to Secure Lucky License Plate Numbers," *Xinwen chenbao*, May 31, 2005.

33   Car clubs have: Ted Conover, "Capitalist Roaders," *New York Times*, July 2, 2006; "A Fleet of 32 Polo Cars Comprise a Wedding Party on the Third Ring Road," Blog ZOL, posted Nov. 13, 2006. See a photo of the procession at www.blog.zol.com.cn/29/article_28866.html.

33   Once, bikes were prized: Throughout the Mao era and even into the 1990s, there were long waiting lists for each of the some forty million bikes manufactured each year. Pan Zhenhua, "A Visit to Shanghai's Phoenix Bicycle Corporation," *Guangcha yu sikao*, Aug. 31, 2007; Hu Libo, "The Original Function of Bicycles Retreats from the Historical Stage and Becomes a Symbol of Health and Environmentalism," *Gongyi shibao*, Aug. 7, 2007.

34   Although traditional brands: Andrew Browne, "A Legend's Bumpy Ride," *Wall Street Journal*, April 29, 2006.

34   The competition at one: Quoted in "China, Land of Bicycles," *China Today*, Feb. 16, 2004.

34   In 2007, Chinese automakers: "Every 100 Chinese to Own 4 Cars in 2010," *People's Daily Online*, April 24, 2006.

34   Even as the government: "Export of Chinese-Branded Cars Encouraged," *Asia Times*, April 2, 2005.

35   Chinese companies such as: Keith Bradsher, "Thanks to Detroit, China Is Poised to Lead," *New York Times*, March 12, 2006; "In 2009, Independent Brands Point Their Swords Overseas," *Beijing shangbao*, Jan. 20, 2009.

35   In 2005, China: "Chinese Autos Gear up for World Market," *People's Daily*, March 1, 2006.

35   The next Asian: Gordon Fairclough, "Chinese Autos Aimed at Mainstream Market," *Wall Street Journal*, March 1, 2006; Peter Hessler, "Car Town," *New Yorker*, Sept. 26, 2005, which also provides an excellent profile of Chery. See also "Geely Marching Forward to '08," *BusinessWeek*, March 21, 2006.

36   While its initial: "Chery Builds a Factory in Turkey to Advance Its Army into the American Market," *21 shiji jingju baodao*, Oct. 21, 2009.

36   A sign at the: Sign quoted and translated in Hessler, "Car Town"; Chris Buckley, "Skepticism Greets Global Ambitions of an Upstart Chinese Carmaker," *International Herald Tribune*, Jan. 7, 2005; Gordon Fairclough, "China Auto Exports May Roil Rivals," *Wall Street Journal*, Feb. 16, 2006.

36   The ascendancy of: On the problems of developing Chinese brands at home, see You Nuo, "The Issue of Branding," *China Daily*, June 20, 2005.

36 Because of the size: In 2006, Toyota, the last of these to enter the world's fastest-growing car market, began production of its first Made-in-China Camry, its best-selling model in the United States. Elaine Kurtenbach, "Camry to Hit China Fast Lane," *Shanghai Daily*, May 22, 2006.

36 For instance, in honor: Huang Xiwei, "BMW Promotes Special Edition of 760Li for Sixtieth Anniversary Celebration," *Nanfang dushi bao*, Oct. 8, 2009.

36 And when Volkswagen: "China on the Right Road," *The Standard*, Sept. 14, 2005.

36 Even as the: www.worldwatch.org/press/news/2004/09/22/. Hearing on Asia's Environmental Challenges: Testimony of Christopher Flavin at U.S. House of Representatives Committee on International Relations, hearing on September 22, 2004.

37 Already China accounts: Howard W. French, "A City's Traffic Plans Are Snarled by China's Car Culture," *New York Times*, July 12, 2005.

37 By the early 1990s: Zijun Li, "Government Encouraging Smaller Cars, Improved Fuel Efficiency," *China Watch*, Jan. 26, 2006.

37 As Lester Brown: Lester Brown, *Plan B 3.0: Mobilizing to Save Civilization* (New York: W. W. Norton, 2008). He estimates that in 2001, each of the United States' 214 million cars required on average 0.18 acres of pavement for roads and parking spaces, and cropland tends to be ideal for roads because it's usually flat and well drained. The United States has paved nearly 4 million miles of roads and enough spaces for all those cars to park, equal to some 50 million acres, or roughly the same amount of land currently devoted to growing wheat in the United States.

37 Countries such as China: If they emulate industrial societies, we can wonder which ones. Japan and Western European countries have fewer cars per capita than the United States, one in two rather than three in four. Likewise, these countries pave less per vehicle, 0.05 rather than 0.18 acres. But even this lower level of per capita car ownership would leave China with 640 million cars (more than 20 times what it had in 2006). And even at the lower rate of pavement (0.05 acres), that many cars would see China pave 32 million acres of land, or half of China's land currently devoted to rice. Lester R. Brown, "They Paved Pears and Rice and Put Up a Parking Lot," www.grist.org/news/maindish/2001/03/01/rice/, 2001.3.1.

38 Between 2000 and 2004: And by 2035 it hopes to surpass the U.S. Interstate Highway System's 46,000 with 53,000 miles of highway. "Cars in China." It's not yet clear, though, how or even when it'll all be used. Despite Beijing's efforts to build and promote a national highway system as the basis of a car culture of weekend holidays and intercity transport, the vast majority of car owners travel only short distances, and less than one fifth drive their vehicles outside their hometowns. Cost is one reason. The ten tolls collected between Beijing and Shanghai alone equal 500 yuan, a cost higher than a discounted air ticket. Likewise, at this point, Chinese may prefer group travel to independent travel. These projects often anticipate government-led demand as the state introduces industrial devel-

opment or population resettlement only after road construction. Interior highways often have national strategic implications as part of the "Go West" policy initiated in 2000, intended to integrate poorer, more remote, less populated ethnic minority regions such as Xinjiang and Tibet. "Cars in China"; Ted Conover, "Capitalist Roaders."

38   They also took: Zijun Li, "Government Encouraging Smaller Cars, Improved Fuel Efficiency," *China Watch*, Jan. 26, 2006; "China Welcomes Small Cars Back to Its Streets," Reuters, Jan. 6, 2006.

38   Cities such as Beijing: "Beijing to Curb Private-Car Ownership," *Asahi Shimbun*, June 18, 2005.

39   By 2008, Beijing: "Cars in China."

39   Beijing officials, facing rising: "Beijing Institutes 'No Car Day' to Clean Up Air Pollution"; "Beijing's Inaugural 'No-Car Day' Fails to Get Out of First Gear," *American Free Press*, June 5, 2006.

39   On the other hand: Li Yunhong, "A Capital Carpool Family," *Falv yu shenghuo*, Aug. 22, 2008; Zhang Guilin, "For Urban Dwellers Frugality Becomes Fashionable: Carpool, House Share, and Group Travel," Xinhua, July 24, 2008.

39   Yet the new tax: Wu Zhong, "China Auto Boom Unfazed by New Taxes," *Asia Times*, May 18, 2006.

40   Thirty years ago: Richard Parker, "The First Post-Oil Society?" *Mother Jones*, Feb./ March 1979.

40   As planned, the: Antoaneta Bezlova, "China Battles Auto Addiction," *Asia Times*, Oct. 5, 2006.

2. WHO GETS WHAT?

45   But by 2005: "China to Rival Top Luxury Consumer in 10 Years," *American Free Press*, Sept. 16, 2005. China's appetite for global luxuries is difficult to measure. To underscore the difficulty of measuring the actual size of the poorly defined "luxury market" in China, the perennially skeptical (and insightful) China-based business consultancy Access Asia compiled a list of estimates of China's share of the global luxury market. The range varied from very low estimates of 2 percent (*Women's Wear Daily*) and 5 percent (*International Herald Tribune*) to significantly higher estimates of like "18% of global sales" (Xinhua) or "29% of all luxury good sales worldwide" (*Taipei Times*) and everything in between, such as *Forbes's* ludicrously precise 21.4 percent and Goldman Sachs's 2008 estimate of 12 percent.

45   By 2005, Chinese tourists: "Chinese Tourists Top Consumers in the US," *Qingnian shibao*, April 16, 2009; Ma Guihua, "England Becomes a Hot Tourist Destination for Chinese Luxury Consumers," Xinhua, Dec. 19, 2008; Wang Fang, "Chinese Visitors Stimulate the French Tourist Industry," *Huanqiu shibao*, May 8, 2004.

45   Take, for example: "China Is the Top Market for the Most Expensive Bentley, the 728," Renmin wang, Sept. 3, 2003.

45 Chinese yuppies, dubbed Chuppies: Jehangir S. Pocha, "China's Hunger for Luxury Goods Grows," *Boston Globe*, March 21, 2006; Wu Qiong, "Chinese Market Demand Is Staggering," *Shanghai zhengquan bao*, Nov. 27, 2006.

46 Since the economic reforms: Cheng Shiming, "Chinese Luxury Consumption Will Soon Surpass Japan, Making It a Paradise for Luxury Goods," *Sanlian shenghuo zhoukan* 24 (2009); Xia Yi, "Chinese Luxury Goods Consumption Exceeds US$3 billion," Zhongguo xinwen wang, Feb. 18, 2009; "Controversial Consumption of Luxuries," *China Daily*, Aug. 6, 2005.

46 As late as 1992: Yu Jie, "Who Bought the Ten Million Yuan Bentley?" *Guancha*, May 27, 2005.

46 International luxury brands: Jia Xiaodong, "Shenyang Becomes a New Market for Luxury Goods," *Wenhui bao*, Oct. 20, 2009.

46 The French luxury jeweler: Jiang Jingjing, "Fit for a Queen," *China Daily*, March 13, 2006; Yang Yan, "Bathrooms Become Luxurious," *Beijing shangbao*, Sept. 20, 2007.

46 In 2006, the *Hurun Report*: Jehangir S. Pocha, "China's Hunger for Luxury Goods Grows."

47 Although China has emerged: "China Gets High on Scotch with a Touch of Green Tea," *Times of India*, Oct. 29, 2005. There are extensive criticisms online of the faux pas of the new rich; for a review of many, see "Misunderstood Consumption and New Illiteracy in the Age of Globalization," *Xin zhoukan* 7 (2007).

47 No less than: Shadow Lau, "Sipping Wine, Chinese-style," *Asia Times*, Nov. 1, 2005.

47 By 2005, China had: Zhu Dan, "Chinese and International Companies Vie for Domestic Diamond Market," *Jingji cankao bao*, Nov. 1, 2004.

47 Likewise, since easing: Geoffrey York, "Gold Rush Grips Chinese Consumers," Bell Globemedia, Jan. 24, 2006.

47 By 2006, China: Hu Xiaohong, "Couples Crowd to Buy Out-of-Stock Wedding Rings," *Jinghua shibao*, Feb. 10, 2006.

47 In fact, most of: Gong Zhen and Li Han, "Research on Chinese Luxury Goods Consumption," *Shangye shidai* 11 (2007).

47 As one newspaper: "Watch Out How Much You Spend," *China Youth Daily*, May 15, 2005.

48 In the mid-1990s: Tim Johnson, "China Hits the Slopes," Knight Ridder, Feb. 3, 2006; Ning Nan, "The Qiaobo Ski Dome: Eight Years of Commercial Success," *Shangwu zhoukan* 23 (2006).

49 Golf is the: Patrick L. Smith, "Did the Chinese Invent Golf?" *New York Times*, Feb. 28, 2006; "The Origins of Golf," Xinhua, March 24, 2009.

49 The country boasts: Sam Ng, "At Golf, China Swings—and Misses," *Asia Times*, May 7, 2004; Tim Yeo, "Home on the Driving Range," *Financial Times*, Nov. 3, 2006.

50   As with elites: Quoted in Charles McGrath, "How Do You Say Shank in Mandarin?" *New York Times*, Feb. 5, 2006.

50   Xiamen University administrators: Wang Qian, "The School Golf Debate," *Xinmin zhoukan*, Nov. 9, 2006; Xu Jitao, "Shanghai School Tees Off with Golf Classes," *China Daily*, Sept. 14, 2006.

50   China remains nominally: For a range of opinions, see "Controversial Consumption of Luxuries."

50   In response to the: "China Slams Cognac Consumption," UPI, July 11, 1994.

50   Similarly, golf's association: Indeed, Zhao Ziyang, the Chinese leader purged in the aftermath of the Tiananmen incident of 1989, includes a lengthy anecdote about how much the CCP hated his playing golf in his autobiography, *Prisoner of the State: The Secret Journal of Zhao Ziyang* (New York: Simon & Schuster, 2009), 233–51.

50   In 2003, former premier: Sam Ng, "At Golf, China Swings—and Misses."

51   And when the: Quoted in "Golf Course Draws Criticism in China," Bloomberg News, Nov. 27, 2006; "Chinese Uni Accused of Elitism with Compulsory Golf Classes," *American Free Press*, Oct. 17, 2006.

51   But shopping sprees: Don Lee, " 'Second Wives' Are Back," *Los Angeles Times*, Nov. 22, 2005.

51   In places such as: Liu Jinling, "The Ripple Effects of Guangdong Punishing Those Maintaining Mistresses," *Shenzhen fazhi bao*, July 18, 2000.

52   As with so many: Wu Jing, "Chinese Law Will Punish Those Maintaining Mistresses," *Liaoning ribao*, Feb. 2, 2001.

52   One of the numerous: Rachel DeWoskin, "Wife Sentence," *The Sunday Times*, Oct. 22, 2006.

52   In rare cases: Li Xi, "Suffering and Fortune Are the Same," *Caifu shibao*, Feb. 29, 2008; Lee, " 'Second Wives' Are Back"; "Mistress Rumors Kill Rich Girl's Internet Auction," *China Daily*, July 15, 2005.

52   The political career: Liang Juan and Song Chang Qing, "Corrupt High Official Pang Jiayu," *Banyuetan*, Aug. 27, 2008.

52   As Rachel DeWoskin: Quoted in DeWoskin, "Wife Sentence," www.timesonline .co.uk/article/0,,2099-2409883,00.html.

53   In a review of: Liu Jinling, "The Ripple Effects of Guangdong Punishing Those Maintaining Mistresses."

53   In perhaps the most: Howard W. French, "Chinese Woman Goes Way Off-message on the Olympics," *International Herald Tribune*, Jan. 11, 2008; Zhong He, "CCTV Family Scandal," *Nanfang dushi bao*, Dec. 29, 2007.

53   The refusal to accept: Wei Minli, "China Faces Serious Population Aging Trend," *Xinjing bao*, May 25, 2009.

53   In addition to the: "China Has the Second Highest Number of Billionaires After the US," *Yangcheng wanbao*, Dec. 31, 2007; Tania Branigan, "Slump in Stockmarkets Wipes out Two Thirds of China's Billionaires," *The Guardian*, Nov. 1, 2008.

54 In the late 1990s: Emma Brockes, "'If I Was a Lowly Official They Would Be Proud,'" *The Guardian*, Nov. 8, 2004.

54 A surprising 65 percent: "Should We Hate the Rich?" *Xinwen shijie* 9 (2007).

55 According to a: Lu Peng, "The Origins of the Rich and Powerful: A Comparison of Wealthiest from China, Russia, and Hungary," *Nanfang zhoumo*, Oct. 9, 2009; "Rich People Feel 'Insecure, Troubled,'" *China Daily*, July 20, 2006.

55 The thirtysomething billionaire: Jonathan Watts, "China's New Rich Learn to Flaunt It," *The Guardian*, Jan. 14, 2006; Brockes, "'If I Was a Lowly Official They Would Be Proud.'"

55 Examples include: Chen Wuqing, "Where Has the Sentiment of Hating the Rich Come From?" *Beijing keji bao*, July 14, 2005.

56 There are four primary: Xiaowei Zeng, "Market Transition, Wealth and Status Claims" in David S. G. Goodman, ed., *The New Rich in China: Future Rulers, Present Lives* (London: Routledge, 2008).

56 According to the sociologist: Thomas Gold, "Urban Private Business and China's Reforms," in Richard Baum, ed., *Reform and Reaction in Post-Mao China: The Road to Tiananmen* (New York: Routledge, 1991), 94.

56 This newly affluent: Zhahui Hong, "Mapping the Evolution and Transformation of the New Private Entrepreneurs in China," *Journal of Chinese Political Science* 9, no. 1 (Spring 2004): 26–27.

57 According to one report: "90 Percent of China's Billionaires Are Children of Senior Officials," Oct. 19, 2006. See www.financenews.sina.com/ausdaily/000-000-107-105/202/2006-10-19/1509124173.shtml.

58 The final, largest: Minxin Pei, "How China Is Ruled," *The American Interest* 3, no. 4 (March–April 2008).

58 The top twenty companies: *China Economic Quarterly* 6 (2008).

59 As the sociologist Xiaowei: Xiaowei Zeng, "Market Transition, Wealth and Status Claims," 69.

59 which explains why: Shen Jie, "An Expert Unscrambles the Psychology of Hating the Rich," *Zhongguo qingnian bao*, Sept. 17, 2006; Yi Jun, "Giving Special Privileges to the Wealthy Is Adding to 'Wealth Hatred,'" *Zhongguo qingnian bao*, March 12, 2003.

59 In 2003, the: "Build an Economic Civilization That Supports the Wealthy," *Zhongguo wenhua bao*, Sept. 4, 2003.

59 Other reported forms: Chen Wuqing, "Where Has the Sentiment of Hating the Rich Come From?"

60 The reaction on the Web: These characterizations comes from journalist He Qinglian, "Bigwigs Create the Sentiment of Hating the Rich," *Kaifang* 9 (2004). Her analysis is repeated verbatim (without attribution) in many places, including in Liu Changfa, "Resolving the Mentality of Hating the Rich," *Zhonggong Zhengzhou shiwei dangxiao xuebao* 1 (2008).

60 In the country's wealthier: Wu Fanglan and Zhu Guodong, "Kidnappings of the Rich and Powerful: The Richer You Get, the More Dangerous? Who's Kidnapping China's Wealthy?" *Liaowang dongfang zhoukan*, Dec. 2, 2005.

60 When Hong Kong factory: Evan Osnos, "Kidnapping Industry Is Booming in China," *Chicago Tribune*, Jan. 22, 2006.

60 As one market begets: "Deciphering the Real Lives of the New Aristocracy in Six Major Chinese Cities," *Renmin wang*, July 30, 2009; Steven Ribet, "Held to Ransom," *The Standard* (Hong Kong), Jan. 21, 2006.

60 One shoe factory owner: Quoted in "The Wealth of the Rich Belongs to Whom?" *Shichang bao*, July 15, 2005.

61 A dramatic increase: Chen Wuqing, "Where Has the Sentiment of Hating the Rich Come From?"

61 After a brutal series: Jonathan Watts, "Charity: New Cultural Revolution," *The Guardian*, Jan. 10, 2006.

61 As with every other: Li Liguo, "Ministry of Civil Affairs Adopts Five Measures to Regulate and Promote the Development of Philanthropy," Xinhua, March 13, 2007; Michael Mackey, "The New Chinese Philanthropy," *Asia Times*, May 14, 2005.

61 The 2007 *Hurun Report*: Zou Hanru, "China's Rich Are Giving It Away," *China Daily*, April 20, 2007.

62 But market reforms: Quoted in He Qinglian, "A Listing Social Structure," Chaohua Wang, ed., in *One China, Many Paths* (London: Verso, 2003), 164. This section on class reformation in China relies on the highly critical and influential article by He Qinglian.

63 The government's attempts: Yingjie Guo, "Class, Stratum and Group: The Politics of Description and Prescription," in David S. G. Goodman, ed., *The New Rich in China: Future Rulers, Present Lives* (London: Routledge, 2008), 40.

64 As Sébastien Noat: Dan Levin, "Beijing Lights Up the Night," *New York Times*, June 15, 2008.

3. MADE IN TAIWAN

68 Taiwanese investments have gone: "Taiwanese Investment and Cross-Strait Trade Continue to Grow," *Guowuyuan bangongting*, March 19, 2007; "The Founding Place of the Communist Party's Regime Becomes a Hot Place for Taiwanese Investment," Xinhua, Sept. 23, 2009.

70 Since the first major: Because many of the Taiwanese businesspeople speak Taiwanese (the Minnan dialect) with a rural accent, Taiwanese living in Shanghai and other cities are known as Tabazi, a term derived from the Shanghaiese term Xiangbazi, which means "country bumpkin." Some Taiwanese living in China even refer to themselves by this term. Official sources most frequently

use the term Taibao, "Taiwanese compatriots" or "the New Shanghaiese" (*Xin Shanghai ren*).

71   Like the treaty ports: On treaty ports as a conduit for Western and Japanese consumer culture in the early twentieth century, see Gerth, *China Made*.

71   In the 1980s: On the growth of Taiwanese chains in China since the late 1990s, see Wang Qi, "Taiwanese Service Sector's Investments in the Mainland," *Zhongguo qiye jia*, Aug. 22, 2007.

71   Take the case of: Ping Lin, "Economic Expectation for Migration to China—Taiwanese Immigrants of Dongguan and Shanghai," *International Journal of Chinese Culture and Management* (forthcoming). Used with permission.

72   As one Taishang: Ibid.

72   The media saturated: Chen Bin, *My Shanghai Experience: Strategies for Travel, Investments and Settling Down in the Mainland* (Taipei: Shengxun wenhua, 2000); Zhang Jinpin, "Chen Bin and Shanghai Fever," *Xinwen zhoukan* 40 (2001).

72   Within five years: Yaping, "Investing in Shanghai: Taiwanese Businesspeople, the New Shanghaiese, Part 1," CCTV, *The Sound of China* program, Dec. 27, 2006; Horng-luen Wang, "How Are Taiwanese Shanghaied," *positions: east asia cultures critique* 18, no. 1 (2009); Jimmy Lee, "Time to Move On? Taiwanese Firms in the Pearl River Delta," *Taiwan Panorama*, Dec. 2004; Zhu Xianlong, "Why Do Taiwanese Businesspeople Favor Shanghai?" *Zhongguo wang*, Sept. 13, 2001; Jiang Yizhi, "Is Kunshan the Next Challenge for Taiwanese Businesspeole?" *Dongfang qiyejia*, April 28, 2006.

72   Unlike their earlier: Yaping, "Investing in Shanghai"; Ji Shuoming, "Taiwanese Businesspeople Are Transforming Themselves and Shanghai," *Yazhou zhoukan*, Aug. 19, 2007.

73   These transplants helped: Yaping, "Investing in Shanghai"; Ji Shuoming, "Taiwanese Businesspeople Are Transforming Themselves and Shanghai."

73   "You can have as . . . ": Translated and quoted in Wang, "How Are Taiwanese Shanghaied?"

74   But now New Shanghai: Yaping, "Investing in Shanghai"; "Taiwan's Unemployment Rate Raises Yearly, Those Looking for Work on the Mainland Make Shanghai the Top Choice," *Fengxianwang*, Nov. 6, 2007.

74   The profound influence: Wen-ting Tsai, "Biting Off as Much as They Can Chew—Taiwanese Restaurants in the PRC," *Taiwan Panorama*, December 2003.

74   The biggest Taiwanese: But this was a product first launched in China and then in Taiwan. "From the Mainland and Back to Taiwan: Master Kang Reflects the Development of Taiwanese Businesspeople on the Mainland," *Xinhuawang*, Oct. 9, 2009.

74   Take Yonghe King: "Taiwan's Yon Ho Soybean," *Capital Magazine*, reposted at *Zhongguo shipin keji wang*, Dec. 12, 2003; "Yonghe King," *Minying jingji bao*, May 29, 2006.

75 A few years ago: "Yonghe King."

75 In Shanghai, Yon: Tsai Wen-ting, "Yon Ho Soybean Conquers Mainland China," *Taiwan Panorama*, Dec. 2003.

75 The chain began: "Yonghe King Challenges 'Foreign' Fast Food," *Texu jingying*, Jan. 18, 2005.

75 The company branched: Ling Huishan, "Yon Ho Soybean Suppresses Yonghe King's Trademark," *Xinxi shibao*, Jan. 12, 2005.

77 The Taiwanese-dominated world: Marc Moskowitz, *Cries of Joy, Songs of Sorrow: Chinese Pop Music and Its Cultural Connotations* (Honolulu: University of Hawaii Press, 2010).

77 This pop revolution: Wang Meng, "Imagination and Outlook," *Wenxue bao*, July 8, 2008.

77 Indeed, among villagers: Guo Sheng, "The Singer Brought by Balloons," *Dongfang jinbao*, May 9, 2005.

77 Smuggled onto the: Thomas B. Gold, "Go with Your Feelings: Hong Kong and Taiwan Popular Culture in Greater China," *The China Quarterly* 136 (1993).

77 Teng's songs introduced: Guo Sheng, "The Singer Brought by Balloons."

77 Her fame even: Coral Lee, "From Little Teng to A-Mei: Marking Time in Music," *Sinorama*, February 2000.

78 Finally, in 1987: Wang Meng, "Imagination and Outlook."

78 The music also: Nimrod Baranovitch, *China's New Voices: Popular Music, Ethnicity, Gender, and Politics, 1978–1997* (Berkeley: University of California Press, 2003).

78 Mandopop allows the: Moskowitz, *Cries of Joy, Songs of Sorrow*, chap. 4. Used with permission of the author.

78 In the early 1980s: Lee, "From Little Teng to A-Mei."

78 At the same time: Ibid.

79 These pop stars: Emily Honig and Gail Hershatter, *Personal Voices: Chinese Women in the 1980s* (Stanford, Calif.: Stanford University Press, 1988), 41–80.

79 It also offered: Baranovitch, *China's New Voices*, 143–48.

79 But Chinese policy makers: Jin Zhaojun, "A Retrospective on Thirty Years of Chinese Pop Music," *Nanfang zhoumo*, Dec. 12, 2008.

80 The dominant Taiwanese: Coral Lee, "The A-Mei Phenomenon," *Taiwan Panorama*, Feb. 2000.

81 In 1993, for instance: Zheng Jianli, Zhou Tingyu, and Wu Xiaoen, *Garden of Sounds: MTV's Spatial Meaning* (Beijing: Huayuan shengyin, 2004). Quoted in Moskowitz, *Cries of Joy, Songs of Sorrow*.

81 Sinification included videos: Baranovitch, *China's New Voices*, 199–206.

81 It is little wonder: Eric Lin, "The Cross-Strait Entertainment Industry: Competition or Complementarity?" *Taiwan Panorama*, Dec. 2002.

81 As one veteran: Blog posting of "The State of Taiwan Pop Music in China," at www.zonaeuropa.com/culture/c20060404_1.htm, which itself is a translation of a

blog post by Massage Milk, "The People Are Dumb. There Is Lots of Money. Come Quickly" (posted April 1, 2006). Massage Milk is a longtime music critic by profession at *Lifeweek Magazine* in China.

81   F4 got its: Hiroshi Aoyagi, "Pop Idols and the Asian Identity," in Timothy J. Craig, ed., *Japan Pop! Inside the World of Japanese Popular Culture* (Armonk, N.Y.: M. E. Sharpe, 2000), 321.

81   Thanks to the highly: Unless otherwise stated, "Korea" refers to South Korea.

82   Sony capitalized on the: Quoted in John Pomfret, "Band Hits a Sour Note in China," *Washington Post*, June 10, 2002.

84   As China lowered: Tsai Wen-ting, "Taiwan's Publishers Stake a Claim in China's Developing Market," *Sinorama*, April 2002.

84   By 2000, things had: Ibid.

85   Likewise, Taiwanese Internet: Tsai Wen-ting, "Transplanted from Taiwan—Yam Culture Catches On in the PRC," *Sinorama*, Jan. 2002.

86   This wave of influence: Zhang Xiuxian, "The Korean Wave and Cultural Communication—The Case of China," *Dangdai wenhua yanjiu wang*, Nov. 11, 2005; "Korean TV Commercial Wave Hits Asia," *Chosunilbo*, April 3, 2006.

86   Likewise, the Chinese: Ng Boon Yian, "The Making of Korean Brands," *Asia Times Online*, Aug. 18, 2005.

86   Korea is now: Helen Leavey, "Taiwan: Sold on Seoul," BBC, Jan. 14, 2002.

86   A cottage industry: John Burton, "A Korean Wave of TV Programmes, Films, and Pop Bands Have Become Hip," *Financial Times*, Oct. 24, 2001.

86   In China, South Korea: For an exploration of this and other interpretations of the popularity of the Korean Wave, see Cho Hae-Joang, "Reading the 'Korean Wave' as a Sign of Global Shift," *Korea Journal* 45, no. 4 (2005).

86   As twenty-eight-year-old: Quoted in Norimitsu Onishi, "China's Youth Look to Seoul for Inspiration," *New York Times*, Jan. 2, 2006.

87   This image, broadcast: Evan Osnos, "Asia Rides Wave of Korean Pop Culture Invasion," *Chicago Tribune*, Dec. 27, 2008.

87   These "set-jetters": Bae Keun-min and Reuben Staines, "'Hallyu' Brings New Travel Trend to Korea," *Korea Times*, Feb. 23, 2006.

87   Chinese pop culture: Hyejin Kim, "South Koreans Find the Good Life in China," *Asia Times Online*, April 8, 2006.

88   In Shanghai, for example: Seo Ji-eun, "In China, It's Not Just Factories," *Joong-Ang Daily*, October 17, 2006.

88   After the widely popular: Chung So-jeong, "Cultural 'Empire' Rides on Korean Wave," *Korea Times*, May 24, 2006; "Zhang Guoli: Oppose Korean and Japanese Dramas and All Foreign Television Programming," *Meiri Gansu*, Sept. 28, 2007.

88   But other observers: Quoted in Osnos, "Asia Rides Wave of Korean Pop Culture Invasion."

89 Ten years after: Burton, "A Korean Wave of TV Programmes, Films, and Pop Bands Have Become Hip."

89 Culture industries, the: Lee Yong-sung, "KOCCA Expects Culture Industry to Lead Business," *Korea Herald*, March 8, 2006.

89 The global: For official government websites on the Korean Wave, see *Hallyu* (Korean Wave Tourist Marketing), Korean National Tourism Organization, www .knto.or.kr/eng/hallyu/hallyu.html, www.knto.or.kr/eng/hallyu/hallyuintro.html; "Korean Wave Sweeps Across Asia," *Korea Herald*, March 8, 2006; "Taiwan, China United in Backlash Against Korean Wave," *Chosunilbo*, Jan. 11, 2006.

4. STANDARDIZING ABUNDANCE

92 According to a 2008: Zachary Karabell, "Thank God for the Chinese Consumer," *Wall Street Journal*, Aug. 8, 2008.

93 Today they spend only: Zhao Weihua, *Status and Consumption: A Study of Consumption of Different Classes in Contemporary China* (Beijing: Shehui kexue wenxian chubanshe, 2007), 2; Jayanthi Iyengar, "In China, Say It with Consumer Goods," *Asia Times*, May 14, 2004; "Research Report: The Current Situation of China's Urban and Rural Household Consumption," *Guangming ribao*, Jan. 1, 2009.

93 China's decision to allow: "Former State-owned Stores," *Shanxi xinwen wang*, Oct. 22, 2008; Brenda Sternquist and Zhou Xi Qiao, "China: The Planned to Free Market Paradigm," *International Journal of Retail and Distribution Management* 23, no. 12 (1995): 21–28.

94 But starting with: Heidi Vernon Wortzel and Lawrence H. Wortzel, "The Emergence of Free Market Retailing in the People's Republic of China: Promises and Consequences," *California Management Review* 29, no. 3 (1987): 59–76.

95 Of course, these budding: On the famous Third Plenary Session of Eleventh Central Committee of the Communist Party, which made these decisions, see *Peking Review* 12, no. 29 (1978): 12.

95 Between 1980 and 1985: Wortzel and Wortzel, "The Emergence of Free Market Retailing in the People's Republic of China."

95 To give but one: John A. Reeder, "A Small Study of a Big Market in the People's Republic of China—the 'Free Market' System," *Columbia Journal of World Business* 18, no. 4 (1983): 74–80.

95 The story of the: "Looking Back at the Re-opening of the Bei Hang Agricultural Market," *Xinhua wang*, Oct. 16, 2008.

97 As one woman: Reeder, "A Small Study of a Big Market," 75.

98 But a decade or so: "Looking Back at the Re-opening of the Bei Hang Agricultural Market."

98 The Bei Hang market: Reeder, "A Small Study of a Big Market," 76.

98 But within a few: Ibid., 79.
98 The end of fixed: Brenda Sternquist and Zhou Xi Qiao, "China: The Planned to Free Market Paradigm," *International Journal of Retail and Distribution Management* 23, no. 12 (1995): 21–28.
99 One way to measure: Gao Wang, Fei Li, and Xi Liu, "The Development of the Retailing Industry in China: 1981–2005," *Journal of Marketing Channels* 15, no. 2 (2008): 145–66.
102 Likewise, a younger: Ann Veeck and Alvin C. Burns, "Changing Tastes: The Adoption of New Food Choices in Post-reform China," *Journal of Business Research* 58, no. 5 (May 2005): 644–52.
102 Of course, Walmart: Cai Yifei, "What Have Supermarkets Changed?," *IT jingli shijie*, March 20, 2008.
104 Within a decade of: H. Frederick Gale, "China's Growing Affluence: How Food Markets are Responding," *Amber Waves* 1, no. 3 (June 2003); "China Promulgates GMO Safety Regulations," *Nanfang dushi bao*, June 14, 2001.
106 Rather, as Chinese: This skeptical opinion is often put forward in the electronic newsletters and reports by the market research company Access Asia (www .accessasia.co.uk).
106 For as we shall: Fuchsia Dunlop, *Shark's Fin and Sichuan Pepper: A Sweet-Sour Memoir of Eating in China* (New York: W. W. Norton, 2009).
107 Perhaps no irony: Jun Jing, *Feeding China's Little Emperors* (Palo Alto, Calif.: Stanford University Press, 2000); Clifford Coonan, "China's New Wealth Threatens to Take Heavy Toll on Health," *The Independent*, May 10, 2006; K. C. Chang, *Food in Chinese Culture* (New Haven, Conn.: Yale University Press, 1977).
108 The effects that: Philip Bowring, "Getting Rich and Fat," *International Herald Tribune*, Oct. 26, 2004.
108 By the end of: For the exact statistics, see www.ncbi.nlm.nih.gov/entrez/query .fcgi?cmd=Retrieve&db=PubMed&list_uids=12075583&dopt=Abstract, "Time Trends of Obesity in Pre-school Children in China from 1989 to 1997." Luo J. Hu, F. B. Takemi Program, Harvard School of Public Health, Boston, Mass.
108 Shanghai alone throws: Wu Yunhe, "Stop Extravagant Resource Consumption," *China Daily*, Sept. 5, 2005.
109 Wu Mingzheng, a manager: "Oppose Conspicuous Consumption, Zhejiang Renews 'New Consumption' Campaign," *Zhonggue qingnian bao*, March 29, 2008.
109 This scene is repeated: Ibid.
109 In 2008, Zhang: Deng Fuyi, "The Blogging Secretary: China Is the Most Wasteful Consumer of Food and Beverages," *Xinkuai bao*, July 7, 2008.
109 In the northeast city: He Xingli, "The Food Wasted by Harbin's Restaurants Startles—Over 20,000 Restaurants Dispose of 400 Tons Daily," *Heilongjiang ribao*, March 12, 2007.
109 In response, Zhejiang: Dong Bishui, "Hangzhou's Waste of Food and Beverages Is

Annually 1.4 Billion Yuan—Zhejiang Renews Its 'New Consumption' Campaign," *Zhongguo qingnian bao*, March 11, 2008.

5. BRANDING CONSUMER CONSCIOUSNESS

111 When David Ogilvy: David Ogilvy, *Ogilvy on Advertising* (London: Prion Books, Ltd., 2007), 187–88.

112 China's ad market: Xiao Yu, "Ad Spending Rises 17% in the First Quarter of 2008, with Steady Increases by Olympic Partners," *Zhongguo xinwen bao*, May 15, 2008.

112 China now has: Xie Genyun, "A Report on the 2006 Chinese TV Ad Market," *Xinwen zhanxian*, May 2007.

112 As one woman: Of course, it's not her imagination. See Ye Feng, "An Analysis of Hidden Advertisements in Movies," *Quanqiu pinpai wang*, April 5, 2009.

113 Advertising in China: "A Million Advertising Employees Face Assessment Examination," Zhongguo xinwen chuban wang, Oct. 29, 2007; Yan Pin and Li Zheng, "The Gap Is Not Small, the Potential Is Great: How Far Off Is Chinese Advertising?" Xinhua; the United States employed about half a million people in advertising and public relations in 2006. See U.S. Bureau of Labor Statistics, "Advertising and Public Relations Services," at www.bls.gov/oco/cg/cgs030.htm.

113 In 2004, one: Yang Wenjin, "Spending on Comestic Advertising Is the Highest," *Xinjing bao*, Feb. 28, 2005.

113 As expressed by: James Borton, "Magazine Licensing Red-Hot in China," *Asia Times*, Dec. 16, 2004.

115 As Chinese marketing: "Official: Consumption of Chinese Products Should Be Encouraged," *China Daily*, Sept. 19, 2003.

115 A useful measure: State Council Information Office, white paper, "New Progress on China's IPR Protection," Xinhua, April 21, 2005.

116 No wonder a: Xuan Yi, "Who Pays for Cool? A Survey of Consumer Sentiment Among Current University Students," *Beijing chenbao*, April 30, 2004.

116 For example, a: Alan Wheatley, "China Starts to Protect Trademarks," *International Herald Tribune*, Sept. 16, 2008.

116 According to China's: Zhang Yi, "Ministry of Commerce: Only 20% of Companies Involved in International Trade Have Their Own Brands," *Beijing chenbao*, Feb. 28, 2007.

117 According to Li: Wen Bin, "Chinese Enterprises Urgently Need to Improve Their Brand Competitiveness," *Zhishi chanquan bao*, Jan. 16, 2004.

117 In 2005, quality: Wang Zhiling, "The Business Logic Behind the Shenzhen Häagen-Dazs Incident," *Ershiyi shiji jingji baodao*, July 6, 2005.

118 In contrast, powerful: "Consumer Rights—Buyers Bite Back," *China Economic Review*, Jan. 23, 1999.

118 Such mixed feelings: Liu Weiling, "Consumers Have Their Say," *China Daily*, Jan. 9, 2004.

118 The city decided: Yu Jinmeng, "Kunming Development Arouses Local Resentment," *Zhongguo qingnian bao*, Aug. 8, 2005; "Kunming Bans Foreign-Sounding Names," *China Daily*, Sept. 14, 2005.

119 According to one: Quoted in Amy White, "Nike Faces China Ire Over 'Fear' Ad," *Media Asia*, Dec. 17, 2004.

119 Chinese companies sometimes: "Chinese Companies Cashing in on Anti-Japanese Sentiment," *Yomiuri Shimbun*, Sept. 29, 2005. For more on Feng Jun, see Fan Yinghua, "Feng Jun: A Patriot's Paranoia," *Xiaokang caizhi*, Aug. 17, 2009.

119 China's aspirations to: For a scholarly history of the origin of national brands in China, see Gerth, *China Made*.

121 This push to: "China's Established Brands: Beijing Has the Most," *Beijing yule xinbao*, Oct. 8, 2006.

121 To help reach: An Li, "A Gathering for 925 Products," *Zhongguo zhiliang yu pinpai* 1 (2006). Cambridge University management professor Peter Nolan has written extensively on the subject of China's "national team." See, for instance, his *China and the Global Economy* (New York: Palgrave Macmillan, 2001).

122 For instance, the: P. Bellabona and F. Spigarelli, "Moving from Open Door to Go Global: China Goes on the World Stage," *International Journal of Chinese Culture and Management* 1, no. 1 (2007): 93–108; "SASAC Director Li Rongrong: Only the Best State-Owned Enterprises Should Make Acquisitions in Europe and the United States," *Zhongguo zhengquan bao*, Sept. 27, 2008.

122 One can find: "China Makes Inroads on Cuban Streets," Reuters, Sept. 30, 2009.

122 China's biggest appliance: Paul Gao, Jonathan R. Woetzel, and Yibing Wu, "Can Chinese Brands Make It Abroad?" *The McKinsey Quarterly*, 2004 Special Edition: Global Directions.

123 For instance, in: "Official: Consumption of Chinese Products Should Be Encouraged," *China Daily*, Sept. 19, 2003.

123 In the summer: "The Guiding Principles of National Intellectual Property Strategy," See www.baike.baidu.com/view/1736822.htm.

123 For example, the China: Matt Young, "Marlboro Country's Borderline with China," *Asia Times*, March 10, 2006.

124 One county in China: Clifford Coonan, "Chinese Workers Urged to Puff Up Economy by Smoking," *Irish Times*, May 5, 2009; on complementary efforts to limit foreign cigarettes, see Wang Jizhou, "Tobacco Monopoly Faces the Impact of International Competition," *Kaifang chao*, Aug. 2003.

124 In anticipation of: "45 Businesses Scoop Top Brand Gongs," Xinhua, Sept. 3, 2001.

124 Laurent Philippe, the head: Jacques Penhirin, "Understanding the Chinese Consumer," *The McKinsey Quarterly*, Sept. 2004; Shi Yunting, "An Analysis of Some Problems Translating Luxury Brand Names," *Jingji yu shehui fazhan*, April 2009.

125 To meet regional taste: See Jing Wang, *Brand New China: Advertising, Media, and Commercial Culture* (Cambridge, Mass.: Harvard University Press, 2008).

126 Today Lenovo offers: Ling Zhijun, *The Inside Story of the Lenovo Group's Management* (Beijing: Zhongxin chubanshe, 2005).

126 In April 2003: "China Steps Up Efforts to Forge World Name Brands," Xinhua, Jan. 6, 2004; Xin Bei, "Lenovo Deal a Huge Step for Chinese Brands," *China Daily*, Dec. 10, 2004.

127 It became the world's: Pepe Escobar, "Selling China to the World," *Asia Times*, Jan. 15, 2005.

127 The decade and a: Robin Kwong, "Luxury Brand Ownership on Rise in Asia," *Financial Times*, April 29, 2008.

128 In contrast, the: Milton Kotler, "Brand Plan Hinges on Distribution," *China Daily*, May 1, 2001; Yu Mingyang, *2008 Report on Chinese Brands* (Shanghai: Shanghai jiaotong daxue chubanshe, 2008), 80.

129 In the early 1970s: "Foreign Brands Replace Chinese Watches as Status Symbols," *Renmin ribao*, April 5, 2006; Luo Yaxian and Zou Qilin, "The Life and Death of the Chinese Watch Industry," *Qiye guanli*, July 2008.

129 Take Maotai, the famous: "Maotai Liquor: From Drink of Officials to Drink of Ordinary People," *China Daily*, Sept. 29, 2002.

130 Cognac is the liquor: Joseph Scarry, "Making the Consumer Connection: Heroes Can Mean Everything When Marketing in China," *The China Business Review* 24, no. 4 (1997); Huang Lichang, "Declining Consumer Demand for Domestic Baijiu: Young People Think Drinking It Is Unfashionable," *Changcheng wang*, Nov. 26, 2009.

130 In 1990 the former: "Brands May Not Live Forever," *China Daily*, May 4, 2004; "Old Firms Need Brand Protection," *China Business Weekly*, Aug. 9, 2004.

6. LIVING IN A WORLD OF FAKES

135 Brand owners in China: Eric H. Smith, Statement for Panel: "Intellectual Property Protection as Economic Policy: Will China Ever Enforce Its IP Laws?" Congressional-Executive Commission on China, May 16, 2005, www.cecc.gov/pages/roundtables/051605/index.php.

135 American hit movies: "Final Petition Heard in Court for Author of *Will the Boat Sink the Water?*" *Boxu xinwen*, Sept. 3, 2004.

135 The variety of fakes: Frederik Balfour, "Fakes!" *BusinessWeek*, Feb. 7, 2005.

135 A fake battery: "A Special Ministry of Public Security Bureau Will Fight IPR and Internet Crime," *Zhongguo keji*, April 3, 2006; Meng Dengke, "Memorandum on Sanlu Milk Powder Incident," *Nanfang zhoumo*, Sept. 17, 2008.

136 Very few consumables: James Doran, "Fake Goods Explosion May Reach $2,000bn," *Times of London*, Feb. 13, 2006; Peter S. Goodman, "China's Killer Headache: Fake Pharmaceuticals," *Washington Post*, Aug. 30, 2002; Chinese offi-

cials routinely reject the accusation that the drugs come from China. See "Chinese Official Rejects Foreign Media Assertion That 'China Is a Major Exporter of Counterfeit Products,'" Xinhua, May 26, 2009.

136 According to Stu: Balfour, "Fakes!"

136 Not surprisingly, then: "U.S. Faults China on Battling Fake Goods," AP, Nov. 7, 2005.

137 No wonder, then: William Glaberson, "6 Are Charged with Selling Millions of Counterfeit Marlboros," New York Times, Feb. 21, 2003.

137 Similarly, while it: Balfour, "Fakes!"

138 Perhaps the most: Andrew Mertha, The Politics of Piracy: Intellectual Property in Contemporary China (Ithaca, N.Y.: Cornell University Press, 2005).

138 Indeed, at times: Jamie Miyazaki, "Faking It Gucci Style," Asia Times, Feb. 6, 2004.

139 Entire cities and counties: Other examples include Hebei's Baigou, Guangdong's Shantou and Shenzhen, and Fujian's Fuzhou.

139 But compare this: Balfour, "Fakes!"

139 For instance, the manufacturers: Bruce Meyerson, "China Gives BlackBerry Maker a Raspberry," AP, April 25, 2006.

140 On August 3, 2005: Zhang Youyi, "Judges Repeatedly Beaten, Sanctity of the Law Challenged," Fazhi zaobao, Aug. 15, 2005.

140 Conflicts of interest don't: Daniel C. K. Chow, Statement for Panel: "Intellectual Property Protection as Economic Policy: Will China Ever Enforce Its IP Laws?" Congressional-Executive Commission on China, May 16, 2005, www.cecc.gov/pages/roundtables/051605/index.php.

140 Even further down: See photo in Mertha, The Politics of Piracy, 4. I have a similar photograph, taken in Kunming, Yunnan province, in 2009.

140 The government has gradually: Ibid., chap. 4, argues that China's copyright law is a consequence of foreign pressure.

141 And because China's: Miyazaki, "Faking It Gucci Style."

141 In IPR legal culture: Lv Wei, "The Competitiveness of China's Intellectual Property," Beijing ribao, July 4, 2005; Brad Spurgeon, "The New Chinese Counterfeit Game," International Herald Tribune, Nov. 15, 2004.

142 In response, Alley vendors: Zhang Jing, "Beijing Has a Silk Alley," Xinmin zhoukan, July 19, 2006.

143 Indeed, actual and fake: Quoted in Balfour, "Fakes!"; Li Yunhong, "Silk Alley: Counterfeits Use High-tech," Falv yu shenghuo, Nov. 17, 2003.

143 Because of the: Jonathan Watts, "European Luxury Brands Challenge Chinese Pirates," Guardian, Nov. 4, 2005.

143 In the spring of: Zhang Muhan, "Silk Alley's Landscape," Shichang bao, April 25, 2007.

143 Although city officials: "Beijing's Silk Street Market Thoroughly Closed," Xinhua, Jan. 7, 2005.

143 Finally, at the end: "Famous Silk Street Faces Tight Check on Fake Goods," *China Daily*, March 31, 2005.

143 Although vendors were: Tim Johnson, "China Clamping Down on Pirated Olympic Merchandise," *The Mercury News* (San Jose), May 6, 2006.

144 Perhaps it's a fitting: Gu Xiaoyu, "Silk Alley Breaks 200 Million in Sales During the Olympics," *Jinghua shibao*, Aug. 22, 2008.

144 In Shanghai, for instance: Cai Ziqi and Li Wei, "An Investigation into the Loss of Business During the Reestablishment of the Xiangyang Market," *Xinmin wanbao*, Aug. 14, 2006.

145 The scandal centered around: Liu Hui, "171 Babies Become 'Big-headed,'" *Beijing keji bao*, April 28, 2004; "Prime Suspect in Fake Milk Powder Scandal Detained," *China Daily*, Nov. 23, 2004.

145 But the scandal was: Liu Weifeng, "Fake Milk Powder Severely Sickens Infant," *China Daily*, April 15, 2005.

145 The scandal shocked: Bai Xu and An Bei, "Crying Shame of the Baby-milk Fraudsters," *China Daily*, Nov. 3, 2004.

145 At over a billion: "Sixty Years of the Chinese Milk Industry," *Nongmin ribao*, Sept. 17, 2009; "On the Anniversary of the Melamine Incident, the Chinese Dairy Industry Still Hasn't Recovered," *Shidai zhoubao*, Sept. 30, 2009.

146 China raised its consumption: You Changqiao, "How Is Milk Condensed?" *Zhongguo yingxiao chuanbo*, March 17, 2003.

146 As one anxious father: Quoted in Lao Jia, "Milk Powder Scam Alters Market Layout," *China Business Weekly*, Aug. 31, 2004.

146 It is a measure of: "'Australian Excellence' Milk Powder Is Not a Foreign Brand Name and Is Only for Sale Domestically," *Beijing wanbao*, Oct. 14, 2009.

146 In Beijing, officials: Wang Ying, "Severe Punishment Vowed for Fake Milk Powder Producers," *China Daily*, April 21, 2004.

147 A store owner: Xin Dingding, "Shopkeeper Punished for Fake Milk Powder," *China Daily*, Aug. 6, 2004.

147 Sha Changban, an unlicensed: Ling Hu, "Shoddy Milk Seller Jailed," *China Daily*, Jan. 8, 2005.

147 Two hundred officials: "In Anhui's Fuyang Inferior Milk Powder Case, 11 Provinces and Cities and 97 People Have Been Investigated," *Renmin wang*, Nov. 5, 2004; Liang Chao, "Forget Substitutes, Mom's Best for Milk," *China Daily*, July 23, 2004.

147 High-pressure marketing even: Liang Chao, "Forget Substitutes, Mom's Best for Milk"; Jin Hai, "Things That Need to Be Done, Need to Be Done Well," *Renmin ribao*, May 8, 2004; Liu Weifeng, "Fake Milk Powder Severely Sickens Infant," *China Daily*, April 15, 2005.

148 Formula advertisements continue: "Who Should Be Held Responsible for the 'Big Head' Tragedy?" *Jinrong shibao*, April 30, 2004; Zhou Renjie and Liu Yuchen, "Fuyang Is Horrified by the Deadly Baby Formula—What Sort of Ill-

ness Is 'Big Headed Baby'?" CCTV's *Economic Half Hour*, April 19, 2004, transcript at www.finance.tom.com.

148 Shortly after the scandal: Ge Subiao, "Is There an Unconscious Numbness over 'Big Head Babies,'" Xinhua, April 17, 2005.

149 Between 2001 and 2005, for example: *China White Paper on Intellectual Property Rights Protection* (Beijing, 2005).

149 The government also established: Wang Ying, "Protecting Well-known Trademarks," *China Daily*, Dec. 5, 2004.

150 The CCA began modestly: For an introduction in English, see www.eng.cca.org.cn:801/page/aboutcca.htm.

150 Its responsibilities include: "Consumer Rights Buyers Bite Back," *China Economic Review*, January 23, 1999.

150 In its first few: Jim Abrams, "Small Group Seeks to Protect a Billion Chinese Consumers," AP, Dec. 9, 1987.

151 In 1991, consumer rights: "Consumers' Day Marked in 2,000 Chinese Cities," Xinhua, March 15, 1991.

151 As a result of: "Sign to Protect Consumer's Rights Makes Its Maiden Appearance," Xinhua, March 13, 2001.

152 Frustrated international and: Tan Loke Khoon, "Counter Feats: The Art of War Against Chinese Counterfeiters," *The China Business Review* 21, no. 6 (Nov.–Dec. 1994).

152 After identifying culprits: Nan Yan, "Pinkerton Detectives Fight Fakes in China," *Zhongguo jingji zhoukan* 16 (2004); Bai Xuan, "The Foreign-Invested Anti-Counterfeit Company, Chengxinchong," *Zhongguo jingji zhoukan* 2 (2004).

152 International owners of: www.qbpc.org.cn/. The site includes a very useful monthly newsletter on IPR enforcement issues and violations in China; "Battle Against Fakes Stepped Up," *China Daily*, Dec. 28, 2001.

153 There are, for instance: "When Idol Was 'Shanzhai-ed,'" *Renmin ribao* (Overseas Edition), Aug. 28, 2008; "The History of Chinese *Shanzhai* Television Dramas," *Xin shiji zhoukan*, Oct. 28, 2008.

153 Although shanzhai products: For photos and a description of a *shanzhai* iPhone, see www.app.cntvs.com/user_center/colorkingphone.aspx.

153 Although shanzhai cell phones: David Barboza, "In China, Knockoff Cellphones Are a Hit," *New York Times*, April 27, 2009.

153 As a twenty-five-year-old salesman: "'Shanzhai': Faking It for Money or Fun?" Xinhua, Dec. 11, 2008.

154 In any case, these: "Protect the Shanzhai Spirit," *Nandu zhoukan*, Aug. 1, 2008.

155 According to a survey: "With Shenzhen Guidance, the *Shanzhai* Industry Spreads," *Renmin zhengxie bao*, Aug. 7, 2009.

155 There are also safety: In any case, the shanzhai culture and economy are growing quickly and spreading into other spheres. There are now even shanzhai shoes

(Adidos) and shanzhai fast-food outlets (Pizza Huh and KFG), but also shanzhai movie stars, a shanzhai Spring Festival gala, an imitation of the officially sanctioned three-hour Chinese New Year's variety show using unknown acts and hosted by CCSTV (China Countryside TV), itself a shanzhai of the powerful state-owned television network CCTV. Li Jie, "The Original Cast Will Again Lead the Shanzhai Gala," *Beijing chenbao*, Nov. 15, 2009.

7. EXTREME MARKETS

157 Thus it created quite: "Nanny Sparks Controversy in Guangdong," Xinhua, June 14, 2006.

158 After yet another baby: "In Chengdu, a Woman Selling Breast Milk Online Makes 300 Yuan a Day," *Chengdu wanbao*, Sept. 21, 2008; "After the Milk Powder Incident, Shenzhen Residents Push the Monthly Salary of Wet-nurses over 10,000 Yuan," *Nanfang dushi bao*, Sept. 19, 2008.

158 Cultural and economic forces: Zhou Zhoujiang and Liu Weidan, "The Undercurrents of Wuhan's Sex Imbalance," *Chutian jinbao*, June 26, 2008; Erik Eckholm, "Desire for Sons Drives Use of Prenatal Scans in China," *New York Times*, June 21, 2002.

159 Since the early 1980s: Andy Newman and Rebeccaa Cathcart, "In an Adoption Hub, China's New Rules Stir Dismay," *New York Times*, Dec. 24, 2006.

160 Of these, 95 percent: Peter S. Goodman, "Stealing Babies for Adoption," *Washington Post*, March 12, 2006. The amount $3,000 is only the donation to the orphanage; total expenses range from $10,000 to $20,000, at least a third less than private adoptions in the U.S. cost.

160 The baby adoption market: Goodman, "Stealing Babies for Adoption."

161 In 2006, however: Newman and Cathcart, "In an Adoption Hub,"

161 Americans have returned to: U.S. Department of State, "Total Adoptions to the United States," www.adoption.state.gov/news/total_chart.html.

161 Because orphanages impose: Goodman, "Stealing Babies for Adoption."

162 The market value: See the very helpful report "The Finances of Baby Trafficking," posted at www.research-china.blogspot.com/2005/12/finances-of-baby-trafficking.html.

162 Stolen babies are worth: Mark Magnier, "Child-Theft Racket Growing in China," *Los Angeles Times*, Jan. 1, 2006.

162 In 2006, for instance: "Sentencing in Case of Hunan Hengyang Welfare Agency Selling Babies," Xinhua, Feb. 24, 2006.

162 Babies have even: "'Babies for Sale' on Chinese eBay," BBC News, Oct. 20, 2005.

162 From 1980 to 1999: "Missing, Presumed Sold: Chinese Parents' Desperate Hunt for Their Kids," Radio Free Asia, May 3, 2006.

162 In 2004 alone: Li Weiwei, "Chinese Public Security Agencies Rescue Nearly 9,000 Trafficked Women and Children in 2004," Xinhua, Feb. 15, 2005.

162 In 2005, police busted: Goodman, "Stealing Babies for Adoption."

163 For example, in 2005: Guan Xiaomeng, "Baby-Selling Orphanage in Hunan Cracked Down," *China Daily*, Nov. 24, 2005.

163 As with its other: Magnier, "Child-Theft Racket Growing in China."

163 Another illegal domestic market: Alexa Olesen, "Rural Chinese Kids Face Trafficking Risk," AP, April 4, 2007; "A Crackdown on Child Abductions Rescues over 3,000 Minors," Xinhua, Feb. 5, 2009.

164 The unintended gender imbalance: Anne E. McLaren, "Marriage by Abduction in Twentieth-Century China," *Modern Asian Studies* 35, no. 4 (2001): 953–84.

164 It was also considered: Angela Ki Che Leung, "To Chasten Society: The Development of Widow Homes in the Qing, 1773–1911," *Late Imperial China* 14, no. 2 (1993): 1–32.

164 Likewise, pre-Communist times: Susan Mann, *Precious Records: Women in China's Long Eighteenth Century* (Palo Alto, Calif.: Stanford University Press, 1997), 42–43.

164 And desperate families: On the selling of girls and women, including kidnapped ones, as brides and maids in Late Imperial China, see Ann Waltner, *Getting an Heir: Adoption and the Construction of Kinship in Late Imperial China* (Honolulu: University of Hawaii Press, 1990), chap. 3. She notes that adoptions included a monetary transaction, particularly when two unrelated parties were involved.

164 While it is difficult: "Missing, Presumed Sold"; Li Bin and Wu Jingjing, "Over Four-Year Period National Security Agencies Free over 50,000 Sold Women and Children," Xinhua, Aug. 16, 2005.

164 According to their own: Jill McGivering, "Vietnam-China Trafficking on Rise," BBC News, Jan. 24, 2006; "Women, Children Smuggling Cases on Rise in SW China Region," Xinhua, Jan. 23, 2006.

164 Periodic high-profile cases: "Public Sentencing of 104 from Major Cases of Abducting and Selling People," Xinhua, May 29, 2002.

165 And in the province: "Mongolian Court in Session to Hear the Biggest Cases of Abductors and Sellers of over a Hundred Women," *Zhongguo xinwen wang*, May 24, 2001.

165 The *New York Times* reporter: Seth Faison, *Beyond the Clouds: Exploring the Hidden Realms of China* (New York: St. Martin's Press, 2004), 184–86.

165 This demand for wives: Howard W. French, "Shanghai Journal: In a Richer China, Billionaires Put Money on Marriage," *New York Times*, Jan. 24, 2006; Li Haipeng, "A Note on the Marriage Proposals of the Wealthy," *Nanfang zhoumo*, Jan. 5, 2006.

166 Nevertheless, the inability: "A Report on Investigations into the Population: By 2020 the Number of Bachelors Will Reach 30 Million," *Guangzhou ribao*, Jan. 12,

2007. On the political implications, see the provocative article by Martin Walker, "The Geopolitics of Sexual Frustration," *Foreign Policy*, March/April 2006.

167 Indeed, one convicted trafficker: Qian Guibao interviewed by Liao Yiwu, *The Corpse Walker: Real-Life Stories, China from the Bottom Up* (New York: Random House, 2008), 16–17.

167 The market for various: Hannah Beech, "Sex and the Single Chinese," *Time*, Dec. 5, 2005; "An Investigation into the Condition of Morality in the Chinese Family," *Beijing ribao*, June 11, 2007.

168 After decades of supplying: "Guangzhou Sex Culture Festival Invites Japanese Porn Stars," *Guangzhou ribao*, Nov. 1, 2009.

169 Many Chinese women: Blog posting: "What Sorts of Advertisements Are 'Hymens'?" posted on 2005.10.11 at www.peacehall.com/news/gb/misc/2005/10/200510111422.shtml and translated at http://www.zonaeuropa.com/20051012_1.htm.

169 Indeed, China now: Lionel M. Jensen and Timothy B. Weston, "Introduction" in Jensen and Weston, eds., *China's Transformations* (Lanham, Md.: Rowman & Littlefield, 2007).

170 A recent scandal: "Henan Man Buys Virginities from 17 Girls," *Shanghai Daily*, May 25, 2006.

170 Although sex workers: Although popularly known as "ducks," in Shenzhen, male sex workers refer to themselves as *nan gongguan, gongguan xiansheng, nanji*, and other terms. In North China, a more common term is *shaoye*.

170 In Shenzhen, the: Fang Gang "Investigating the Lives and Place of Shenzhen's Male Sex Workers," *Nanfang wang*, Dec. 25, 2007. Fang Gang, who wrote a Ph.D. on the subject, argues that male prostitution as a profession is a new phenomenon and not simply an extension of the "favored males" (*nanchong*) who appear in Chinese historical records.

171 One twenty-six-year-old woman: Quoted in Tom Miller, "Boys Flocking to Be 'Ducks' for China's Bored Housewives," *The Guardian*, May 7, 2006.

171 As one duck: Quoted in Zhang Huimin, "Urban Shadows," *Zhongguo siwei wang*, Sept. 11, 2004.

171 On their first: "Beijing Cleans Up Entertainment District," *Beijing chenbao*, June 6, 2006.

171 According to the: "China Taking in North Korean Sex Slaves, Says US," Reuters, Dec. 9, 2005.

171 In Malaysia, rich: Baradan Kuppusamy, "Malaysia's Hot New Import: Chinese Sex Slaves," *Asia Times*, July 16, 2003.

172 Over the past: Bruno Philip, "At the Heart of China's Organ Trade," *Guardian Weekly*, May 10, 2006.

173 In 2004, for instance: "Fu Biao's Complicated Medical Procedure, Organs Come from an Executed Prisoner," *Nanjing ribao*, Sept. 17, 2004.

173 One source long: "China Donor Drive Aims to End Prisoner Organ Trade," Reuters, Aug. 26, 2009.

173 China does not: Mark Magnier and Alan Zarembo, "China Admits Taking Executed Prisoners' Organs," *Los Angeles Times*, Nov. 18, 2006.

173 Whatever the number: Thomas Diflo, "Use of Organs from Executed Chinese Prisoners," *The Lancet* 364, suppl. 1 (Dec. 18, 2004): 30–31.

173 In 2006, an: "China Denies Death Row Organ Sale," BBC News, Sept. 28, 2006.

174 Authorities also banned: "China Bans Corpse Trade," *Aljezera*, July 15, 2006.

174 The price for: "Drop in Executions Leads to Organ Shortage," Reuters, March 28, 2007.

174 In wealthy countries: Moises Naim, *Illicit: How Smugglers, Traffickers, and Copycats Are Hijacking the Global Economy* (New York: Anchor, 2005), 160.

174 Areas in and: Philip, "At the Heart of China's Organ Trade."

174 Those advertising this: Jo Revill, "UK Kidney Patients Head for China," *Guardian*, Dec. 11, 2005.

174 As with traded: Magnier and Zarembo, "China Admits Taking Executed Prisoners' Organs."

175 High-end pharmacies and: Clifford Coonan, "Endangered Wildlife Moves Up Wealthy Chinese Menus," *The Independent*, April 28, 2006.

176 But the biggest bust: Ibid.

176 And Chinese consumers: Jonathan Watts, "'Noah's Ark' of 5,000 Rare Animals Found Floating Off the Coast of China," *The Guardian*, May 26, 2007.

176 The range of: Ibid. On the role of Chinese turtle farms in the black market, see Shi Haitao, James F. Parham, Michael Lau, and Chen Tien-His, "Farming Endangered Turtles to Extinction in China," *Conservation Biology* 21 (2007): 1, 5.

176 Among these products: For an overview of bear farming and bile extraction, see Peter J. Li, "China's Bear Farming and Long-Term Solutions," *Journal of Applied Animal Welfare Science* 7, no. 1 (2004): 71–81.

176 The bile, which: Tim Johnson, "China Refuses Calls to Shut Bile Farms," *Chicago Tribune*, Jan. 15, 2006.

177 The World Wildlife Fund: Clifford Coonan, "Chinese Bid to Lift Ban on Tiger Trade Will Result in Extinction, Say Conservationists," *The Independent*, May 18, 2007; K. Nowell and Xu Ling, *Taming the Tiger Trade: China's Markets for Wild and Captive Tiger Products Since the 1993 Domestic Trade Ban* (Hong Kong: TRAFFIC East Asia, 2007).

178 The impact of: Juan Forero, "Letter from South America: Asia's Love for Shark Fin Comes at a Brutal Price," *International Herald Tribune*, Jan. 6, 2006.

178 The international kung fu: The graphic video for Jackie Chan and the other Chinese stars are posted at the WildAid website: www.wildaid.org/index .asp?CID=7&PID=507.

179 The consumption of: Coonan, "Endangered Wildlife Moves up Wealthy Chinese Menus"; "Origins of SARS Found," *Nanfang ribao*, Jan. 12, 2009.

179 There is some: "China Seizes Bear Paws, Dead Pangolins," Reuters, April 27, 2006; Zhang Qian, "Think Fin, Save Sharks," *Shanghai Daily*, July 28, 2009.

8. ENVIRONMENTAL IMPLICATIONS

181 Even such small: Chen Hang, "The Disposable Hidden Concern," *People's Daily* (overseas version in Chinese), July 11, 2009.

181 In socialist China: Judith Shapiro, *Mao's War Against Nature: Politics and the Environment in Revolutionary China* (New York: Cambridge University Press, 2001). On the late imperial environmental record, see the classic by Peter Perdue, *Exhausting the Earth: State and Peasant in Hunan, 1500–1985* (Cambridge, Mass: Harvard University Press, 1987), and Mark Elvin, *Retreat of the Elephants: An Environmental History of China* (New Haven, Conn.: Yale University Press, 2004).

182 To the growing: Wei Jingjing, "Say 'No' to Disposable Chopsticks," *Zhongguo renkou bao*, April 23, 2000; Li Ying, "Technology Is Changing Life," *Keji ribao*, July 16, 2005.

182 Growing prosperity allows: Mia MacDonald and Sangamithra Iyer, "Skillful Means: The Challenges of China's Encounter with Factory Farming" (New York: Brighter Green, 2008), downloaded at www.brightergreen.org/files/brightergreen chinaprint4.pdf, accessed on Jan. 23, 2010.

183 With four times the: Lester Brown, "Why the World Needs a Plan B for China," *The Guardian*, Feb. 5, 2006.

183 If, as already: Of course, these sobering estimates do not include the cars added to India, whose population will surpass China by 2030, or other countries. Brown, "Why the World Needs a Plan B for China."

184 To cite just one: Wang Xi, "Expert: Abnormally High Proportion of Coal Pressures China to Achieve Energy-Saving Emission Reduction," Xinhua, June 17, 2009.

184 The country burns: Jacques Leslie, "The Last Empire: China's Pollution Problem Goes Global," *Mother Jones*, Dec. 10, 2007.

184 Furthermore, it: Lester R. Brown, *Plan B 2.0: Rescuing a Planet Under Stress and a Civilization in Trouble* (New York: W. W. Norton, 2006), 9; Keith Bradsher and David Barboza, "Pollution from Chinese Coal Casts a Global Shadow," *New York Times*, June 11, 2006.

184 One consequence of this: The World Bank and State Environmental Protection Administration (China), *Cost of Pollution in China: Economic Estimates of Physical Damages* (Washington, D.C.: The World Bank, 2007); "China's Environment: A Great Wall of Waste," *The Economist*, Aug. 19, 2004.

185 Across the country: William Mellor and Allen Cheng, "China's Rising Entrepreneurs," *Sydney Morning Herald*, May 27, 2006.

185 In fact, cement: And, unfortunately, it's a notoriously difficult industry to green. Also, China's cement output per person, 5.1 metric tons, is still only about a fourth of the American rate of 19.4 tons and is gaining on the EU's 8.6 tons. Elisabeth Rosenthal, "Cement Industry Is at Center of Climate Change Debate," *New York Times*, Oct. 26, 2007; Elisabeth Rosenthal, "China Increases Lead as Biggest Carbon Dioxide Emitter," *New York Times*, June 14, 2008.

186 Since the 1990s: Li Zhang, *In Search of Paradise: Middle-Class Living in a Chinese Metropolis* (Ithaca, N.Y.: Cornell University Press, 2010).

186 The aquifers: Elizabeth Economy, *The River Runs Black: The Environmental Challenge to China's Future* (Ithaca, N.Y.: Cornell University Press, 2005), 68.

187 Water shortages have been: Brown, *Plan B 2.0*, 55. See also Maude Barlow and Tony Clarke, *Blue Gold* (New Delhi: Earthscan, 2003).

187 All across China: Brown, *Plan B 2.0*, 52–53; Xiao Hua, "What Sort of Signal Is the Disappearance of a Thousand Lakes," Xinhua, Nov. 4, 2009.

187 Shanghai, which was built: Leslie, "The Last Empire: China's Pollution Problem Goes Global"; Rujun Shen, "Shanghai Highrises Could Worsen Rising Seas Threat," Reuters, Oct. 6, 2008.

187 Likewise, by the: Barlow and Clarke, *Blue Gold*, 22.

187 Already some sixty: Leslie, "The Last Empire: China's Pollution Problem Goes Global."

187 As a result: Economy, *The River Runs Black: The Environmental Challenge to China's Future*, 68; Editorial, "Clean Water: Still Elusive," *New York Times*, Oct. 21, 2009.

188 Even more than: "Misunderstood Consumption and the New Illiterate in the Era of Globalization," *Xinzhou kan*, July 2007.

188 The habit of buying: John G. Rodwan, Jr., "U.S. and International Bottled Water Developments and Statistics for 2008," *Bottled Water Reporter*, April/May 2009.

188 If Chinese consumers drink: Abid Aslam, "Bottled Water: Nectar of the Frauds?" OneWorld website, Feb. 4, 2006.

189 A quarter of China: "The Chinese Miracle Will End Soon," *Der Spiegel*, March 7, 2005.

189 If the disappearance of: Jehangir Pocha, "China's Growing Desert," *In These Times*, Oct. 2006, 32–33.

189 In fact, Russian officials: Christian Lowe, "Expansive China Faces Grass-roots Resentment," Reuters, Aug. 7, 2009.

190 As of 2008: MacDonald and Lyer, "Skillful Means: The Challenges of China's Encounter with Factory Farming."

190 Chinese investors have: Shapi Shacinda, "Zambia Wins Chinese Investment, Opposition Snubbed," Reuters, Feb. 3, 2007.

190 Take cashmere sweaters: Evan Osnos, "That Low-Priced Cashmere Sweater Has a Hidden Cost," *Chicago Tribune*, Dec. 28, 2006.

191 Already, residents of some: Brown, *Plan B 3.0: Mobilizing to Save Civilization*, (New York: W. W. Norton, 2008), 88–96.

191 Deforestation along the: Feng Yuanli, "Why Is the Yangzi River Flooding Every Year?" *Nanfang dushi bao*, July 5, 2002; Economy, *The River Runs Black: The Environmental Challenge to China's Future*, 66–67.

192 The suburbs of: Brown, *Plan B 3.0*, 116; see the documentary *Manufactured Landscapes*, which examines the work of photographer Edward Burtynsky and includes many photographs of massive garbage dumps in China.

192 Your last computer: "Seventy Percent of Global E-waste Pours into China, Most Secondhand Goods Are Foreign Garbage," *Beijing chenbao*, Jan. 9, 2007.

192 Entire towns such as: Mark Chisholm and Kitty Bu, "China's E-waste Capital Chokes on Old Computers," Reuters, June 11, 2007.

192 What can't be resold: Zhang Miaomiao and Zhu Wei, "Chinese Mobile Phone Waste Is Extremely Serious, on Average Nearly 70 Million Are Discarded Yearly," Xinhua, Nov. 8, 2005.

193 By 2000, one: Tian Xu, "Some Arrogant Advice on 'Disposable Products,'" *Zhongguo maoyi bao*, July 6, 2000.

193 Within a few years: The Northwest province of Heilongjiang alone uses an estimated one hundred million boxes annually. Wang Ce, "Heilongjiang Prohibits the Use of Disposable Tableware," *Zhongguo shipin bao*, Nov. 6, 2000.

193 In late 1999: Zheng Jianling, "Consumer Goods: Say 'No' to Disposable Styrofoam Tableware," *Zhongguo zhiliang bao*, July 13, 2000; Xiang Yan, "Disposable Chopsticks Is the Touchstone for Environmental Inspection," *Zhongguo baozhuang bao*, June 6, 2001.

193 The Chinese have given: Jiang Jianhua, "Disposable Tableware: 'White' Is Prohibited and 'Green' Is Difficult to Promote," *Zhongguo huagong bao*, Oct. 13, 2000.

193 The capital of Zhejiang: Xu Zhengfeng, "Putting an End to a Plastic Plague," *Asia Times*, Aug. 17, 1999.

193 Although the Chinese Communist: Allen T. Cheng, "China Pushes to Establish Recycling Industry," Bloomberg News, Dec. 20, 2004; T. J. Zheng, "China's Green Quandary," *EE Times*, Jan. 5, 2005.

194 Sales of products that: Hirotaka Yamaguchi, "Quality of Chinese Products," *Asahi Shimbun*, Oct. 29, 2005; "A Concern: Why Are Environmentally Protective Electronic Products Sold in Europe and America but Not Domestically?" Xinhua, July 6, 2006.

195 A task force: "NPC Debates Limiting Air-conditioning to 26°," *Guangzhou ribao*, July 27, 2007; "Another City to Have 'Energy Police,'" *China Daily*, June 11, 2007.

195 But such efforts: Jing Zhiqiang, "Why Have Efforts to Limit Air-condition Use Amounted to Nothing?" *Dazhong ribao*, July 30, 2008; "Beijing 'Energy Police' to Patrol Shopping Malls," Reuters, Jan. 19, 2006.

195 But in 2006 the: "National Bureau of Statistics Officials Say the Success of the Green GDP Accounting System Is Very Unlikely," *Diyi caijing ribao*, May 11, 2006.

197 Chinese environmentalists have: "China's Forest Coverage Rate Reaches 20.36 Percent," Xinhua, Nov. 17, 2009.

197 One activist, for instance: Zhong Xia, "How to Deal with 'Disposable Chopsticks,' " *Renmin zhongxie bao*, Nov. 28, 2000.

197 Anti-chopstickers also appeal: Hou Yuanzhao, "The Problem with Disposable Chopsticks," *Zhongguo lüse shibao*, June 23, 2004.

197 Environmentalists also attack: For example, see Long Yun, "Disposable Chopsticks 'Coloring': The Whiter the More Dangerous," *Jiating daobao*, June 3, 2005; Han Guangwen, "Consumer Guide: Refuse to Use Disposable Chopsticks," *Zhongguo shiyou bao*, May 27, 2001.

197 One food industry: Zhou Zhiguo, "Disposable Chopsticks Are Not Without Merit: Disposable Chopsticks Should Be Used Rationally," *Zhongguo shipin zhiliang bao*, July 4, 2000.

198 Consumers justified their: Qiu Xiang, "Disposable Chopsticks: Why Are They Prohibited Yet Still Used?" *Shaanxi ribao*, June 8, 2001.

198 In 2005, perhaps: "National Standards for Disposable Chopsticks Issued," *China Daily*, Oct. 11, 2005.

198 The following year: "China Introduces Chopsticks Tax," BBC News, March 22, 2006.

198 These efforts have: Jane Spencer, "Banned in Beijing: Chinese See Green over Chopsticks," *Wall Street Journal*, Feb. 8, 2008.

199 Likewise, reports in the: Zhang Zuhui, "The Consumer Market," *Dazhong keji bao*, March 27, 2001. In the Hubei provincial city of Ezhou, for instance, one reporter found shortly thereafter that retailers and wholesalers had unlimited supplies of disposable chopsticks. Song Zhexian, "The Municipal Government's Order to 'Ban White Pollution' in the End Is Ineffective," *Hubei ribao*, Jan. 14, 2002.

FURTHER READINGS
AND RESOURCES

This book tries to fill the gap between the broad journalistic accounts of contemporary China and specialized literature, which is often less accessible to nonexperts because it assumes prior knowledge. Here I've provided suggestions for extending the analysis offered in this book in many different directions.

CHINESE HISTORICAL SOURCES

For a succinct and highly readable account of China's modern history, see Rana Mitter, *Modern China: A Very Short Introduction* (New York: Oxford University Press, 2008). For an interpretive history of the same, see that author's *A Bitter Revolution: China's Struggle with the Modern World* (New York: Oxford University Press, 2005). For an economic overview, see Barry Naughton, *The Chinese Economy: Transitions and Growth* (Cambridge, Mass.: The M.I.T. Press, 2007). Good political overviews include Kenneth Lieberthal, *Governing China: From Revolution to Reform* (New York: W. W. Norton, 2003), and Joseph Fewsmith, *China Since Tiananmen: From Deng Xiaoping to Hu Jintao* (Cambridge, U.K.: Cambridge University Press, 2008). Maurice Meisner's *Mao's China and After: A History of the People's Republic* (New York: Free Press, 1999) remains an excellent political and intellectual history of China since 1949, especially the Mao years. For an ambitious attempt to link the economic rise of China with the simultaneous changes around the world since the early 1980s, see David Harvey, *A Brief History of Neoliberalism* (New York: Oxford University Press, 2007). Two books with informative essays intended for general readers are Kate Merkel-Hess et al., eds., *China in 2008: A Year of Great Significance* (Lanham, Md.: Rowman & Littlefield, 2009), and Lionel Jensen and Timothy Weston, eds., *China's Transformations: The Stories Beyond the Headlines* (Lanham, Md.: Rowman & Littlefield, 2007).

For those interested in more scholastic historical analyses of consumerism in modern China, I am currently writing a history of the rise, fall, and reemergence of consumerism in China since 1900. Those particularly interested in the early twentieth-century history of consumerism in China may wish to consult my *China Made: Consumer Culture and the Creation of the Nation* (Cambridge, Mass.: Harvard University Press, 2004). Although not explicitly about consumerism, many books touch on complementary aspects. For an entertaining and sumptuously illustrated history of clothing, see Antonia Finnane, *Changing Clothes in China: Fashion, History, Nation* (New York: Columbia University Press, 2008). Readers particularly interested in business history should consult the work of Sherman Cochran, starting with his classic study, *Big Business in China: Sino-Foreign Rivalry in the Cigarette Industry, 1890–1930* (Cambridge, Mass.: Harvard University Press, 1980). Also see anything by art historian Craig Clunas, including his latest, *Empire of Great Brightness: Visual and Material Cultures of Ming China, 1368–1644* (Honolulu: University of Hawaii Press, 2007). For a stimulating history of when and why China fell behind northwest Europe in consumption, consult Kenneth Pomeranz's instant classic, *The Great Divergence: China, Europe, and the Making of the Modern World Economy*, rev. ed. (Princeton, N.J.: Princeton University Press, 2001).

The books most similar to mine in approach are not about China. Since the "consumerist" turn in academic studies in the 1990s, a growing number of popular and academic books about consumerism in the Western world have appeared. Two of the best of these are Lizabeth Cohen's *A Consumers' Republic: The Politics of Mass Consumption in Postwar America* (New York: Knopf, 2003), and Lawrence Glickman, *Buying Power: A History of Consumer Activism in America* (Chicago: University of Chicago Press, 2009). On modern Western Europe, see Victoria de Grazia's *Irresistible Empire: America's Advance through 20th Century Europe* (Cambridge, Mass.: Harvard University Press, 2005). Frank Trentmann, a leading historian of global consumerism, has a handy bibliography of thousands of books on the global history of consumerism and consumption here: www.consume.bbk.ac.uk/index.html.

NEWS WEBSITES/LISTSERVS

The most important website for keeping up-to-date on English-language writings on China published in newspapers and magazines is the China Digital Times (www.chinadigitaltimes.net/). There are also specialized English-language webpages devoted to one or another aspect of China. The most important site for environmental news and discussions is the bilingual site run by the British journalist Isabel Hilton, see www.chinadialogue.net. On the Chinese media, see www.danwei.org. For an entertaining site devoted to tabloid-like news emanating out of China, see www.chinasmack.com. For in-depth commentary by China specialists on current events and intended for nonspecialists, see www.thechinabeat.org. For an invaluable resource for modern Chinese culture, literature, and history, see the Modern Chinese Literature and Culture site run by Kirk Denton, www.mclc.osu.edu/default.htm.

There are also specialized Web Listservs; most are open to nonspecialists. I have found two particularly useful. The Professional Association for China's Environment (PACE) distributes an "electronic newsletter devoted to giving interested readers a comprehensive update of news concerning China's environment" (www.tech.groups .yahoo.com/group/PACELISTSERVER/join). For a highly recommended, free, and acerbic newsletter on the Chinese market, sign up for market research company Access Asia's e-newsletter here: www.accessasia.co.uk. Finally, readers may be surprised to see the occasional citation of rather unusual news sources (e.g., *The Hindu*). Kudos to Google alerts (www.google.com/alerts) for providing many odd but occasionally useful leads by daily searching the combined terms *China* and *consumer*.

POPULAR ACCOUNTS OF CONTEMPORARY CHINA

Even as English-language newspapers come under increased financial pressure and close foreign offices, China remains well served by excellent reporters, particularly those at the *New York Times*, *Washington Post*, the *Guardian*, and the *Financial Times*. Books by their correspondents are always must-reads. This book complements the terrific first-person accounts of contemporary China written by journalists, such as *Financial Times* reporter James Kynge's wide-ranging *China Shakes the World: The Rise of a Hungry Nation* (London: Phoenix, 2007), and *Washington Post* correspondent Philip Pan's *Out of Mao's Shadow: The Struggle for the Soul of New China* (New York: Simon & Schuster, 2008), which focuses on human rights through biographies, and the classic by *New York Times* correspondents Nicholas Kristof and Sheryl Wu-Dunn, *China Wakes* (New York: Vintage, 1995). Likewise, recommended is anything by *New Yorker* correspondent Peter Hessler, especially *Oracle Bones: A Journey Between China's Past and Present* (New York: HarperCollins, 2006), and NPR correspondent Rob Gifford's *China Road: A Journey into the Future of a Rising Power* (New York: Random House, 2008), which focuses on contemporary life along the ancient Silk Route. *Newsweek* correspondent Duncan Hewitt's *Getting Rich First: A Modern Social History* (New York: Pegasus Books, 2008) provides a collection of his reporting on a vast range of topics. *Financial Times* reporter Alexandra Harney provides a critical overview of why Chinese products are so competitive globally in *The China Price: The True Cost of Chinese Competitive Advantage* (New York: Penguin, 2009). And finally, *Washington Post* correspondent John Pomfret's *Chinese Lessons: Five Classmates and the Story of New China* (New York: Henry Holt, 2007) documents the Reform Era through divergent lives.

There are also a growing number of terrific memoirs, too numerous to list, by a new generation of writers and slackers living, reflecting, and writing on China. For a particularly entertaining account of her culinary adventures, see Jen Lin-Liu, *Serve the People: A Stir-Fried Journey Through China* (New York: Mariner Books, 2009). For the growing number of translations of fiction and nonfiction, consult, www.mclc .osu.edu. Or begin with these two: Yiwu Liao, *The Corpse Walker: Real-Life Stories, China from the Bottom Up* (New York: Random House, 2009), and Ye Sang, *China Candid: The People on the People's Republic* (Berkeley: University of California Press, 2006). I am grateful to these people for illuminating so many diverse aspects of contemporary China.

ACADEMIC AND BUSINESS BOOKS

There is also extensive social science scholarship focusing on contemporary China. Elisabeth Croll, *China's New Consumers: Social Development and Domestic Demand* (London: Routledge, 2006), focuses on social classes. Academic titles, including collections of essays or case studies, are again much more narrowly focused. These include Deborah Davis, ed., *The Consumer Revolution in Urban China* (Berkeley: University of California Press, 2000); James Watson, ed., *Golden Arches East: McDonald's in East Asia* (Palo Alto, Calif.: Stanford University Press, 2007); and David Goodman, ed., *The New Rich in China* (London: Routledge, 2008). Each one of the topics covered in this book—from cars to advertising to environmental issues—has a specialized literature. See, for instance, Eric Thun, *Changing Lanes in China: Foreign Direct Investment, Local Governments, and Auto Sector Development* (Cambridge: Cambridge University Press, 2006); Jing Wang, *Brand New China: Advertising, Media, and Popular Culture* (Cambridge, Mass.: Harvard University Press, 2008); and Robert Weller, *Discovering Nature: Globalization and Environmental Culture in China and Taiwan* (Cambridge: Cambridge University Press, 2006).

Because consumerism is a wide-ranging business topic, this book addresses many topics covered more thoroughly in other books. A huge number of books, for instance, discuss marketing to China, which I think of as the "how to crack the China market" books. The best of these include James McGregor, *One Billion Customers: Lessons from the Front Lines of Doing Business in China* (New York: Free Press, 2007); Ted Fishman's *China Inc.: How the Rise of the Next Superpower Challenges America and the World* (New York: Scribner, 2005); Tom Doctoroff's *Billions: Selling to the New Chinese Consumer* (New York: Palgrave, 2005); and Oded Shenkar's *The Chinese Century: The Rising Chinese Economy and Its Impact on the Global Economy, the Balance of Power, and Your Job* (Philadelphia: Wharton School, 2005).

ACKNOWLEDGMENTS

For the first five years I worked on this book, I did so alone—trawling Chinese and English-language newspapers and magazines, reading scholarly writings and business reports, visiting stores and traveling to markets throughout China, discussing shopping experiences with all kinds of consumers, and, above all, grappling with how to render the huge topic of Chinese consumerism into discrete chapters and topics. But as a historian accustomed to working with the past, I was unprepared for how to write about a topic that continually changes. These cycles of reading, writing, learning more, and expanding chapters might have continued forever without the numerous people who helped me finally pull this book together.

My thanks must begin with Rana Mitter, who read drafts, made publishing contacts, and set an example of collegiality that inspires all who know him. A few fellow academics read the entire book and provided honest, direct, and thorough criticism: John M. Carroll, Laura Kissel, Hyung Gu Lynn, and Anne Reinhardt. And I probably need a special category of acknowledgment for Patricia M. Thornton, who not only cheerfully read every chapter but kept asking for more drafts. Another colleague dropped everything and provided comments on three chapters within twenty-four hours: Anna Lora-Wainwright. Many busy academics gave feedback on one or more chapters or helped with related issues: Kate Blackmon, Felix Boecking, Peter Carroll, Jean-Pascal Daloz, John Darwin, Victoria de Grazia, Prasenjit Duara, Rosemary Foot, Matthew Johnson, Toby Lincoln, Marc Moskowitz, Annie Nie, Peter Perdue, Ruth Rogaski, Eric Thun, Frank Trentmann, and Zhao Fang. I also continue to enjoy the wise counsel of trusted friends, especially Frank Bechter, Ken Chase, and Mike Rogers, and the support of my former graduate school advisers William Kirby and Philip Kuhn. Similarly, I received helpful research assistance from Cheng Linsun, Li Chenghong, Ryan Manuel, Parichehre Mosteshar-Gharai, Joseph Richardson, and above all, Jeanne Barker-Nunn, who also greatly helped make the book more readable.

The most important sources for this book have been the countless and unnamed Chinese who shared their insights with me over the past quarter-century—everyone from cabdrivers sharing opinions about the best shopping spots in town while stuck in traffic jams to the head of a state-owned bank who explained why the world needn't worry about Chinese pollution. I also had direct assistance from Chinese friends and researchers who tolerated endless requests for help finding material on one subject or another and shared their own experiences of living in China. These include Cao Dongmei, Huang Zhenping, Jiang Jin, Li Zhen, Qu Jun, Shi Jianfeng, Xu Jilin, and Yu Dan, who despite their invaluable help are obviously in no way responsible for my interpretations.

I completed this book at Oxford University as a tutor and fellow of Merton College. Thanks to its retiring head, Dame Jessica Rawson, Merton has been a wonderful place to write, teach, dine, and discuss ideas. I am grateful to the other fellows of the college for their probing questions and tolerance for my inchoate, if enthusiastically delivered, answers. I am particularly indebted to the other history tutors in the college, Matthew Grimley and Steven Gunn, and our now-retired colleague Philip Waller for showing me the ropes, repeatedly and patiently. I am also grateful to the Oxford history faculty staff, particularly Sue Henderson, Jacqui Julier, Aileen Mooney, and the former chair, Christopher Haigh. But I began the research for this book while teaching at the University of South Carolina, where I was fortunate to have the support of an inspiring provost, Mark Becker, and wonderful colleagues, particularly the chair of the history department, Patrick Maney, and the director of the Walker Institute, Gordon Smith.

Then there are others who provided critical but indirect help. Early on, Herrick Chapman and Lizabeth Cohen encouraged me to try to write for a broader audience; Stacey Millner-Collins taught me many things; Chris Haworth resolved countless knotty problems; Simon MacKinnon suggested how to make the book more appealing to business readers; and Yu Jie taught me the advantages of knowing a management consultant—instant answers to any questions, delivered at any hour. Susan Rabiner, my agent and the author of one of the finest ruminations on the writing process, found the perfect editor, Thomas LeBien, whose faith in the project and clear vision for it (even when my own eyes went blurry) exceeded even his high reputation. Likewise his staff, especially Dan Crissman, and colleagues at Farrar, Straus and Giroux worked hard to produce the book promptly and publicize it. I am also grateful to Jenna Dolan for copyediting the manuscript and to the production editor, Wah-Ming Chang.

Finally, I am indebted to my family, particularly my brothers, Erich Gerth and Paul Gerth, who provided frank advice, on both the book and personal matters. My sisters Monica and Claudia and their families were also supportive, as was my extended family, including Pamela Gerth and Bruce and Susana Erling. My early exposure to the ideas of my father, an international trade adviser, and the compassion of my mother, the director of a charity, have undoubtedly shaped my understanding of the world, so it is to my parents, Judy Valentine Gerth and Roger Gerth, that I dedicate this book.

INDEX

private investigators, 53, 152
privatization, 58, 62, 63
profiteering, 57
property speculation, 57–58, 186
prostitution, 52, 72, 166–72, 179–80;
    international market for, 171–72;
    male, 170–71
public transportation, 22, 23, 25, 29, 30,
    39, 150
publishing, 83–85

Qiaobo Ski Domes, 48
Qinghai province, 187
Quality Brand Protection Committee
    (QBPC), 152

racketeering, official, 57
Rain, 86
Reagan, Ronald, 65
recycling, 181–82, 188, 193–94
RedBerry, 139
Reform Era, 7, 11, 26, 45, 49, 51, 53,
    56, 60, 63, 77, 93, 115, 167, 190
Republic of China, 66
restaurants, 73, 74–76, 90, 96; brand-
    name, consistency among, 128;
    chopsticks in, 181, 182, 184, 198;
    endangered species and, 178, 179;
    waste in, 108, 109
retirement, 12, 56, 159
rice, 102, 103–104, 107, 196
road-building, 38, 102, 185
rural areas, 4, 11, 63, 185

Samsung, 117
sand, 183, 189, 191
SARS, 179
Save the Children, 163

saving, 9, 10, 11, 12
Seagram, 130
second wives, 51–53
7-Eleven, 92, 105
Sex Culture Festival, 168
sex trade, 51–52, 166–72, 179–80;
    international market, 171–72; men in,
    170–71
sexual revolution, 167–68
Sha Changban, 147
Shanda Network Development, 55
Shanghai, 51, 66; building in, 185, 186,
    204; cars in, 25, 31–32; convenience
    stores in, 105; counterfeits in, 144;
    electricity use in, 194; food waste in,
    108; Nanjing Road in, 101; Taiwanese
    and, 72, 73, 74; underground railway
    in, 39; water table and, 187; wet
    markets in, 105
Shanghai Automotive, 26
Shanghai VW, 40
Shanghai Yangjing Juyuan Experimental
    School, 50
shanzhai products, 152–55
shark fin soup, 177–78
sheep, 191
Shenyang, 46, 95, 96, 97, 169
Shenzhen, 170
Shenzhen Mobile Communication
    Association, 155
Shenzhen, Zhongjia Household
    Services, 157
Shiseido, 4–5
shopping, 92, 106, 202; bags for, 193;
    bargaining in, 98, 99; at chain stores,
    101–107; choice in, 92, 96–100, 106,
    107, 124; at convenience stores,
    101–102, 104–105; at marketplaces,
    94–98, 102, 105, 106; at
    supermarkets, 92, 93, 101–105
shopping malls, 24, 46, 71, 101, 106

INDEX